Fast Track
to **FCE**

Longman

Jane Allemano

Teacher's
Book

Pearson Education Limited
Edinburgh Gate Harlow
Essex CM20 2JE England
and Associated Companies throughout the world

www.longman.com

First published 2001
Seventh Impression 2006

ISBN-13: 978-0-582-40577-6
ISBN-10: 0-582-40577-7

Set in 9.5/11.5pt Zapf Humanist

Printed in Malaysia, KHL

Project managed by David Francis
Designed by Michael Harris

Acknowledgements

We are grateful to the following for permission to reproduce copyright material:

ACT Ice Hockey Association for an adapted extract from 'Hi my name is Brendan' on http://www.icehockeyact.asn.au/brendon; Express Newspapers for an adapted extract from 'Julia and Ben' in SUNDAY EXPRESS Magazine 19.3.00; Geographical Magazine. The Magazine that explores the World for an extract based on 'Climb Every Mountain' by Fabrizio Zangrilli in GEOGRAPHICAL November 1999; Gruner & Jahr Ltd for an adapted extract from 'Wright brothers' in FOCUS Magazine March, 2000; Guardian Newspapers for an adapted extract from the article 'How to get through your first day in the job' by Hilary Freeman in THE GUARDIAN 17.6.00; Highbury House Communications for text based on 'Bermuda Triangle' in CARIBBEAN UNCOVERED magazine Autumn/Winter; Hotcourses.com for information from 'Filling the gap' in 'What University or College?' 99/2000 on www.oncourse.co.uk; Independent Newspapers Ltd for an adapted extract from 'The Fantasy Builder' in THE INDEPENDENT ON SUNDAY 1.8.99; Minx Magazine for an adapted extract from 'Is your boyfriend...' in MINX magazine; News International Syndication for adapted extracts from 'Muzak' by Candida Crewe in THE TIMES Magazine © Candida Crewe/Times Newspapers Limited 27.5.00, 'Tree Tops' in MEGA Saturday Magazine in THE TIMES 15.4.00 © Times Newspapers Limited 2000 and an adapted extract from the article 'Dogs for the disabled' in SUNDAY TIMES magazine 19.7.98; Premier Media Partners listening text based on '21st Century World' in British Airways HIGH LIFE Magazine December 1999; Redwood Publishing Ltd for an adapted extract from the article 'Global Shopper' in AA magazine Autumn/Winter 2000; Sustrans Ltd for a listening text - prepared with material supplied by SUSTRANS Ltd (a charity), and Telegraph Group Ltd for an adapted extract from 'Case History' by Clare Thomson in SUNDAY TELEGRAPH 4.6.00

We have been unable to trace the copyright holder of the article 'The football agent' in HOTLINE magazine and would appreciate any information that would enable us to do so.

Sample OMR answer sheets are reproduced by permission of the University of Cambridge Local Examinations Syndicate.

Contents

Coursebook Contents map

Introduction to the course

The *Fast Track to FCE* course comprises a student's *Coursebook*, a set of two class cassettes, an *Exam Practice Workbook* (available with or without Answer key) and this *Teacher's Book*.

Also available for use with this course is *First Certificate Practice Tests Plus,* a collection of eight tests in the exact format of the exam. Exam strategies and tips in the first two tests remind students of what they have learned during their course.

Key features

The material in *Fast Track to FCE* Coursebook can be covered in one year, and provides everything your students need to help them get an A grade in the exam. The twelve units each provide practice for all five Papers in the exam, and the tasks are at FCE level from the start.

• Effective exam training

The **Exam overview** at the front of the *Coursebook* gives information about each Paper, including the test focus of each task type. **Exam files** in the units summarise key information to help you introduce each new task type as it appears in the course. *Exam strategy* boxes offer guidelines on how to tackle each task while *exam tips!* offer additional useful pointers. The boxes are colour-coded, making it easy for students to revise in the run-up to the exam.

Step-by-step guidance is provided in initial units to build up students' confidence and ensure they understand how to apply the recommended strategies.

A **Practice exam** at the end of the *Coursebook* provides the opportunity for timed practice, and allows you and your students to evaluate which areas may need further practice and revision before the exam.

• Extensive coverage of exam topics and vocabulary

The key topic areas tested in the FCE exam are all covered in depth, ensuring that students are well prepared for the range of texts they will be faced with. Each unit contains a wealth of topic-related vocabulary, which is practised in Speaking and Use of English formats, as well as in Writing. Unit-by-unit **vocabulary files** at the end of the *Coursebook* allow students to revise key vocabulary easily.

• Thorough consolidation of FCE grammar

The grammar syllabus revises all areas tested in the exam, and the approach ensures that the relevance of each grammatical area to Paper 2 and Paper 3 of the exam is apparent. **Grammar files** present the key grammar covered in each unit, and further information is provided at the end of the *Coursebook*. There are useful cross references from the units to the extra reference material.

• Extra support for Speaking and Writing

Each unit contains a Paper 5 task. In Units 1–4, there are recorded models for analysis of students' performance in Parts 1–4 of the test. Task-related vocabulary is presented in colour-coded boxes, which also allows for easy revision. At the end of the *Coursebook*, a **Functions file** contains useful expressions for comparing and contrasting photos, expressing opinions, agreeing and disagreeing, etc. Students should be referred to this when doing Paper 5 tasks.

Writing sections contain sample answers for analysis of the key features of each type of writing, plus a focus on the grammar needed for the task. A **Writing file** at the end of the *Coursebook* provides a model for each type of writing tested in the exam, plus useful language and tips.

• Enables students to take responsibility for their learning

The course explains to students what skills the tasks in the exam are designed to test, and provides them with the opportunity consciously to practise and improve their own skills. They are also encouraged to record useful vocabulary in a vocabulary notebook. *Study tips* suggest ways they can organise their notebooks – which will allow them to review and memorise the language more effectively.

• Regular opportunities for revision and testing

Progress reviews and tests in the *Coursebook*, *Exam Practice Workbook* and *Teacher's Book* provide you and your students with regular opportunities to monitor progress. There is also a complete practice exam at the end of the *Coursebook*.

Organisation of the *Coursebook*

The *Coursebook* contains 12 theme-based units. There are three **Progress tests**, after Units 4, 8 and 12. These use Paper 3 formats to test the grammar and vocabulary that has been covered in all units up to that point. There is a complete **Practice exam** after the last Progress test. Opportunities for revision are also provided after every two units in the *Exam Practice Workbook* and there are photocopiable **Unit** and **Progress tests** in this *Teacher's Book*.

At the end of the *Coursebook* you will find the following reference sections:

- **Grammar reference**: contains 26 grammar files which complement the files in each unit and add further information about the grammar point.
- **Writing file**: contains grade A model answers to each task type, with notes and useful language for each type of writing.
- **Vocabulary file**: unit-by-unit vocabulary lists.
- **Functions file**: functional language for Paper 5.

Unit organisation

Each unit in the *Coursebook* provides training and practice for all Papers of the exam, as well as grammar consolidation and vocabulary development work. The units are organised into double-page spreads as follows:

- Lead-in and Reading 1
- Grammar and Use of English 1
- Listening and Speaking
- Lead-in and Reading 2
- Vocabulary and Use of English 2
- Writing

Reading 2 introduces a new aspect of the unit theme. For example, in Unit 1, *Entertainment*, the topic of Reading 1 is films, while Reading 2 introduces the topic of art for young people.

Approach

Lead-in

The Reading texts are always preceded by a **Lead-in** which requires students to discuss questions or talk about photos related to the topic of the Reading. Discussing a topic before reading about it allows the students to bring their own background knowledge and expectations to the text, facilitating comprehension. In addition, it allows you to check how much vocabulary students know, and to teach any new items relevant to the topic. The discussion tasks also practise skills useful for Paper 5.

The **Lead-in** sections usually contain a box of useful expressions for the task. Here are some ways to make best use of this:

- Ask students to decide which words match which pictures (when talking about photos).
- Brainstorm topic vocabulary on the board with books closed, then compare their ideas with the ones in the book.
- Give students definitions and ask them to decide what items in the box they refer to.

Reading

In Units 1–4, **Reading 1** and **Reading 2** both practise the same exam task type. **Reading 1** introduces the task and shows students how to tackle it step by step. **Reading 2** tests their ability to apply the strategy introduced in **Reading 1**. In this way, students are thoroughly familiarised with the skills tested and the best reading strategies to use for each reading task type. From Unit 5 onwards, the second reading task is always different from **Reading 1** and students are reminded of the recommended strategies introduced in earlier units. The *Exam Practice Workbook* always contains a third reading task related to the unit theme.

For all task types except Part 4 (multiple matching), it is recommended that students skim the text first. The *Coursebook* provides questions to check students' general understanding after this first rapid reading. Encourage the students to skim by setting a time limit, and making it into a competition to see who can answer the questions first. You can reduce the time limit as the students progress through the course.

It is best not to pre-teach new words in a text, as students need to develop ways of coping with new vocabulary they meet in the exam, so the Course does not normally include such exercises. Encourage students to use the context to work out the words they need to do the task (see Unit 1 page 10). Tell them to ignore words they don't need to understand because they are not tested or not necessary for understanding of the general meaning. Such items are often focused on in follow-up vocabulary tasks (see Unit 7 page 86).

Over to you tasks provide an opportunity for students to respond to the content of the text on a personal level and to put to use some of the vocabulary in the text to express their ideas.

Vocabulary tasks focus on collocations, prepositional phrases and such like from the text. (The *Exam Practice Workbook* provides additional follow-up work on vocabulary.)

Grammar

The approach to grammar in the course takes into account the fact that the FCE year is a year of revision and students have previously studied the major grammatical areas. The aim is to remind students of those areas tested in the exam and familiarise them with how they are tested. Therefore each grammar section is followed by a Use of English section which tests the grammar point. (Other points are also included.)

The key information about the grammar point is summarised in a **grammar file**. Further details are given in the reference section at the back of the book. Practice is provided through contextualised tasks, and there are opportunities for freer practice and personalisation. There is further consolidation of the grammar point, plus exam style practice in the *Exam Practice Workbook*.

The **grammar file** may be used as follows:

• For presentation of grammar

1 Ask different students to read out an example sentence each from the box.

2 Ask students to explain when we use the forms given and/or to explain the difference between alternative forms.

3 Ask prompt questions to practise the point.

See Unit 1, TB page 18.

• For checking answers

1 Use your own method of presenting the grammar point.

2 Students do the exercises in pairs or individually.

3 Tell students to check their answers by looking at the information in the **grammar file** before you check answers as a class. This should be done in pairs, because discussion, even in the mother tongue, is a useful way of encouraging students to work things out for themselves. If necessary, they can also refer to the information in the reference section at the back of the *Coursebook*. This will help to develop their reference skills.

Use of English 1

The task in this section is always either Part 2 (open cloze), Part 3 (key word transformation) or Part 4 (error correction). It includes examples of the grammar point in the preceding section as well as training in exam technique.

Except for Part 3, all tasks in Paper 3 are text-based, and the texts all have a title. It is important to train students to use the title to start thinking about the content, and to read and understand the whole text before attempting the task. The *Coursebook* always provides tasks which get students used to doing this, and help you to check their understanding before they start the task itself.

In early units, clues are provided to help students with the task (see Unit 3, page 37). As the course progresses, students are encouraged to keep a checklist of typical grammatical points tested, to help them become more independent in their preparation for the exam.

Listening

Note: The Listening and Speaking sections can be taught independently of the other sections.

For all parts of the Listening Paper, students should be trained to read the instructions and the questions carefully to help them predict what they are going to hear. The Coursebook always supplies pre-listening tasks to encourage them to do this (see Unit 2 page 20, Unit 10 page 120).

Vocabulary is not normally pre-taught in the course, as students need practice in coping with unknown words to prepare them for the exam. Vocabulary can be taught as a follow-up if desired. One way to do this is to photocopy the tapescript at the back of this *Teacher's Book* and use it for training in guessing meaning from context and/or dictionary work.

Earlier units provide guidance on tackling each task type, focusing on particular problems thrown up by the task. For example, for Part 3 multiple matching, it is especially

important to train students to review their answers, as one wrong answer can lead to another (see Unit 6 page 71).

As a follow-up, there is usually a task which asks students to respond personally to the content of the Listening text (see Unit 2 page 20, Unit 7 page 83).

Speaking (Paper 5)

The Speaking sections contain additional topic vocabulary related to the theme of the unit. Vocabulary to describe photographs is always provided in a colour-coded box. There may be exercises which focus on the vocabulary before the actual exam task (see Unit 3 page 33, Unit 5 page 59). Otherwise, you can follow the procedures recommended for the Lead-in above.

For all tasks, students are encouraged to refer to the **functions file** at the end of the *Coursebook*, which is introduced in Unit 2 (see page 21).

The practice simulates exam procedures. Students are encouraged from the start to work in groups and do timed practice, with one student acting as the examiner, and the others as candidates. For Part 2 Speaking tasks (individual long turn), the photographs for Candidate B are found at the end of the Coursebook. The examiner's scripts for Part 2 and 3 tasks are also at the end of the book. Ensure that students know exactly what they have to do. It is recommended that you put students into different groups each time and make sure that the roles of candidate and examiner are rotated.

Vocabulary

This section provides consolidation and extension of topic-related vocabulary, as well as regular and systematic practice in those lexical areas tested in Paper 3, for example: words with similar meanings, collocations, phrasal verbs, prepositions, word formation. (See Unit 1 pages 12–13 and Unit 2 page 24 for an introduction to lexical cloze and word formation.) It is always followed by a Use of English task which tests the types of vocabulary presented and practised. There is further consolidation work in the *Exam Practice Workbook*.

Recording and reviewing vocabulary

The *Coursebook* contains a great deal of vocabulary and students should be encouraged to record useful phrases and collocations that they meet during the course in their own vocabulary notebooks. Remind them to write an example sentence to help them remember the meaning. It is also a good idea for students to write down the different forms of a word to help them prepare for Paper 3 word formation (see Unit 2 page 25, **study tip!**).

It is very important that students organise their vocabulary notebooks in a way that helps them retrieve, review and memorise the vocabulary they record easily. They can divide their notebooks into sections, for example:

• topic-related expressions
• phrasal verbs – listed under the particle (e.g. *at, up,* etc.) or by topic (see Unit 3 page 28, Reading 1, Exercise 6)
• prepositional phrases by preposition (see Unit 5 page 54, Reading 1, Exercise 4), etc.

The *Coursebook* contains regular reminders to record vocabulary plus suggested ways of doing this.

It is a good idea to spend five minutes at the beginning of a lesson reviewing key vocabulary from a previous lesson. Here are some suggestions:

- Remind students of the topic of the text they read or listened to last lesson. Ask them to recall five new phrases or expressions they learned. Put them on the board as students call them out. Ask other students to give an explanation, example or definition.
- Choose your own set of phrases, and give students a quiz. Give them definitions, synonyms or antonyms. Students have to guess the items.
- Photocopy the text from the *Coursebook* and delete various items. Hand out copies to students, to fill in the gaps.
- Get students to test each other regularly. For homework, students choose words and phrases from the text, and prepare gap-fill sentences, using their dictionary to help them. Then they test each other in class.

Use of English 2

The task in this section is always either Part 1 lexical cloze, or Part 5 word formation. The content of the text is related to the unit theme. As with the other text-based parts of Paper 3, exercises are provided to encourage students to read the title and the whole text for general understanding before doing the task itself. In earlier units, clues are provided to help students with the task.

When students do the task, make sure they read the whole sentence before and after the gap to be sure of the meaning, before they make their choice.

When checking answers to lexical cloze tasks, focus on the reasons why one answer is correct. Ask for example:

Which word/phrase expresses the right meaning in this context?

Which word fits into the grammar before and after the gap? (Direct students' attention to collocation, dependent prepositions, verb patterns, etc.)

The Answer keys in this *Teacher's Book* often provide explanations of why answers are right or wrong.

Follow-up tasks in this section include suggestions for students to record lexical patterns in their vocabulary notebooks (see Unit 6 page 75, Unit 8 page 99).

Writing

The Writing sections cover all the types of writing used in the exam, with a special emphasis on the obligatory transactional letter (Part 1). The content of the writing task relates to the theme of the whole unit, so students should not have too much trouble with ideas or vocabulary.

Writing sections follow this pattern:

1 Students read a writing task, highlight key points to bear in mind when answering the task, and decide what register is appropriate.

2 They read and analyse a sample answer to the task. Each Writing section focuses on a key aspect relevant to the type of writing, for example:

Unit 1: style and register (for formal letters)
Unit 2: identifying what points to include in transactional letters
Unit 3: expanding notes into sentences (for transactional letters)
Unit 4: writing good introductions and conclusions (for articles)
(See **Coursebook Contents map.**)

Note: The sample answers are not perfect. In suggesting how they may be improved, students are developing awareness of the task requirements, which will help them review their own work more effectively. The **writing file** at the end of the *Coursebook* provides A grade model answers for each type of writing.

3 Students revise a key grammatical point relevant to the specific writing task, presented in a **Focus on grammar** section, for example:

Unit 2: polite questions – transactional letter asking for information
Unit 5: reported statements – transactional letter of complaint
Unit 9: participles – increasing range and variety of structures in a story
(See **Coursebook Contents map.**)

4 They plan their answer to a parallel writing task.

5 They write their answer.

We recommend that the preparation is done in class, while the writing is done for homework.

Students are always reminded to check their work for errors when they have finished writing. You can encourage this by providing time in the next writing class for students to exchange and check each other's work and suggest improvements. The *Exam Practice Workbook* provides another task for extra practice.

Organisation of the *Exam Practice Workbook*

The *Workbook* contains 12 eight-page units that mirror the themes of the *Coursebook* units. Each unit contains the following sections:

Vocabulary: This section provides recycling and consolidation of the vocabulary in Reading 1 of the *Coursebook*.

Grammar and Use of English: This section provides further practice of the grammar point, leading up to a Use of English task (open cloze, key word transformation or error correction).

Vocabulary: This section provides recycling and consolidation of the vocabulary in Reading 2 of the *Coursebook*.

Vocabulary and Use of English: This section provides recycling and consolidation of the material in the *Coursebook* Vocabulary section, and additional Use of English practice.

Reading: Every unit contains an exam style reading task, linked to the unit theme, for extra practice of reading skills and exam techniques. In Units 1–4, the reading task is the same as that in the *Coursebook*. From Unit 5 onwards, there is a third task type, which ensures students have regular opportunities to revise skills and techniques presented in previous units.

Writing: The *Workbook* provides another writing task related to the theme of the unit. It is usually the same type of writing as the task in the *Coursebook*, to ensure that students get maximum practice of each style of writing.

The consolidation exercises are intended to be set for homework after students have completed the relevant section in the *Coursebook*. There are cross-references from each *Workbook* section to the relevant *Coursebook* section, so that it is easy to see which exercises relate to each section.

The exam style **Reading task** may be allocated for homework at any point while students are working through the unit. Alternatively, it could be done in class to provide timed exam practice, for example as a follow-up to the photocopiable **Unit tests** provided at the end of this *Teacher's Book*.

After every two units, there is a **Progress review**, which provides further practice of the grammar and vocabulary in the previous two units. After every four units, there is a **Progress check**, which helps students to prepare for the **Progress test** in the *Coursebook*.

Organisation of the *Teacher's Book*

As well as this Introduction, the *Teacher's Book* contains the following sections:

Guide to the FCE exam: This includes an overview of each paper plus marking and assessment criteria. In addition, there is a detailed description of each task type, with suggestions on general ways of preparing for FCE.

Unit-by-unit teaching notes: These explain the rationale behind the exercises in the *Coursebook*, with annotated answers for all exercises and exam tasks.

Tapescripts (photocopiable): The tapescripts for all the listening tasks are at the back of the book for ease of photocopying. You may wish to photocopy them to do further work on analysing the Listening task, or for vocabulary teaching.

Unit tests (photocopiable): These test the grammar and vocabulary covered in the unit. There are five exercises in each test and a total of 25 items. The items reflect the five Paper 3 tasks, but for ease of administration and checking, they use discrete sentences rather than full-length texts.

Progress tests (photocopiable): These test the material covered in the previous units and are in the format of Paper 3. The answers to the tests are also provided in the *Teacher's Book*.

Sample OMR Answer sheets: In Papers 1, 3 and 4 of the exam, students indicate their answers by shading in the correct lozenge on an Answer sheet, which is then marked by an Optical Mark Reader (OMR). It is very useful preparation to give students practice in transferring their answers to the answer sheet before the exam. The sample sheets can be photocopied and used for this purpose. You may wish to use them with the Practice exam at the end of the *Coursebook*.

Guide to the First Certificate in English

Paper 1 Reading
(1 hour 15 minutes)

Format

Paper 1 consists of four parts. Each part contains a text with comprehension questions. The total number of questions is 35. The texts range in length from 350–700 words and may be taken from a range of sources, including newspaper and magazine articles, non-fiction and fiction.

Answering

Candidates indicate their answers by shading in the correct lozenge on an answer sheet which is then marked by an Optical Mark Reader (OMR). (See TB page 142.)

Marks

Two marks are given for each correct answer in Parts 1, 2 and 3. There is one mark for each question in Part 4.

Part	Task description and focus	Number of questions	Task format
1	Multiple matching: reading for the main points in a text	6 or 7	A text preceded by multiple-matching questions. Candidates must identify the main idea of a paragraph by matching paragraph headings or summary sentences to each paragraph.
2	Multiple choice: reading for detail and global understanding e.g. author's attitude, purpose of text etc.	7 or 8	A text followed by 4-option multiple-choice questions
3	Gapped text: understanding text structure	6 or 7	A text from which paragraphs or sentences have been removed and placed in jumbled order after the text.
4	Multiple matching: reading for specific information	13–15	A text preceded by multiple-matching questions. Candidates must match a series of prompts to the right parts of the text.

Preparing for Paper 1

In order to tackle Paper 1 successfully, students should be familiar with a range of different types of reading material. In addition to working through their *Coursebook*, they should be encouraged to read widely outside the classroom. As many exam texts are taken from newspapers and magazines, students should read these as often as possible to familiarise themselves with their style.

In the exam, the instructions specify the text type (e.g. magazine article, etc.) and the texts always have a title. Students should get into the habit of reading the instructions and the title to help them predict content. They should also draw on their own experience and knowledge of the topic.

Students also need to be familiar with different reading techniques, such as skimming, scanning and reading for detail, and should be able to use the appropriate technique for the given reading task.

Reading widely will help students to further develop their reading skills and broaden their knowledge of the world. To encourage reading outside class, they could be asked to bring articles to class regularly for discussion. They could also be encouraged to use Penguin *Graded Readers* for extensive reading practice.

Part 1 Multiple matching

The main reading skill required by this task is the ability to understand the main points of a text. The task should be done relatively quickly. Students are recommended to:

- skim the whole text for general meaning first. For non-fiction texts, this generally involves reading the whole of the first and last paragraph, and the first and last sentence of the other paragraphs (these usually contain the key information).
- read through the list of headings given to get an idea of the topics.
- read each paragraph in turn and highlight key words and phrases that express the main idea of the paragraph.
- look for the heading or summary sentence which paraphrases the main idea, i.e. uses different words to say the same thing.

Extra activities which can be used with any text to help students prepare for this task include the following:

- students write their own heading for sections of a text.
- students identify the topic sentence of each paragraph and rewrite it in their own words.
- students summarise each paragraph of a text in a given number of words.

Part 2 Multiple choice

This task requires more detailed reading of the text than Part 1. There are two types of question:

1 The stem is an incomplete sentence and the correct option completes the sentence in accordance with the content of the text.

2 The stem is a question and the correct option provides the answer.

The questions may test understanding at word, phrase, sentence, paragraph or whole text level. Most of the questions are about content. There may also be:

- a question testing reference, e.g. What does 'it' in a given line refer to?
- a question testing inference of meaning from the context, e.g. What does the writer mean by a word in a given line?
- a question testing global understanding, for example the purpose of the text, the writer's opinion, the source, etc. A question of this type would always be the last question.

Students are recommended to:

- read the whole text once quite quickly.
- look at the question stems without looking at the options.
- identify the part of the text that each question is referring to and try to answer in their own words.
- look at the options and choose the one that most closely matches their own answer.

In class, encourage them to discuss why the other three answers are not correct as this will help them to become aware of the possible traps, e.g. options that use words from the text but do not answer the question, or contain a word that changes the meaning of an otherwise correct answer, etc.

Part 3 Gapped text

This task tests understanding of text structure and organisation. The text requires detailed reading and is likely to take longer to complete than other tasks.

In order to do the task successfully, students need to develop a good grasp of:

- coherence – how ideas are developed either chronologically or logically through a text.
- cohesion – grammatical and lexical links between sentences and paragraphs. Grammatical links include use of tenses, pronouns, linking expressions and conjunctions. Lexical links include synonyms, repeated words and phrases.

When tackling the exam task, students are recommended to:

- read the whole of the base text first, without looking at the extracts, to get an idea of the development of ideas.
- read the text again paragraph by paragraph, try to predict what information comes in the gap, and look for an extract that fits the meaning.
- look for grammatical and lexical links before and after the gap.

Extra activities that can be used to help train students for this task include the following:

- ask students to identify all the cohesive devices in a text and the items they refer to.
- give students a text from which the cohesive devices have been removed and ask them to insert the missing items.
- cut up a text into separate paragraphs and ask students to work out the correct sequence using clues supplied by meaning, grammar and lexis.
- give students a text from which one paragraph has been removed and ask them to write the missing paragraph.

Part 4 Multiple matching (questions)

This is the longest text in the paper. However, the task does not require students to read the whole text in detail, and they should be discouraged from doing so. Instead, it requires scanning skills. Students are recommended to:

- read the questions first.
- scan the text to find the part that contains the answer to each question.
- read only that part carefully to check it answers the question correctly.

If students are not very proficient at scanning, it may be useful to give them easy tasks such as the following early in their course:

- tell students to look for all the numbers or proper names in a text.
- tell students to look for words in a text connected to a particular topic.

These can be done with any text.

Also, set a more generous time limit at first and then reduce it as the students become more proficient.

Paper 2 Writing
(1 hour 30 minutes)

Format

The Writing paper is in two parts and candidates have to complete two writing tasks using 120–180 words for each task. Part 1 is a compulsory question. In Part 2, candidates choose from four tasks.

Answering

Candidates write their answer in the question booklet.

Marks

Both questions carry equal marks.

Assessment

Each question is marked on a scale of 0–5. There is a 'general impression' mark scheme that applies to all questions and refers to general features such as:

- completion of the task
- the effect on the target reader
- accurate use of language
- use of a range of vocabulary and grammatical structures
- clear organisation of the material

This is used in conjunction with a 'task-specific' mark scheme, which focuses on criteria relevant to a particular task. These include relevance, register and presentation.

Part	Task description and focus	Number of tasks	Task format
1	Question 1: a transactional letter (formal/ informal)	1 compulsory task	Candidates are given input material of up to 250 words, which may include graphic and pictorial material. Input texts may include adverts, letters postcards, etc.
2	Questions 2–4: a choice from the following types of writing: an article; a non-transactional letter; a report; a discursive composition; a descriptive/ narrative composition; a story. Question 5 (set text): writing one of the above on a prescribed background reading text.	1 task from a choice of 4. Question 5 has a choice of 2 options	A writing task described in no more than 70 words.

Preparing for Paper 2

Part 1

In Part 1, the main focus is on completing the task fully, and on the use of appropriate style and register for the target audience. Students should:

- read the question very carefully and highlight the points that they must include in their letter.
- identify the target reader and choose the appropriate register required for the letter.
- plan how to organise the points that must be included, and identify any areas where they can expand on them without introducing irrelevant material.

When preparing students for Paper 2, the stages above are best done in class before setting a writing task for homework. It should be emphasised to students that planning before starting to write is far more effective than writing a draft then copying it out again.

When they write the letter, students must use the appropriate opening and closing formulae (e.g. *Dear Sir or Madam* in a formal letter when the recipient's name is not known). They should be encouraged to use their own words as far as possible and not 'lift' from the input. (There may sometimes be certain key words which are impossible to paraphrase, and it is acceptable to repeat these.)

Part 2

In Part 2, students are advised to select the question they answer carefully, bearing in mind their own experience and knowledge. They should only attempt Question 5 if they have a good knowledge of one of the set books listed.

The main test focus is on range of language as well as appropriacy of format and register. However, it is still essential for students to complete the task and keep the content relevant.

A **composition** should clearly answer the question set and should show a logical development of an argument. Paragraphing is very important here.

An **article** should have an eye-catching title and be written in a style that will attract the reader.

A **report** should be clearly organised and in an impersonal style. Headings may be used for each section of the report. It is not recommended to write a report in letter format.

A **story** should develop naturally from or lead to the given sentence. Candidates should be discouraged from trying to match a previously prepared story to the given sentence.

A **letter of application** must include all the points asked for and be written in a style and tone suitable for a prospective employer.

An **informal letter** should come to the point of the task quickly and not contain too much general exchange of news.

Paper 3 Use of English
(1 hour 15 minutes)

Format

Paper 3 contains five parts and a total of 65 questions.

Answering

Candidates write their answers on an answer sheet (see specimen OMR sheets on TB page 143).

Marks

Questions in Parts 1, 2, 4 and 5 carry one mark. Questions in Part 3 carry two marks.

Part	Task type and focus	Number of questions	Task format
1	Lexical cloze (multiple choice): emphasis on vocabulary	15	A modified cloze text containing 15 gaps and followed by 15 multiple-choice questions.
2	Structural cloze: emphasis on grammar and vocabulary	15	A modified cloze text containing 15 gaps.
3	Key word transformations: emphasis on grammar and vocabulary	10	Discrete items with a lead-in sentence and a gapped response to complete in 2–5 words using a given key word.
4	Error correction: emphasis on grammar	15	A text containing errors. Some lines contain an extra and unnecessary word.
5	Word formation: emphasis on vocabulary	10	A text containing 10 gaps. The stems of the missing words are given beside the text and must be changed to provide the missing word.

Preparing for Paper 3

To be successful in Paper 3, students need to have a good command of grammar and vocabulary at this level. To prepare for this paper, it is important that they record and learn words as parts of whole phrases rather than individually, e.g.:

advise somebody to do something
NOT
advise

This will help them to become aware of the grammar and collocational range of words as well as the meaning. Without this awareness, they will not be well equipped to deal with Paper 3 tasks.

Students should be able to use a monolingual dictionary such as the *Longman Dictionary of Contemporary English* to find grammatical information about words, as well as their meaning, typical collocations and fixed phrases. Encourage them to use dictionaries in class when doing Paper 3 exercises and to keep vocabulary notebooks.

Four of the five parts in Paper 3 are text-based and all the texts have a title to help students predict the content of the text they are about to read.

Part 1 Lexical cloze

This task tests not only the meaning of the words but also an awareness of the 'grammar' of words, for example, what preposition or verb form a word is followed by. Knowledge of collocations and fixed phrases is also tested.

Part 2 Structural cloze

This part tests structural accuracy. The gapped items are all words that will be well known to the students and include auxiliary verbs, prepositions, linkers, articles, pronouns, verb forms, etc. It is their usage in specific contexts that is being tested. Students should be trained to identify parts of speech in preparation for this task.

Part 3 Key word transformations

A wide range of structures and lexical phrases can be tested here, including conditionals, verb tenses, modal verbs, reported speech, the passive, phrasal verbs, verb/noun + preposition, gerund and infinitive, etc. Students must not change the word given and must not write more than five words. Students need to be aware of alternative ways of expressing ideas as preparation for this task.

Part 4 Error correction

The text for this task is at a level at which the students themselves might write and the task focuses on errors that FCE candidates typically make. The extra words may include auxiliary verbs, prepositions, articles and pronouns. Students should be aware that the clue to an extra word may not always be in the same line, so they need to look at each sentence as a whole. Having students find errors in their own work and that of their classmates is useful preparation for this task, and it should also help to improve their own accuracy when writing.

Part 5 Word formation

The types of word building in this exercise involve:
- the addition of prefixes and suffixes.
- internal changes (e.g. *long* → *length*).
- compounds (e.g. *time* → *timetable*).

Students should be aware of the uses of the main prefixes and suffixes and also the internal changes that can result from the addition of a suffix (e.g. *explain* → *explanation*). Train the students to use dictionaries to research the different forms of a word.

Paper 4 Listening
(approximately 40 minutes)

Format

The paper contains four parts with a total of 30 questions. Each part consists of a recorded text or texts and comprehension tasks. Each text is heard twice. Recordings contain a variety of English native speaker accents as well as non-native speaker accents that approximate to the norms of native speakers.

Text types

Recorded texts include both:
- monologues such as phone messages, commentaries, instructions, talks or lectures, news, advertisements, etc.
- conversations, discussions or interviews

Answering

Candidates transfer their answers to an answer sheet (see specimen OMR sheet on TB page 144).

Marks

Each question carries one mark.

Part	Task description and focus	Number of questions	Task format
1	Multiple choice: understanding gist, main points, detail, function, location, relationships, roles, mood, attitude, intention, feeling or opinion	8	Eight short unrelated extracts, approximately 30 seconds each. They may be monologues or dialogues. Multiple-choice questions with three options.
2	Note-taking or sentence-completion: understanding gist, main points, detail or specific information, or deducing meaning	10	A monologue or text involving interacting speakers and lasting approximately three minutes.
3	Multiple matching: as for Part 1	5	Five short related extracts, of approximately 30 seconds each. They may be monologues or interacting speakers. The questions require selection from a list of six options.
4	Selection from two or three possible answers: as for Part 2	7	A monologue or exchange between interacting speakers, lasting approximately three minutes. The questions require a selection, e.g.: true/false; yes/no; 3-option multiple choice.

Preparing for Paper 4

To prepare for Paper 4, students should be given the opportunity to hear as much spoken English as possible, from a range of sources.

In the exam, candidates are given time to read the questions. They should use this time to try and predict what they are going to hear, using the clues given by the task as well as their own knowledge of the subject and/or the situations. Pre-listening tasks in class can help students get used to doing this.

Part 1

In this part, the questions are all unrelated, so students can make a 'fresh start' on each one. They can both read and listen to the questions so they have plenty of time to think about the clues they are listening for. The question always makes the focus clear. It may require students to listen for: where the speaker is, the subject of the extract, the relationship between the speaker and listener, function (e.g. criticism, complaint, etc.), emotion, attitude, opinion or intended outcome.

Careful listening to meaning is required, as merely listening for words may lead to the wrong answer.

Part 2

In preparation for Part 2, students should be given ample practice in listening and note-taking.

For this task, students do not normally have to write more than three words. Paraphrasing is not expected, so students can expect to write words that they hear on the recording. The gaps follow the order of information in the recording, so if students have difficulty with one part, they should leave it and move on; otherwise they will not be able to fill subsequent gaps.

In the exam, candidates are given time to write out their answers on the answer sheet at the end, and students therefore do not need to worry about presentation while they are listening.

Part 3

This part consists of five separate extracts on a related topic. The task is to match each speaker to the correct item in a list, which contains one distractor, or false item.

Before listening, students should read the questions carefully to help them identify the main focus of each extract. It is important to train them to review their answers constantly, as one wrong answer can lead to another.

Part 4

In this part, there are three possible task types: multiple choice, true/false or matching. The matching task may involve choosing from two or three options, e.g. choosing A or B or both, or choosing A or B or neither. Students should be prepared for any of the possible task types.

Paper 5 Speaking
(approximately 14 minutes)

Format

The Speaking test has four parts. The standard format is two candidates and two examiners. One examiner acts as both interlocutor and assessor, and asks questions or provides instructions. The other acts as assessor and does not intervene.

Assessment

Candidates are assessed on their performance throughout the test according to the following criteria:

Grammar and vocabulary (accuracy and appropriacy): candidates are expected to know enough grammar and vocabulary to produce accurate and appropriate language to meet the task requirements without continual pauses to search for words and phrases.

Discourse management: examiners are looking for evidence that candidates can express themselves coherently in connected speech.

Pronunciation: candidates are expected to produce individual sounds, link words appropriately and use stress and intonation to convey the intended meaning.

Interactive communication: this refers to the candidate's ability to interact effectively with the interlocutor and the other candidate by responding and initiating appropriately and at the required speed and rhythm. Candidates should also show sensitivity to turn-taking and an ability to develop the task and move it towards a conclusion.

Part	Task description and focus	Length of part	Task format
1	Social interaction: giving personal information	3 minutes	Interlocutor interviews candidates.
2	Individual long turn: talking for a minute uninterruptedly, comparing, contrasting and commenting on photographs	4 minutes	Each candidate talks uninterruptedly for 1 minute in response to visual and verbal prompts. Each candidate is then asked to comment briefly on what the other has said (approximately 20 seconds).
3	Collaborative task: negotiating an outcome, problem solving	3 minutes	Candidates talk to each other in response to visual and verbal prompts.
4	General discussion	4 minutes	The interlocutor ask for the candidates' opinions on wider issues connected with the topic in Part 3.

Preparing for Paper 5

Each Part of the test focuses on a different type of interaction: between the interlocutor and each candidate, between the two candidates and among all three. In preparation, students need to practise talking individually and in small groups. To do well, they will need to be aware of the norms of turn-taking and of tactics for moving a conversation forwards.

Students should listen carefully to the interlocutor's instructions. Asking for repetition of instructions will not affect their marks in any way, whereas not answering the task set will lose them marks.

Part 1

The interlocutor asks the candidates questions in turn and there is not necessarily any interaction between the candidates. Here, one-word answers are not enough, so students should be ready to give full and informative answers. On the other hand, prepared speeches should be avoided as they are not part of good interactive communication.

Part 2

The candidates should listen carefully to the task and not merely describe the pictures. They are advised not to talk about each picture in turn, but to talk about the similarities and differences straightaway and then move on to the final part of the task. Timed classroom practice will help them to judge how much they can say in a minute and to pace themselves accordingly.

Part 3

Again, the candidates should listen carefully to the task set and remember that they will not be penalised if they ask for the instructions to be repeated. They should attempt to bring the other candidate back to the task if he/she moves away from it.

They are recommended to discuss as fully as possible the suggestions given to them in the form of visual cues, then try and reach an agreement. However, it is not necessary for them to agree, as it is the discussion and negotiation that are more important than the outcome.

Candidates should show that they are able to express their opinions, agree and disagree, respond to their partner's opinions, encourage their partner to contribute and move the conversation towards an outcome. It is important to make students aware that if they dominate the conversation, they will lose marks. Frequent classroom practice of discussion skills will prepare students for this part of the test.

Part 4

Here, candidates are asked for their opinions on different aspects of the topics in Part 3. The interlocutor may direct the questions towards individual candidates or to both. Students should be prepared to offer full responses with reasons and examples. They will also be given credit for developing the topic. Regular practice in backing up and expanding on their opinions is useful.

1 Entertainment

Lead-in (CB page 4)

The **Lead-in** is designed to start students thinking about the topic of the text and to introduce the vocabulary area. Focus attention on the photographs and discuss the questions as a whole class. Encourage students to use the expressions in the vocabulary box to help them answer the questions. Explain any items that are new. Teach any further items students need for the discussion.

PHOTOS

The top photo is from the American thriller, *Jaws*, about a man-eating shark.
The second photo is a still from the popular British romantic comedy *Four Weddings and a Funeral* starring Hugh Grant and Andie MacDowell.

Reading 1: *multiple matching*

(CB pages 4–5)

Focus attention on the **exam file** to introduce the task type. Explain that the exercises that follow will show students step by step how to do this kind of task.

1 Predict

Explain that the instructions and the title of the text are designed to help the candidate in the exam to predict the content of the text. Students should, as far as possible, take advantage of what they know about the subject to help them understand the text.

ANSWERS

1   The instructions tell you that this is an article about how a film is made.
3   Possible words:
types of film: thriller etc.
people: director, scriptwriter, actor
aspects of filming: special effects, scenery, costumes, make-up etc.

2 Skim for gist

Explain to students that it is always a good idea to skim read the text before they read it more carefully, just to get a general sense of the content and the organisation.

Draw students' attention to the **exam tip!**. Remind them that they can understand a lot about a text just by reading the introduction, conclusion and the first and last sentence of the other paragraphs.

Encourage students to skim the text for the answers, rather than reading for detail, by setting a time limit of 2–3 minutes.

Note: The question numbers refer to the paragraphs.

ANSWERS

0   False. 'the film-maker must have a clear idea of what the film is trying to say' (lines 2–3) 'the film-maker must be sure that the theme of the film will attract an audience.' (lines 11–13)
1   True. 'Unlike ... films in Britain usually begin with a script' (lines 14–17)
2   True. 'A film-maker has to show that he or she is able to put together a group of technicians ... '. (lines 30–32)
3   False. 'Directors usually form their own company.' (lines 34–35)
4   True. 'There are several organisations which provide financial support ...' (lines 41–42)
5   False. 'After the money has been raised, filming does not begin immediately ...' (lines 52–53)
6   True. 'Many people that you do not see in the film play a vital role.' (lines 60–61)

3 Reading task: *match headings*

The first part of the exercise draws students' attention to the fact that the headings will paraphrase the text. The multiple-matching task does **not** involve matching single words in the headings and text. Students need to learn how to look for ideas expressed in different ways.

ANSWERS

Ex. 3.1
1   what the film is trying to say
2   Different: the heading paraphrases the main idea.

Ex. 3.2
G   The first step. The key word in the text is 'begin'. The heading paraphrases this idea with the word 'first'.

Ex. 3.3
2A   'Able to put together a crew' (line 31)
3D   'Usually form their own company' (lines 34–35)
4B   'Organisations which provide financial support' (lines 41–42)
5F   'The film-maker plans the shoot' (lines 53–54)
6E   'Many people that you do not see in the film' (line 60)

Over to you

4 Vocabulary search/Discussion

The students can do this exercise in pairs. The aim is to encourage students to re-use language from the text. The discussion work is good practice for Speaking Paper 5, Parts 3 and 4.

Homework: ▶▶ *Exam Practice Workbook* page 4

Grammar: *present and future* (CB page 6)

Note: The **grammar file** summarises the key points practised in the lesson. Further information is included in the reference section at the back of the *Coursebook*.

See **Introduction** page 7 for suggestions on how to use the **grammar file**.

Presentation (1): *present tenses*

Here is a suggestion for presenting the present simple and continuous using the **grammar file**.

A/B Present simple/present continuous

Ask different students to read out an example sentence each from the file.

Ask further questions to practise the language point, e.g.:

How often do you go to the cinema?
Do you watch movies on TV or satellite?
What movies do you usually watch?
What are you doing right now?
What are you studying this term?

C *always*

Ask students to explain the difference between 'always' with the present simple and continuous. Emphasise that 'always' with the continuous usually implies annoyance on the part of the speaker.

D State verbs

Point out that some verbs, such as 'know, understand' etc., 'like, dislike', etc., are not used in the continuous form because they describe permanent states, not actions. But others, such as 'have, think, feel, see', can be used in either form, but with a change in meaning.

Read out the following examples and ask students to explain the difference in meaning.

*I **think** 'Titanic' is the best film ever made.*
(= opinion)
*I **am thinking** of going to see a film tonight.*
(= considering, planning)
*I **see** what you mean.* (= understand)
*Tom **is seeing** a lot of Mary these days.*
(= spending time with)

1 Practice: *gap fill*

Let students work in pairs to do the exercise. Encourage them to use the **grammar file** to help them. Looking out for key words such as adverbs and time expressions will be useful.

2 Practice: *question and answer*

This task provides oral reinforcement of the contrast between present simple and continuous in a personal context.

Presentation (2): *future tense forms*

Focus on the **grammar file**. Explain that the choice of verb form to refer to the future depends very much on the speaker's attitude about how likely it is that the future event will really happen.

Ask different students to read out the examples in **A–C** and ask: *What's the difference?* (See **grammar file** 5, CB page 178 for the answers.)

3 Practice: *gap fill*

Let students work in pairs, using the **grammar file** to help them. When you check answers, ask them to match each answer to an example in the grammar box.

4 Practice: *question and answer*

This exercise provides another chance for students to use the language in a personal context.

Homework: ▶▶ *Exam Practice Workbook* pages 4–5, Exercises 1–4

Use of English 1: *transformations*

(CB page 7)

Note: This lesson covers a number of structures tested in Paper 3 of the FCE exam. You can use it as a diagnostic lesson, to find out about the ability of your class. The structures are all practised in later units of the *Coursebook*.

Refer students to the **exam file** and the **exam strategy**.

1 Guided key word transformations

Students could do this exercise individually and then compare their answers in pairs before the class check.

2 Analysis of answers

The aim of this exercise is to help students identify what the grammatical transformation is. Being aware of what the question is testing will help them in the exam.

ANSWERS

Exs. 1/2
1 am thinking of recording (verb tenses – present continuous)
2 are you going to/planning to (verb tenses – future)
3 don't have to (modal verbs)
4 does not belong to me (change from one structure to another)
5 were you I would (conditionals)
6 last time I went (verb tenses – present perfect vs past simple)
7 do you pronounce (change from one structure to another)
8 must be followed (passive)

---

3 Identify common errors

The aim of this exercise is again to raise students' awareness of errors to avoid when doing this task type.

ANSWERS

1 am responsible for checking (c)
2 whether she was interested (d and e)
3 are included in (b)
4 doesn't feel like going (e)
5 works as hard as (a)

▶▶ *study tip!*

Focus attention on the *study tip!*. Point out that in order to do exam tasks successfully, students need to know how to use words accurately in sentences. When they note down new words, they should always record their grammatical pattern.

ANSWERS

study tip!
Further examples on CB pages 6/7:
verb + preposition
to look at, to complain about, to take over, to wait for (p. 6, Ex. 1); *to think of* (p. 7, Ex. 1)
expressions with gerunds / infinitives
to advise sb (not) to do sth (p. 7, Ex. 1)

Homework: ▶▶ *Exam Practice Workbook* page 5, Exercise 5

Listening: *extracts (multiple choice)*

(CB page 8)

Tapescript: ▶▶ TB page 105

Focus attention on the **exam file** to introduce the task type. Point out:

- this task is quite easy, as they hear the questions as well as the extract on the recording, and they hear each 30-second extract repeated immediately.
- each of the short extracts is completely separate, so they can focus on each new text individually, and don't need to think about the one before.
- each question focuses on one type of information only, depending on the content of the extract.

1 Strategy: *identify key words*

1 Explain that in the exam, candidates are given time to read through the questions. They should use this time to identify what they need to listen for by underlining key words in the questions and thinking about what they might hear.

ANSWERS

What does the speaker's friend <u>want to do</u>?

---

2 Explain that the recorded extract may contain misleading information, that could make them choose the wrong answer. They need to listen carefully for key words or phrases that will rule out all the options but the correct one.

ANSWERS

1 The conversation could be about buying tickets for a trip or for the theatre.
2 All the words might occur except 'scriptwriter', which relates to the topic of film.
3 Words for all the topics: ticket, seat, sold out, ticket agency, in advance, to cancel
4 theatre only: last night;
   trains or flights only: timetable, delay, departure

---

3 Let students listen to the extract twice, then elicit the answer.

ANSWERS

1 The correct option is B. The phrase that rules out every option except B comes at the end of the recording: 'Friday is the last night!' References to 'booking a flight or a train ticket' are designed as 'distractors' to mislead anyone who is not listening carefully.
2 The words in the recording are different from the questions.

2 🔲 Listening task

Focus attention on the **exam strategy** before playing the rest of the recording.

ANSWERS

2A 'They wouldn't give us the funding'
3C 'I began to make records, perform in public' ... 'The New Mozart'
4C 'I watched him on my favourite video'
5B 'Your own copy of the director's cut, a special version' ... 'material which has never been seen before'
6B 'They haven't started playing yet'
7A 'You can't hear them performing – it's completely soundproof'
8C 'I really think you have to give me what I paid for' ... 'I want to have the tickets that I paid for.'

3 🔲 Task analysis

Play the recording again section by section, and elicit the key phrases. Tell the students to shout 'STOP' when they hear the key phrase. Pause the tape to discuss.

Speaking: *interview* (CB page 9)

Tapescript: ▶▶ TB page 106

Refer students to the **exam file**. Point out that this part of the Speaking Test is important as it allows the examiner to form a first impression of the candidate.

1 🔲 Model interview: *content*

Play the recording a first time, to give students the chance to hear the type of questions that will be asked in Part 1 of the Speaking Test.

2 🔲 Model interview: *exam strategy*

Focus students' attention on the **exam strategy**. Play the recording again, and ask students to identify which candidate performed better.

ANSWERS

Maria's responses are too short. Carlos's responses provide the right amount of detail.

3 Error correction

Note: These answers would be too short in the real Speaking Test. They are used here to focus attention on common errors.

ANSWERS

1 I come from ... (present simple for permanent states)
2 I like the river very much. ('very much' should come after the object)
3 There are four (of us/people) in my family. ('There are' is used to answer the question 'How many?')
4 This answer is insufficient – the candidate should offer further details about his family, e.g. what his parents do, etc.
5 I need English to get a good job. (In a result clause 'for' is not used. It is used when followed by a noun, e.g. 'I need English for my job.')
6 I have been learning English for five years. (present perfect for activities happening up to the present + 'for' to express duration of time)
7 This answer is insufficient. 'Anything' as an answer to a question means 'I don't mind', e.g. What would you like to drink?' 'Anything.'
8 I prefer (to go to) the cinema. ('rather' and 'prefer' are not used together)
9 I like action movies best. ('the' is not necessary here)
10 I hope/I'm hoping to become an engineer. ('hope' is a verb here and therefore not preceded by 'to be')

4 Speaking task: *groupwork*

Role-play to simulate the exam is a regular feature of the course, and gives students the chance to practise to a time limit. Suggest that the 'examiner' stop the role-play after three minutes.

After they have prepared their own questions, students can change roles.

▶▶ *exam tip!*

Focus attention on the **exam tip!**. Emphasise that students should not give prepared speeches, but listen to the examiner's questions and answer accordingly.

Pictures at an exhibition

Note: The reading text in this section of the unit always introduces another aspect of the unit theme, in this case, the Arts.

Lead-in (CB page 10)

As before, the **Lead-in** is designed to start students thinking about the topic of the reading text and to introduce the vocabulary area. Focus attention on the pictures and discuss the questions as a whole class. Encourage students to use the expressions in the vocabulary box to help them answer the questions. Teach any further items students need for the discussion.

If the students don't have any ideas in answer to question 3, tell them two of the pictures (by Richard Smith and Gwen John) are mentioned in the reading text. One link between all three therefore is that they have an appeal for teenagers. Tell them they will find out more when they read the text.

> ### PICTURES
>
> The abstract painting is Riverfall, by Richard Smith. The painting of the girl is by Gwen John. These are both contemporary British painters.
> The surrealist painting is by Salvador Dali (b. 1904 in Figueras, Catalonia d. 1989).

Reading 2: multiple matching

(CB pages 10–11)

> ### BACKGROUND INFORMATION
>
> Liverpool is a large city in the north-west of England, and was an important port. The Liverpool Tate Gallery opened in 1988 as the first branch of the main Tate Gallery to be opened outside London. It houses one of the best selections of contemporary art outside the capital.

Explain to students that they are going to do a reading task like the one they did on pages 4–5. Before you focus attention on the **exam strategy**, ask them if they remember the strategy they used to do the task.

1 Predict

Discuss the questions as a class. Stress that there are no right or wrong answers here.

2 Skim for gist

Set a time limit of about three minutes for this task. Then discuss any differences between students' predictions and

the text. Tell students that they should always be prepared for their predictions to be different from the content of the text.

> ### ANSWERS
>
> **Exs. 1/2**
> According to the text, the answers are:
> 1 The management wanted to attract more young people to visit the gallery. (lines 24–27; lines 77–80; final paragraph)
> 2 The teenagers didn't know much about art and had to learn a lot about the background. (paras. 4, 5) They were worried about what their friends would think. (para. 5 lines 56–58) They had to agree on what works of art to put on show. (para. 5 lines 59–61)
> 3 They learned about art and about the work that goes into preparing an exhibition. (paras. 5, 7)

3 Reading task: match headings

Ask students to complete the task using the clues given.

> ### ANSWERS
>
> 1C 'The teenagers made their final <u>selection</u>' (line 17); 'A collection ... all related to the <u>topic</u> of adolescence.' (lines 19–20)
> 2E '<u>There</u> is still a <u>gulf between</u> them and the world of the art gallery' (lines 31–33)
> 3H 'I began to <u>understand</u>' (lines 42–43); 'I began to <u>find out more</u>' (lines 45–46)
> 4A 'Effort and commitment the teenagers had put into selecting the most <u>appropriate</u> works' (lines 52–54)
> 5B 'They all loved it' (line 61)
> 6D 'The Liverpool teenagers <u>learned</u> ... .' (line 74); 'the Tate management now have a better idea of how teenagers think.' (lines 88–90)
> 7F 'We are getting closer to that goal' (lines 104–105)

Vocabulary: using context

4 Meaning from context

The aim of this exercise is to show students what kind of clues to meaning are provided in any text. Awareness of context clues and the ability to use them are vital exam skills. Students should not use a dictionary to do the task. However, they could use one to check their guesses afterwards.

> ### ANSWERS
>
> 1 = to be allowed to look at
> 2 = attract (this synonym occurs in line 79)
> 3 = all of them agreed
> 4 = making you think of something similar. Word formation clues: <u>remember</u>, <u>rem</u>ind. It is not really a painting of water and reeds, but it reminds you of these things.
> 5 = calm

Over to you

5 Discussion

The students can discuss these questions in pairs or small groups. They are good practice for Part 4 of Paper 5 (Speaking).

Homework: ▶▶ *Exam Practice Workbook* page 6

Use of English 2: *lexical cloze*

(CB pages 12–13)

Focus attention on the **exam file** to introduce the task type. Point out that the task on page 13 is a lexical cloze task.

Emphasise that knowing the areas of language tested in the lexical cloze will help them to:

- tackle the task more confidently
- organise their vocabulary learning better.

Explain that they should learn whole phrases not just individual words.

1 – 6 Introduction to areas tested

These exercises introduce and practise each lexical area tested in this part of the exam. Students should work in pairs as this will encourage them to justify their answers. Encourage students to use dictionaries.

ANSWERS

Ex. 1.1
1 spectators (used for someone who watches an event or game)
2 viewers (used mainly for television)
3 onlookers (usually used for people watching unofficially)
4 audiences (for people who watch or listen to a performance – play, concert, show, etc.)

Ex 1.2
1 view (for everything you can see from a place)
2 glimpse (you glimpse something that comes into sight briefly)
3 task (a piece of work)
4 fee (an entrance fee is paid to enter a place)

Ex. 2.1
1 tells the story
2 extremely funny
3 different from
4 believed passionately
5 a huge success

Ex. 2.2
1b); 2e); 3d); 4c); 5a)

Ex. 3.1
1 mentioned that (informed/told *me* that)
2 advised him to (suggested, said *that he should*)
3 let him sit (allowed, permitted, authorised him *to* sit)
4 intends auditioning (want, hope *to* audition)
   Note: 'intend *to audition*' is also correct

ANSWERS

Ex. 3.2
a) verb + *that*: mention, suggest
b) verb + object + bare infinitive: let
c) verb + object + *to*-infinitive: advise, allow, permit, tell
d) verb + object + that: inform, tell
e) verb + *to*-infinitive: intend, want, hope
f) verb + *-ing*: intend
Notes:
'intend' can be used with *-ing* or *to*-infinitive

Ex. 4
1B; 2A; 3D; 4C

Ex. 5.1
1 look round
2 set out
3 gave up

Ex. 5.2 Possible answers
1 I *looked up* the new word in the dictionary.
   I was *looking through* an old photograph album and I found this picture of you on holiday.
2 It took a long time to *set up* the exhibition.
   It's a good idea to bring the plants in before the winter *sets in.*
3 Please *give* your homework *in* on Tuesday. OR I didn't want to go, but I finally *gave in.* When they moved, they *gave away* all their old books to friends.

Ex. 6
1A; 2C; 3A; 4D

7 Use of English: *lexical cloze*

Refer students to the **exam strategy** before they begin. Emphasise how important it is to understand the general meaning of the whole text before they try to fill in the gaps. Point out that the clues indicating which word is correct are not always in the same sentence as the gap, but may be in the sentence before or after.

Lead students through the task.

Tell them to look at the title and ask:

What information do you think a paragraph about video games might contain?
What are the good and bad aspects of video games?

Tell the students to read the first paragraph. Ask:

What may not be true?

Tell them to finish reading the text, then ask:

Why do companies want to sell violent video games?
What is the link between these games and our culture?

The students should then do the task. Ensure that they read the text through to check their answers before you do a class check.

ANSWERS

1D The other words don't make sense in the context. Also, they would be followed by prepositions: *result* in, *respond* to, *relate* to

2D Students must read the whole sentence to realise that the gap requires a linking word introducing a contrast. 'However' is not possible grammatically because it cannot link two clauses. So 'Although' must be the answer.

3C The only word with the right meaning in the context.

4B Collocation = 'increasing number'

5D The only word with the right meaning in the context.

6A The only word that fits grammatically and in terms of meaning.

7D The gap requires a linking word that adds something to the previous sentence.

8D 'take off' has the idiomatic meaning of 'be successful'

9C 10C 11B Students need to read the whole sentence to work out the meaning before they can fill in the gaps.

12B The other verbs require the preposition 'to'.

13A 'afraid' is the only option that can be followed by 'of'

14C 'fail' is the only option that can be followed by the *to*-infinitive

15B 'play a part' is a collocation.

Homework: ▶▶ *Exam Practice Workbook* pages 6–7

Writing: *formal letter of application*

(CB pages 14–15/179)

Use the **exam file** to tell students briefly what to expect in the Writing paper.

Before focusing attention on the **exam strategy**, ask students what they think are the key things to think about when writing:

a) a formal letter

b) a letter of application for a job.

Elicit that a formal letter should:

• have appropriate opening and closing formulae
  e.g. Dear Sir, Yours sincerely.

• not contain any colloquial expressions.

A letter of application should contain enough information to make the reader consider the writer for the job.

When going through the **exam strategy**, emphasise that a letter of application in Part 2 of the Writing paper must include all the points asked for. It should be set out like a letter, with a line space between each paragraph, or an indent, but candidates are not expected to write postal addresses.

1 Understand the task

Stress that students must read the question very carefully. Tell them they can highlight or underline key points on the exam paper.

ANSWERS

Ex. 1.1

Points to keep in mind:

• 'must be able to communicate in English'

• 'a full description of yourself'

• 'why you would like the job'

• 'when you would be available'

Ex. 1.2

Points e) and g) are not suitable for inclusion.

2 Read a sample answer

Students check if the sample answer:

• has covered all the necessary points

• sounds positive.

ANSWERS

1 Missing information: when the student would be available. (This answer would therefore not be given a pass grade.)

2 The following phrases suggest that the writer would like the job:
I would very much like ... , I love drama ... , I think it would be a fascinating experience. I have been dreaming of an opportunity like this for years.

Focus on style and register

3 Analyse the sample answer

The sample answer contains examples of formal and informal language. The aim of this exercise is to make students aware of the difference between appropriate and inappropriate language.

ANSWERS

Ex. 3.1

a) 'Dear Sir or Madam'

b) 'I have just read your advertisement ... '

c) 'I would like to be involved in your show because I think it would be a fascinating experience.'

d) 'I look forward to hearing from you.'

e) 'Yours faithfully,'

Refer students to page 186 of the **Writing file** for other expressions.

Ex. 3.2

Expressions that are too informal:

para. 2: 'I am off to university'

(better = I am going to university)

'... and guess what – I was the star performer!'

(better = and I played the main part.)

'I am also a great dancer.'

(better = I can also dance very well.)

para. 3: 'So you can see why my English is excellent, can't you?'

(better = As a result, I speak excellent English.)

Homework: ▶▶ *Exam Practice Workbook* pages 10–11

Focus on grammar

4 Present perfect/past simple

1 Students find examples of the grammar point in the sample answer.

2 Ask students to try to explain why each tense is used in the context before referring them to the **grammar file**.

ANSWERS

Ex. 4.1/4.2
Examples of present perfect tenses:
para. 1: 'I have just read' (recent past)
para. 2: 'I have acted in a lot of school productions.' (time **when** is not important)
para. 3: 'My family has spent a lot of time living abroad' (**when** is not important)
para. 4: 'I have always wanted to appear' (this is still true)
'I have been dreaming of an opportunity like this for years.' (focus on activity)
Examples of past simple:
para. 2: 'Last year we made a video film' (completed action at a stated time in the past)
'I was the star performer' (finished at a fixed time in the past)

3 Let students do the error correction task in pairs.

ANSWERS

Ex. 4.3
1 have just seen (recent past)
2 have played/have been playing (an action begun in the past that is still true)
3 have given (time not important)
4 Correct.
5 have appeared (when is not important)
6 recorded (at a fixed point in the past)
7 have ever taken (when not important)
8 have been trying (activity still continuing)
9 wanted ('want' is not usually used in the continuous)
10 have had (in our life)

Over to you

5 Writing task

Set this task for homework after preparing students in class. Do this by telling them to read the task, and asking:

1 What information will you include?
2 What style will you use?
3 How many paragraphs will you write? What will you include in each one?

You could put up a paragraph plan on the board for them to use.

ANSWERS

Dear Sir or Madam
para. 1: short introduction: reason for writing
para. 2: personal details/experience/reason for interest
para. 3: preferred dates
Close
Yours faithfully,

CRITERIA FOR MARKING

Content: personal information, experience, date preferred, reasons for wanting to be in the show.
Organisation: Letter format, clear organisation of points, suitable opening and closing formulae.
Register: Formal.
Effect on target reader: Would consider the writer for the job.

Homework: ▶▶ *Exam Practice Workbook* pages 10–11

Unit 1 Test ▶▶ TB page 117

2 Challenges

Lead-in (CB page 16)

The **Lead-in** prepares students for the reading text by giving them background information and helping them to predict the content.

Students can find the answers to Questions 1 and 2 in the caption to the photo on page 16. They should try to guess what happened to Shackleton and his crew on the basis of the caption and the photo of the ship. To encourage students to bring their knowledge of the subject to their reading, ask them to predict the kinds of conditions that explorers face in Antarctica.

PHOTOS

The first photo shows Ernest Shackleton dressed for an expedition to the frozen Antarctic.
The second photo shows his ship, the *Endurance*, in the Antarctic.

ANSWERS

1 Shackleton was an explorer.
2 He hoped to cross Antarctica on foot.
3 Accept any sensible guesses based on the photo caption and photos, e.g.: His ship got stuck in the ice/sank. Shackleton and his crew managed to reach safety.

Reading 1: *multiple-choice questions*

(CB pages 16–17/199)

Focus students' attention on the **exam file** to introduce the task type.

1 Skim for gist

Explain that the first reading is for general understanding. Tell students that they should not worry about understanding the parts they find difficult at this stage. Set a time limit of about three minutes for the first reading of the text.

ANSWERS

1 It got stuck in the ice.
2 By keeping occupied and therefore cheerful.
3 By taking them to Elephant Island and then going on to South Georgia.
4 Because she was impressed by his courage and leadership skills.

2 Strategy: *focus on the questions*

Tell students that a useful technique for this type of task is to read and try to answer the questions themselves, before they look at the multiple-choice options. In this way,

they are less likely to get confused by the options. For this reason the options have been separated for this task. (They are on page 199 of the *Coursebook*.)

Let students discuss Exercises 2.2 and 2.3 in pairs. Check answers as a class.

ANSWERS

2 Key words: greatest threat
    Lines 24–25: he would have to keep the 27 members of his crew in good spirits if they were going to survive
3 Key words: dragging ... small boats
    Line 38: the same words appear.
4 Key words: feel, reached
    Line 48: almost hysterical with joy
5 Key words: Why ... leave
    Lines 50–51: uninhabited and no ships ever visited it
6 Key words: It ... refer to
    Line 53: Taking one boat, he decided to set sail
7 Key words: How did the writer feel ... saw the small boat
    Lines 67–68: I was overcome by emotion and I wept
8 Key words: phrase ... summarises ... writer's opinion
    Line 79: ... knew how to motivate and inspire others

3 Reading task: *multiple-choice questions*

Students should now look at the multiple-choice options on page 199 and choose the ones that are closest to their own answers in Exercise 2. They could do the exercise in pairs using the clues given. Remind them to try to work out the meaning of words they don't know from the context.

ANSWERS

1B 'It has the power to move people deeply' (lines 7–8)
2D 'He paid great attention to the psychological condition of his men and responded immediately to any signs of depression or despair.' (lines 31–33)
3A
4D 'They were almost hysterical with joy' (line 48)
5B 'No ships ever visited it' (line 50)
6A
7D 'I was overcome by emotion and I wept' (lines 67–68)
8C '... is a tribute to Shackleton's leadership skills' '... knew how to motivate and inspire others' (lines 77–80)

Over to you

4 Discussion

Students can do Exercise 4.1 in pairs first. Let them use a dictionary if necessary to check the meaning of the adjectives. Alternatively, use the definitions below (page 26). Give them the definition and ask them to identify the correct adjective.

Exercise 4.2 allows them to respond to the content of the text.

Definitions

courageous – very brave

romantic – imagining life the way you would like it to be rather than the way it really is

reckless – doing something dangerous without thinking about the harm you could do to yourself or to others.

admirable – something or someone that deserves to be praised or admired

sensible – showing good judgement

inflexible – not able or willing to change

irresponsible – not thinking about the negative results of what you do

strong-willed – determined to do what you want

ambitious – determined to be successful

unconventional – behaving in a way that is different from the way people usually behave

selfish – caring only about yourself and not about other people.

ANSWERS

Ex. 4.1

Positive	Negative	Both
courageous	reckless	strong-willed
admirable	selfish	romantic
sensible	irresponsible	unconventional
ambitious	inflexible	

Ex. 4.2
Possible adjectives: ambitious, courageous, sensible, strong-willed, admirable

Homework: ▶▶ *Exam Practice Workbook* page 12

Grammar: *the past* (CB page 18)

Presentation

See **Introduction** page 7 for suggestions on how to use the **grammar file**.

Tell students to look at the **grammar file**. To prepare for Exercise 1, tell them to find and underline the time expressions that are used with each tense. Then ask them to give you further time expressions.

A **Past continuous**: In the (1760s), when, while, as

B **Past simple**: when, after that, later, next, then, before, + expressions referring to a fixed time, e.g. yesterday, in 1999, last week, in July, etc.

C **Past perfect**: As soon as, by the time, after, already, just, ever

1 Practice: *matching*

Tell students to read the left-hand column first, and make sure they understand what the text is about: *the race to put the first man on the moon*. Ask some questions to check general knowledge and comprehension, e.g.:

Who put the first astronaut on the moon? (The Americans)
Can you name the first man? (Neil Armstrong)

When did the first moon landing take place? (1969)
What was the name of the rocket? (Saturn)
How did the astronauts get from their rocket to the surface of the moon? (In the lunar module 'Eagle')
etc.

Let students do the matching exercise in pairs so that they can discuss the answers. Then check as a class.

ANSWERS

1d); 2i); 3g); 4b); 5e); 6f); 7a); 8h); 9j); 10c)

2 Practice: *gap fill*

Make sure students read the whole text first before they do the gap fill. Emphasise that this will help them do the gap-fill task more effectively.

BACKGROUND INFORMATION

Victoria Riches was a member of the first all-female expedition to the North Pole in 1997.

Ask comprehension questions to check understanding, e.g.:

Why did Victoria Riches want to go on the expedition to the North Pole? (She was bored with her job.)
Where did she read the article? (On the Underground train.)
What was her mother's reaction? (She was very interested.)
Why do you think the applicants had to take a selection test? (To find out if they were physically fit and psychologically suitable.)

Let students do the gap-fill task in pairs.

ANSWERS

1   was making (an action in progress)
2   had been doing (an action which happened over a period of time up to the action in 1)
3   happened (a single completed event)
4   was reading (an action in progress)
5   saw (a single completed event)
6   were looking (an action in progress)
7   were planning (an action in progress)
8   had ever achieved (referring to a time before 6 and 7)
9   was (referring to a state in the past)
10 had never wanted (referring to a time before 9)
11 did she wish (referring to a state in the past; 'wish' is not normally used in the continuous – see stative verbs, **grammar file 4 section 3**)
12 rang (a single completed event)
13 told (a single completed event)
14 was thinking (an action in progress)
15 had imagined (referring to a time before 12, 13)
16 (had) heard (an action happening before 16. The past perfect is not always used here as 'after' makes the meaning clear)
17 decided (a single completed event)
18 had to (the verb 'have to' is not used in the continuous)
19 finally heard (a single completed event)
20 had passed (an event happening before 19)
21 felt (a single completed state)
22 was just beginning (an action in progress)

Over to you

3 Discussion

This activity is useful practice for Paper 5 (Speaking), Part 4.

> ▶▶ **extra activity**
>
> Tell students to write about an experience that changed their lives, paying particular attention to past tenses.

Homework: ▶▶ *Exam Practice Workbook* pages 12–13, Exercises 1–6

Use of English 1: *structural cloze*

(CB page 19)

Refer students to the **exam file** to introduce the task. Stress that the missing words are all words that they will know, but the task tests whether they can use the words correctly in sentences. Throughout their course, students should pay attention to how these 'grammatical' words, particularly prepositions, are used.

Exercises 1–4 show students how they should tackle this task type.

1 Read the title and text

Stress to students the importance of reading the title. It contains clues to help them get a general understanding of what the text is about. Explain that they should always read the whole text first and make sure that they have understood the meaning before they start the exercise. There may be important clues later in the text to help them fill earlier gaps. (See the **exam tip!**.)

> **ANSWERS**
>
> 1 Gerow was a pilot, Griffiths an engineer.
> 2 To check that it was working properly.
> 3 Griffiths fell through the open door of the plane.
> 4 Gerow flew low over a frozen lake so Griffiths could jump off.
> 5 Because he slid a long distance over the ice.

2 Identify word types

It is important to train students to identify the kind of words they are looking for before they attempt to fill in the gaps.

> **ANSWERS**
>
> 2 The missing word is a preposition after 'responsible'.
> 3 Needs a preposition (a set phrase).
> 4 Infinitive with 'to' (because it is followed by 'carry' not 'carried').
> 5 Here the linking word must be a preposition.
> 6 A linking word of time is needed.
> 8 The sentence is about Griffiths.
> 11 A modal verb is followed by a bare infinitive.

3 Gap fill

Students can do the exercise in pairs to encourage them to justify their answers. Tell them that it is not necessary to fill in the gaps in sequence. They should first fill in the words they are sure of. This may help them with the more difficult words.

> **ANSWERS**
>
> 1 had; 2 for; 3 in; 4 to; 5 on/of; 6 when; 7 out; 8 his;
> 9 were; 10 what; 11 could; 12 above/from; 13 and;
> 14 was; 15 towards

4 Check answers

Students should always read the whole text again to check for meaning and spelling. Always allow time for checking answers so that they get into the habit of doing this.

Homework: ▶▶ *Exam Practice Workbook* page 13, Exercises 7–8

Listening: *sentence completion*

(CB page 20)

Tapescript: ▶▶ TB page 106

Focus students' attention on the **exam file** to introduce the task type. You can tell them that:

- in the exam they are given time at the end to transfer their answers onto a mark sheet so they don't need to worry about writing neatly when they are listening.
- they will hear the recording twice so they should not worry about information they have missed on the first hearing.

The first two exercises are designed to help students predict the content of the recording and to use their previous knowledge of the subject.

1 – 2 Strategy: *predict content*

Tell students that in the exam they are given time to read the questions before they hear the recording. They should use this time to get an idea of what they are going to hear.

Students can discuss the questions in pairs. Remind them that there are no right or wrong answers, they are just guessing at this stage.

ANSWERS

Ex. 1
1 Mountaineer
2 The questions possibly included:
   'What was your worst experience?'
   'Who do you like to travel with?'
   'Who was your worst travelling companion?'
   'What is your opinion of climbers?'
   'What do you do to relax?'

Ex. 2
1   A book/TV documentary
2   Some kind of activity holiday, possibly a school trip
3   Leg, back, neck
4   On a wall in his house
5   A place
6   Contract/deal/plan
7   A job
8   Negative (the word 'too' indicates this)
9   Travel/climbing/adventure
10 A place

3 **Strategy:** *writing correct answers*

Although students only have to write words they hear on the recording, they still have to make sure the words fit the framework of the gapped sentence. The task is not a listening dictation. This exercise focuses attention on the mistakes they should avoid.

ANSWERS

1   magazine
2   skiing

4 🔊 **Listening task**

1 Play the recording once and ask students to complete as many sentences as they can. They can then compare their answers in pairs and identify exactly what they each need to listen for during the second hearing.

2 When students have completed the listening task, ask them to check their own answers in the same way as in Exercise 3.

ANSWERS

1	magazine	6	plan
2	skiing	7	journalist
3	back	8	selfish
4	desk	9	science fiction
5	tent	10	parks/the park/a park

Speaking: *individual long turn*

(CB page 21)

Tapescript: ▶▶ TB page 107

Refer students to the **exam file** to introduce them to the task type. Then go through the *exam strategy*. Emphasise that:

• they should not just describe each picture in turn, but should concentrate on the similarities and differences between them and then make comments about the content according to the instructions.

• when asked to comment on his/her partner's photographs, the second candidate should talk for a maximum of 20 seconds and should not launch into a long speech.

1 🔊 **Understand the instructions**

Tell students that it is very important to listen carefully to the instructions and not be distracted by the photos. Play the first part of the recording (Exercise 1) which goes up to 'You have only about a minute for this.' Elicit answers to the questions.

ANSWERS

1   The theme is 'travelling in remote areas'.
2   The task is to compare and contrast the photographs and say what dangers people face in those areas.

2 **Compare and contrast photos**

As this is the first time students have done this task, do this exercise with the whole class. Begin by focusing attention on the vocabulary box. Ask students to identify which words and expressions relate to which photo.

Then ask one student to do the first part of the task, saying what is similar and what is different in the two photos. Ask another student to say what dangers people face in places like these, using some of the expressions in the box.

PHOTOS

Photo 1 shows an icy landscape. A team of huskies is pulling a sledge over the frozen snow (huskies are a breed of dogs specially bred for this type of work in icy conditions). There are three men on the sledge.
Photo 2 shows a man on horseback. He is in the Australian outback, a very dry area, almost desert.

3 – 4 🔊 **Model interview:** *exam strategy*

Students can now listen to two candidates talking about the same photos and analyse their performance. Remind them of the *exam strategy* in the box.

Play the recording for Exercise 3 once, and give students the opportunity to discuss Question 1. Questions 2–5 focus on how well the candidate performed in the listening task. Play this part again if necessary.

Play the next part of the recording for Exercise 4 and discuss the questions.

ANSWERS

Ex. 3
2–4   The candidate completes the task fully and speaks
       without too many pauses.
5   She didn't know 'sledge' and paraphrases it: 'something
     for transport that is pulled by dogs'. Paraphrase is an
     important exam technique.

Ex. 4
1   The examiner asks: 'In which place is it more difficult to
     survive?'
2   Various answers possible.
Note: Iannis's answer is a good one. He answers the question
and he does not say too much.

5 **Speaking task:** *pairwork*

Tell students to turn to the photos on CB page 202. Put
them into pairs, and allocate roles: Candidates A and B.

PHOTOS

Photo 1 shows a man wearing cycling gear. He is running up
a hill, carrying his mountain bike over his shoulder.
Photo 2 shows a mountaineer climbing a mountain. It looks
as if it is snowing.

1 Play the next section of the recording, which
contains the Speaking task for Candidate A: *'Compare and
contrast these photos, saying why people choose to do
activities like these.'* Tell the As they have one minute to
talk about their photos. Point out that they have some
vocabulary in a box to help them.

Stop the pairwork after one minute, but let students
continue if they wish to.

2 Play the instructions for Candidate B: *'Can you tell
me which of these activities you would prefer to do?'* Give
the Bs 20 seconds to respond.

Note: Giving students this kind of timed practice will
prepare them effectively for the exam, in which they have
to say as much as they can in a short time.

Adventure sports

Note: The reading text introduces another aspect of the
unit theme, and moves on to the topic of adventure sports
and activities.

Lead-in (CB page 22)

The exercises in the **Lead-in** focus on key vocabulary for
sports and equipment that students may not know, and get
them thinking about the topic of the text they are going to
read.

For the scanning task in Exercise 2, set a time limit of
1–2 minutes, then ask who has found the most answers.
Stress that students are not being asked to read the text in
detail but merely to find the words referring to sports and
equipment.

PHOTOS

From the left:
In the first photo, the people are shooting arrows from a bow.
They are probably shooting at a target which is not shown in
the photo. The sport is archery.
In the second photo, the girl is exploring an underground
cave. She is wearing a helmet with a torch, and waterproof
jacket. The sport is caving.
The girl in the third photo is abseiling from a bridge. She is
wearing a helmet and safety harness. (Abseiling = going down
a cliff, rock or other vertical surface by sliding down a rope
and letting your feet touch the side of the cliff or other
surface.)
In the fourth photo, the man is climbing a rockface, wearing a
helmet and safety harness. The sport is rock-climbing.

ANSWERS

Task 1
See PHOTOS for information for discussions.
Task 2
a) Caving, abseiling, archery, hillwalking, an assault course,
    canoeing, orienteering, rock-climbing
b) Helmets with torches, harness, safety rope

Reading 2: *multiple-choice questions*
(CB pages 22–23)

Tell students that they are going to do a multiple-choice
task like the one they did for Reading 1 on pages 16–17.
Elicit what they remember about the best way to tackle this
type of task, then refer them to the **exam strategy** box to
check.

1 **Predict**

The aim of this exercise is to encourage students to bring
their own knowledge and ideas to their reading. Ask

students to read the sub-heading and the first paragraph and not to read any further. They should then answer Questions 1–3.

> **ANSWERS**
>
> 1   The members of the group were a social worker, an engineer, an aromatherapist (someone who uses massage with pleasant-smelling oils to reduce pain and make you feel well), a student
> 2, 3   Various answers possible.

2   Skim for gist

Set a time limit of 2–3 minutes for reading the rest of the text and ask students if their predictions in Exercise 1 were correct.

3   Reading task: *multiple-choice questions*

Students should follow the exam strategy to do the task. Set a time limit of 15 minutes. When you check answers to the reading task, get students to justify their choices.

> **ANSWERS**
>
> **Ex. 3**
> 1D   'an escape from our everyday life.' (lines 2–3)
> 2A   'hard work.' (line 25)
> 3C
> 4B   'different wind conditions ... different story.' (lines 55–56)
> 5C   'there was no way she was doing it' (lines 61–62)
> 6D   'just when we thought ... any more challenging.' (lines 75–76)
> 7B   'I lost my nerve.' (line 85)
> 8A   'pumping adrenaline' (line 99) (adrenaline is a chemical produced by your body when you are afraid, angry or excited; it makes your heart beat faster so that you can move quickly)

Vocabulary: *idiomatic expressions*

4   Vocabulary search

The aim of the exercise is to focus students' attention on the style of a text, and how style differs depending on the target reader and the type of publication. Awareness of this will help them both with Paper 1 and Paper 2 Writing, where they have to produce writing in an appropriate style.

1 Students can do the word-search exercise in pairs. Let them use their dictionaries if necessary. During the class check, ask them if the words in the text are formal or informal and idiomatic (they are informal and idiomatic).

2 Students should have identified the words in the text as informal and idiomatic. This will help them to answer these questions about style and target reader.

> **ANSWERS**
>
> **Ex. 4.1**
> 1   bunch   5   have a go
> 2   take a swig   6   my knees turned to jelly
> 3   got round to   7   he had to be kidding
> 4   have a great time   8   raved about
>
> **Ex. 4.2**
> 1   a) Quite informal, shown by use of idiomatic expressions and phrasal verbs. Other examples include, e.g.: 'had in store for us' (line 5), 'let themselves in for' (line 18)
>   b) personal – written in first person with personal reactions, e.g. 'That's my excuse, anyhow!' (line 56)
>   c) humorous
> 2   The article was written for a magazine aimed at young people from teens to late twenties.

Homework: ▶▶ *Exam Practice Workbook* page 14

Vocabulary   (CB page 24)

This section prepares students for the word formation task in Paper 3 Use of English.

1   Word-formation rules

Go through the information in the box with the class. For each point, 1–3, elicit some more common prefixes, suffixes and internal changes. You could choose some words from Reading 2.

For example:

1 Adding a suffix
Ask students to give you
- the adjective from 'adventure' (adventurous)
- two nouns from 'perform' (performer, performance)

2 Adding a prefix
Ask students to tell you the negative form of
- appear (disappear)
- friendly (unfriendly)

3 Internal changes
Elicit the adjective forms of
- broad (breadth)
- high (height)

2 – 7   Practice

Let students do Exercises 2–7 in pairs and use their dictionaries where necessary. You can check as a class after each exercise, or after students have completed all the tasks.

Before checking their answers, draw students' attention to the **! spelling** box. Do the exercise, then ask students to spell some of their answers to the exercises to emphasise the importance of correct spelling.

Ex. 2 Nouns from verbs
1 exploration
2 decision
3 entrance
4 equipment

Ex. 3 Names of jobs
1 navigator – the person who plans what direction a ship or plane travels in.
  Other jobs – actor, doctor, sailor, author, instructor, solicitor
2 engineer – the person who designs roads, bridges, machines, etc.
  Other jobs – mountaineer
3 historian – someone who teaches and/or studies history.
  Other jobs – musician, technician, mathematician
4 therapist – someone who provides therapy or treatment.
  Other jobs – artist, psychologist, typist

Ex. 4 Adjectives from nouns
1 courageous
2 romantic
3 ambitious
4 sensible/sensitive
For definitions of these words, see Reading 1, Exercise 4, TB page 26.

Ex. 5 Nouns from adjectives
1 activity
2 ability
3 ingenuity
4 reality
Note the spelling changes in 1–3; all end in -ity.

Ex. 6 Negative prefixes
A uninhabited/unfortunate
B dishonest/disagreeable
C impatient
D irresponsible
E incredible/inhospitable

Ex. 7 -ed/-ing endings
1 bored
2 stimulating
3 interesting
4 challenging
5 terrified
6 frightened

8 Learner training

Students can do Exercise 8 for homework and write their lists in their Vocabulary notebooks. Point out that each word class has a limited number of typical endings, and becoming aware of these will help them in the exam. They should take their examples from the exercises in this section. They should add to their lists as they come across more endings.

1 -ance, -ment, -ity, -or, -ian, -ist
2 -able, -ible, -ous, -ic, -ing, -ed
3 in-, dis-, im-, il-, ir-

! Spelling
The correct spellings are:
1 explanation
2 attendance

Use of English 2: *word formation*

(CB page 25)

Refer students to the **exam file** to introduce them to the task type. Point out that the text is written as a paragraph, so this gives them more context clues to help them with the task.

1 Read for general understanding

Highlight the importance of reading the text through first. Students will need to understand the general meaning in order to identify the correct form of the words.

Elicit answers to the questions. Ask students to identify the activities in the photos.

1 An advertisement/a brochure
2 An activity holiday

PHOTOS

Clockwise from the top left, the photos show young people:
sitting round a campfire on the beach, cooking food over the fire
cliff walking (walking along a cliff by the sea)
horseriding
canoeing
painting
white water rafting

2 Word-formation task

Emphasise to students that they should think about the type of word needed in the gap. They also need to be aware that the word could be singular or plural, positive or negative, first person or third person, etc.

Students can do this exercise in pairs to encourage them to justify their answers.

1 mountaineering (noun)
2 inexpensive (adjective, negative)
3 qualified (adjective)
4 interested (adjective)
5 unfit (adjective, negative)
6 instructors (noun, plural)
7 ability (noun)
8 active (adjective)
9 musicians (noun, plural)
10 discouraged (adjective, negative)

3 Check answers

Remind students of the importance of correct spelling.

4 Analysis of answers

Identifying what they had to do to form the missing word will help students gain a greater awareness of what the task is testing.

ANSWERS

a) 0, 1, 2, 3, 4, 6, 7, 8, 9, 10
b) 2, 5, 10
c) 6, 9
d) 1, 2, 6, 10

▶▶ *study tip!*

Focus attention on the *study tip!*. For practice, you could tell students to note in their Vocabulary notebooks the other possible forms of the words in the Use of English task:

verb	adjective	noun
vary	varied	
	various	variety

Homework: ▶▶ *Exam Practice Workbook* page 15

Writing: transactional letter

(CB pages 26–27)

Refer students to the **exam file** to introduce Part 1 of the Writing paper. Then go through the **exam strategy**. Emphasise that:

- they must read the task very carefully, and include all the points of the information they are told to include. They should not change such information as dates or times, etc., that are in the task.
- the style should be suitable for the intended reader and should be the same throughout the letter.
- they will lose marks if they do not include a suitable greeting and ending, e.g. Dear Sir/Mr Brown.

Ask what style would be appropriate for a letter to:

a) a friend (informal)
b) a person they have never met but are going to stay with (formal)
c) a businessperson (formal).

Discuss what 'a positive effect on the reader' means:

a) the reader should not be made to feel angry or insulted even if it is a letter of complaint.
b) the reader should have all the information they need.

1 Understand the task

1 Elicit the answers from the class. Ask what the Centre Manager will be required to do as a result of the letter (reply to all the queries and reserve a place on the chosen course).

2 Tell students that they should look at all parts of the input, not just at the advertisement to find the points they need to include.

ANSWERS

1 The letter is to the manager of the activity centre; the style should be formal.

2 Points to be underlined:
 a) In the Manager's letter:
  - which type of break
  - the date you wish to come
  - any more information?
 b) In the brochure:
  - someone to meet me at the station?
  - any single rooms?
  - beginners too?
  - suitable clothing?

Focus on planning and organisation

2 Make a paragraph plan

Point out that students need to organise the information they must include in a logical way, and not just cover the points in the order in which they appear in the task. Students could discuss these exercises in pairs or you could do them as a class, and put up the paragraph plan on the board.

ANSWERS

1 Missing points: the date, beginners too?

2
Information to supply:	*Questions to ask:*
· type of break I want	· Will someone meet me at the station?
· the date I wish to come	· Are there any single rooms?
	· Can beginners take part?
	· What clothing should I bring?
	· Any other questions?

3 Possible order:
 Para. 1 Introduction: type of break I want
 Para. 2 date I will come; someone to meet me at the station?
 Para. 3 single rooms?
 Para. 4 beginners? clothing?
 Conclusion

3 Analyse the sample answer

By analysing a sample answer and identifying how well the writer has completed the task, students are shown how to plan and check their own work.

Note: Point out that this is only part of the answer and therefore the task is not complete.

ANSWERS

Ex. 3.1
1 Five points are covered in the extract.
 They are: type of break, date, 'someone to meet me at the station?', 'any single rooms?', suitable clothing.
2 The writer has not copied more than is necessary from the input material.
3 The sentence 'I have some queries about sleeping arrangements and clothes' introduces a new topic, so there should be a new paragraph here.
4 Answers will vary.

Ex. 3.2

1   The style is mostly in an appropriate neutral style. 'Thanks a million' is too informal.
2   The letter should end 'Yours sincerely'.

Focus on grammar

4   **Indirect questions**

Discuss the questions. Ask students to rewrite the indirect questions in the sample answer as direct questions and then elicit the changes in word order and punctuation.

Refer students to the **grammar file** to confirm their answers to Exercise 1 before telling them to do Exercise 2 in pairs.

Ex. 4.1

Indirect questions in the sample letter:
I wonder whether someone could possibly meet me at the station.
Could you tell me if there are any single rooms?
I wonder if you could also tell me what sort of clothes to bring.

1   The writer uses indirect questions to make the letter more polite and the tone less abrupt.
2   The following expressions are used to introduce the indirect questions: *I wonder whether/Could you tell me ... ?/I wonder if you could tell me ...*
3   The word order is the same as a statement. There is no question mark unless the introductory phrase is a question (see **grammar file** 14 CB page 181).

Ex 4.2

1   I was wondering if it's possible to go caving without any previous experience.
2   I'd be grateful if you could tell me what the maximum number of people in each activity group is. OR ... what the maximum number of people is in each activity group.
3   Possible answers are: I'd like to know if/whether there is a fitness room in the activity centre.
4   Could you tell me if/whether I can hire walking boots at the centre or whether I have to bring my own?
5   I was wondering if you could tell me whether you offer discounts for groups. OR Could you tell me whether you offer discounts for groups?

Over to you

5   **Writing task**

Set the writing task for homework.

Content: type of break, date; queries about being met at the station, single rooms, suitable clothing, beginners.
Organisation: letter format, clear organisation of points, suitable opening and closing formulae.
Register: Formal or neutral. Must be consistent.
Effect on target reader: Would be able to reserve a place and would be able to answer all the questions.

Homework: ▶▶ *Exam Practice Workbook* pages 18–19

Progress review 1 (Units 1–2) ▶▶ *Exam Practice Workbook* pages 20–21

Unit 2 Test ▶▶ TB page 118

3 Education

Lead-in (CB page 28)

Focus students' attention on the photos at the top of page 28. Ask them what school subjects are illustrated. Elicit names of more school subjects. Ensure you cover the subjects in the vocabulary box. Discuss Question 1.

Tell students to do activity 2 individually, then compare their answers in pairs. As a class, find out if there are any differences in the rankings for each question. It may be that one subject is at the top of one list, but at the bottom of another list.

Alternatively, simply ask students to say which two subjects:

• are their favourite/least favourite.
• are most enjoyable/least enjoyable.
• are most useful/least useful.

PHOTOS

From the left, the photos on page 28 illustrate: Design Technology, Biology and Geography.
The photo on page 29 shows fashion models on a catwalk in a fashion show.

Reading 1: *gapped text (sentences)*

(CB pages 28–29)

Refer students to the **exam file** to introduce the task type. Tell students to read the task instructions on page 29 and find out if sentences or paragraphs have been removed from this text. (Texts where paragraphs have been removed will be practised later in the book.)

Ask students what they think is meant by 'language links' and 'topic links' (**exam file**).

Language links include: link words like *but/however*, pronouns (*he, she*, etc.), articles (*a, the*).

Topic links: this phrase refers to the way the ideas in the text are developed.

1 Predict

The aim of this exercise is to pre-teach some key vocabulary items, as well as to start students thinking about the topic of the text.

Discuss the questions as a class. Elicit all the information that students learn from the title, sub-heading and first paragraph. Elicit or explain the meaning of the vocabulary items.

Ask students what information they expect the article to contain, e.g.: a description of Susan's modelling work, her reasons for wanting to continue her studies.

ANSWERS

1 The text is about a young British model who is still at school. She is modelling in her holidays. She doesn't want to give up her school work for a modelling career and so she is modelling in the holidays ('holiday job').

2 a) a 'supermodel' is a fashion model who is very famous and earns much more money than ordinary models.
   b) 'catwalk': the long stage that models walk down in a fashion show.
   c) a 'contract' is a work agreement; 'six-figure' refers to the sum of money that is offered: if it is six figures, it must be $100,000 or more.

2 Read the base text

Emphasise to students that they should read the **whole** of the base text **before** they look at the sentences that have been removed. If they have a good understanding of what the text is about, they will find it easier to do the task.

Students should be allowed longer to read the gapped text than the other task types as it requires more detailed study of the text. Allow them about five minutes before discussing the answers to the questions, which check comprehension of key points in the text.

ANSWERS

1 Susan was discovered at the age of 14.
2 School has been more important than modelling.
3 By paying for her studies at university.
4 Paras. 2–5 refer to the past, paras. 1, 6–8 refer to the present, para. 9 refers to the future.

3 Strategy: *identify language links*

These exercises show students what kind of language links to look for between the text and the sentences that have been removed. They are best done as a class.

ANSWERS

Ex. 3.1
1 Reference words – pronouns, link words, articles.
2 Sentences A, C, D, F, I are in the past; B, E, H are in the present; G is in the future tense.

Ex. 3.2
1 How and where she was discovered.
2 Susan.
3 Because the agent must have been mentioned before.

4 – 5 Reading task: *match sentences to gaps*

Set a time limit of about 10 minutes. Let students compare their answers in pairs before checking as a class.

ANSWERS

1F This refers back to 'tiring and confusing' and the fact that the other girls had no work.

2A 'There' refers back to New York, and the sentence introduces the next paragraph where she begins to be successful.

3C 'Them' refers to the talent scouts; 'instead' refers to staying in London rather than going to the States; 'the job' is for Cover Girl; 'so' indicates that the sentence is a consequence of the previous one.

4G 'The contract' refers to the job with Cover Girl. The topic links with the main subject of the sentence, which is Susan not wishing to miss school.

5H 'This' refers to fitting work into the school holidays.

6B 'But' connects the main idea of the paragraph, i.e. Susan is constantly being offered work, with the fact that she turns it down. 'She' refers to Susan.

7E 'On the other hand' introduces an advantage to follow a disadvantage. 'Also realises' refers to 'knows her own mind' in the previous sentence.

Vocabulary: *phrasal verbs*

6 Vocabulary search

Tell students to look at the sentences that have been removed when looking for the phrasal verbs in Exercise 6.1.

Encourage them to try and work out the meaning of the phrasal verbs from the context rather than use dictionaries. Point out that they will not have dictionaries in the exam and so they need to practise working out meanings for themselves.

Remind students to write an example sentence when they add the verbs to their Vocabulary notebooks. Students can do this for homework.

ANSWERS

1 'to sign someone up' – to give someone work (line 9)
2 'to whisk someone off' – to take someone away quickly (line 14)
3 'to insist on doing something' – to be determined to do something (line 40)
4 'to catch up on something' – to finish something that you were not able to do earlier (line 47)
5 'to get through something' – to finish (line 59)
6 'to turn something down' – to refuse an offer (sentence B)

Over to you

7 Discussion

This activity provides useful practice for Paper 5 (Speaking), Part 4. You can do it as a pairwork discussion or as a class.

Homework: ▶▶ *Exam Practice Workbook* page 22

Grammar: -ing *forms and infinitives*
(CB page 30)

See **Introduction** page 7 for suggestions on how to use the **grammar file**.

Presentation

Tell students to look at the **grammar file**.

A *-ing* forms

- Elicit verbs or expressions with similar meanings to 'enjoy' and 'hate' that also take *-ing*:
  like, love, adore, dislike, loathe, can't bear, don't mind, etc.

- Point out that the *-ing* form of the verb is always used after prepositions. Ask what the difference is in these two sentences:
  I'm looking forward to going on holiday.
  (*to* = preposition)
  I want to go on holiday. (*to* = part of the infinitive)

- Tell students to choose one of the set expressions and make their own sentences using it.

B/C *to-infinitive, bare infinitive*

Point out that sometimes the infinitive is used with 'to' and sometimes without. Ask students to complete these sentences in their own way:

My family wants me … .
It isn't very easy … .
My parents make me … .
I think I'd better … .

D *-ing* form or infinitive?

Ask different students to read out an example each. Then tell them the verb 'try' also has two different meanings. To prompt the different meanings, ask students to answer these questions, using 'try':

Why didn't you let me know you would be late?
(Example: *I tried to phone but …*)

I want to get fit. What should I do?
(Example: *Why don't you try going to the gym?*)

Elicit the difference in meaning (make an effort; do something and see what happens).

1 Practice: *choose the correct verb*

1 Ask students to guess what the story is about by looking at the cartoon. This shows a Chemistry lesson. One boy has created a nasty-smelling combination of liquids. The other students are holding handkerchiefs to their noses.

Let students work in pairs and use the **grammar file** to check their answers in pairs before doing a class check.

2 The aim of getting students to predict the next part of the story is to make it easier for them to do the gap-fill task in Exercise 2.1.

ANSWERS

Ex. 1.1
1 to do; 2 to be; 3 to believe; 4 spending; 5 doing;
6 memorising; 7 to study

Ex. 1.2
1 Tom loves science while the writer hates it.
2 The next part of the story will probably give an example of how Tom is different from the writer: something Tom did that is connected with science.

2 Practice: *gap fill*

1 Make sure students read the whole text before filling in the gaps, and discuss this question as a whole class.

2 Students complete this exercise in pairs.

ANSWERS

Ex. 2.2
8 studying; 9 discovering; 10 doing; 11 to prevent; 12 making; 13 blowing up; 14 to specialise; 15 (and didn't mind him) asking; 16 to let; 17 demonstrate; 18 permitting; 19 to use; 20 to think; 21 to put; 22 teaching; 23 go; 24 stay; 25 scrub

Over to you

3 Practice: *gap fill/question and answer*

This exercise gives students the chance to use the language in a personal context, by asking and answering the questions in pairs.

ANSWERS

1 going, doing
2 playing, canoeing or abseiling
3 playing, doing
4 learning, to learn, to cope with
5 leaving, to do
6 getting, to do

Homework: ▶▶ *Exam Practice Workbook* pages 22–23, Exercises 1–2

Use of English 1: *transformations*

(CB page 31)

Tell students to read the instructions to the **exam task**, to remind themselves what they have to do. Refer them to the ***exam strategy*** before they do the task.

Tell them that in this task, all the sentences are related to the subject of school. Ask students what school subjects they can see in the photos.

PHOTOS

From the top these illustrate the following school subjects: Art, Chemistry, Gym/Physical Education

1 Transformations

Students should do the exercise individually.

ANSWERS

1 was the price of/price did you pay for
2 enjoys doing his homework
3 of mobile phones is prohibited
4 keeps borrowing Phil's
5 going to school for the
6 rarely hands her homework in
7 see the point in
8 years since Graham (has) looked
9 to put off revising for
10 had difficulty (in) understanding
11 regrets not studying hard(er)

2 Analyse answers

Let students compare their answers in pairs. If they have different answers, they should try and decide which one is right. This will encourage them to think critically about their own work.

Refer them to the **exam file** in Unit 1 page 7 if necessary, to remind them of the names of typical structures tested in this task.

ANSWERS

Structures tested in the task are: gerund and infinitive forms, noun/verb transfer, past simple/present perfect

Homework: ▶▶ *Exam Practice Workbook* page 23, Exercises 3–5

Listening: *multiple matching* (CB page 32)

Tapescript: ▶▶ TB page 107

Refer students to the **exam file** to introduce them to the task type. Point out that there is one extra option in the task that they will not need to use.

1 – 3 Strategy: *identify the topic*

Emphasise that students should always read the task and the questions before listening to identify the main topic of the extracts. The aim of these exercises is to encourage students to think about what they are going to hear, and to take advantage of anything they already know about the topic (in this case, Shakespeare).

Before they do the quiz, ask students if they can identify what play is illustrated in the photos, which are stills from the film version. (They are from *Romeo and Juliet*, in the film by Zeffirelli – this is the scene where Juliet wakes from her sleep to find Romeo has killed himself, and takes her own life as well.)

Note: In the exam the instructions are read out on the recording as well as being printed on the exam paper.

Ex.1
Shakespeare

Ex. 2
1b; 2a; 3c (This play was written by Oscar Wilde, a famous playwright of the 20th century.); 4a (Hamlet was killed by the son of a man whom he had killed earlier in the play.)

4 🔊 **Strategy:** *listen for the main idea*

The aim of these exercises is to train students to use the first listening to focus on the main idea of each extract. This will help them to differentiate between the speakers.

1/2 Students should do Exercises 4.1 and 4.2 without looking at the exam task, so that they are not distracted from focusing on the content of the recording. Play the recording once through and discuss the questions in Exercise 4.2.

ANSWERS

Ex. 4.2
1   People want to read the plays after seeing the films.
2   The speaker mentions Stratford-upon-Avon and the Globe Theatre – they are places associated with Shakespeare that tourists often visit.
3   He doesn't like the plays because they contain violence and dishonesty, so they are too much like what he sees in his everyday life.
4   His pupils.
5   Because they show how popular Shakespeare still is.

3 Having understood the main content of each extract, the students should find it easier to match the speakers and the options. Don't confirm their answers at this stage.

ANSWERS

1C   She says 'it really makes you want to read the original texts in class'.
2D   She says 'we all went on a coach trip to Stratford-on-Avon'.
3F   He says 'in my job, I see enough violence and dishonesty'.
4B   He says 'Maybe we can perform it on stage for the parents at the end of term'.
5A   She says 'we always need to keep plenty of titles in stock'.

5 🔊 **Strategy:** *confirm answers*

Tell the students to read the questions, which provide further clues to the right answers. Play the recording again so that students can confirm their answers in Exercise 4 before you reveal the key.

ANSWERS

Speaker 1 is young. She reads the plays in class.
Speaker 3 key words: violence and dishonesty – police officer
Speaker 5 key words: best-sellers, different editions, titles in stock – bookseller
Speaker 4 key words: term, parents – teacher

Over to you

Students can discuss this point in pairs before reporting their views to the class. Encourage them not only to describe their own reactions to studying the classics but also to consider young people in general.

Speaking: *collaborative task*   (CB page 33)

Tapescript: ▶▶ TB pages 107–108

Use the **exam file** to introduce the task type.

1 **Vocabulary presentation**

The aim of this exercise is to activate the vocabulary provided in the box. Students do this exercise in pairs. First ask them to match the expressions in the box to the questions, e.g.: Question 1: a traditional classroom.

PHOTOS

Photo 1 shows a traditional classroom with rows of desks. The students are putting their hands up.
Photo 2 shows students working in a small group in a Physics class. They are learning practical skills and using up-to-date technology (a computer). Their teacher is explaining something to them.
Photo 3 shows a small group sitting round a table with their teacher. It is an English class. They are discussing something and the students have their notebooks open.
Photo 4 shows students working on their own in the school library.
Photo 5 shows a student in a self-study situation. He is working on his own, and has a computer.
Photo 6 shows students using laptop computers. They are probably doing project work.

2 🔊 **Model interview:** *content*

1 Play the first part of the recording and elicit answers to the questions.

2 Students should listen for content only this first time, and comment on the candidates' discussion.

ANSWERS

Ex. 2.1
1   The task is to look at the photos and discuss the positive and less positive aspects of each way of learning, then to decide which two ways you think are the most effective.
2   'Sorry, I don't understand very well what I have to do. Could you repeat it, please?'

Ex. 2.2
1   They seem to agree on one way of learning (in a group). They have to stop before they can agree on another.

3 🔲 Model interview: *functional language*

The aim is to focus students' attention on functional language that they can use themselves for this type of task in the exam.

ANSWERS

Ex. 3.1
(Numbers refer to the **Functions file** on CB pp. 200-201.)
 4 Starting a discussion: ✔ Shall I start? ✔ Would you like to start?
 7 Involving the other person: ✔ What do you think?
 10 Reacting to your partner's ideas: ✔ Do you?
 9 Agreeing/disagreeing: ✔ Yes, I agree and ...
 5 Expressing opinions: ✔ I think

Ex. 3.2
 1 The candidates expressed themselves clearly. They stuck to the task and were on the way to achieving it. They incorporated the descriptions of the pictures into the discussion, which is good.
 2 They listened to each other and developed each other's ideas well.

4 Speaking task: *groupwork*

Before students do Exercise 4, remind them of the points in the **exam strategy**. Encourage them to use some of the expressions from the **Functions file** on CB pages 200–201 during their discussion.

Put students into groups of three. The third student should time the other two and then comment on their performance. Put this list of points on the board for them:

• Did they respond to each other's point of view?
• Did they keep to the task?
• Did they complete the task?
• Did they vary their language enough? etc.

Young entrepreneurs

Note: The reading text introduces another aspect of the unit theme. The subject here is a schoolboy who has set up a business while still at school.

Lead-in (CB page 34)

The quiz provides the opportunity to discuss the influence of the World Wide Web (Internet) on life today, and find out how many students are familiar with and use the Internet.

During the discussion, take the opportunity to make sure students know the meaning of the following items:

Definitions

World Wide Web – a huge computer network of files of information available through the Internet
webpage – one of the computer files ('pages') which are accessed through a website (an Internet address)
website – an address on the World Wide Web set up by an organisation or an individual to provide information about themselves or to provide e-mail access; it usually contains a collection of web pages

ANSWERS

Ex. 1
No. 5 is not true.

Reading 2: *gapped text (sentences)*

(CB pages 34–35)

Tell students that they are going to do a gapped-text task like the one they did for Reading 1 on pages 28–29. Elicit what they remember about the best way to tackle this type of task, then refer them to the **exam strategy** box on page 33 to check.

1 – 2 Preparation

The first two exercises ensure students understand the base text before they try to do the exam task itself.

Remind students that they should not worry about unfamiliar words unless they are important in completing the task. They should try to guess meaning from the context as far as possible. You could check comprehension of the following items.

Definitions

advanced for his age – able to understand and do more than most children at that age
aptitude for – if you have an aptitude for something, you are good at it
shuffle a pack of cards – to mix playing cards into a different order before you start playing a game with them

wired up (slang) – able to get onto the Internet; for this you
need a computer and a modem (a piece of equipment
that connects a computer to a telephone line)
postpone – put something off until later

ANSWERS

Ex. 1

1 The article is about a schoolboy called Tom Hadfield, who
set up an Internet business before the age of 16. The
article is written by Tom's father.

2 The text has seven gaps to be filled.

Ex. 2

1 He liked chess, memorising the sequence of playing cards,
working things out. This indicated that he was very intelligent.

2 He was bored, possibly because the work was too easy.

3 At age 7 or 8 when he started to make money by washing
cars.

4 Soccernet is a football website. Tom thought of the idea
while he was daydreaming (not paying attention, thinking
about other things) in class.

5 He could pursue a career in business or as a footballer.

6 They are pleased that he is learning useful skills through
his other activities.

3 Strategy: *identify language and topic links*

These exercises show students what they should be looking
for when they do the exam task. They are best done with
the whole class.

ANSWERS

Ex. 3.1

1 He = Tom; the computer = his first computer,

2 *The program* = the chess program; *declare checkmate* =
a move in chess.

Ex. 3.2

1G

2B 'No answer'. (**Note:** 'they' refers back to 'the teachers'.)

3H 'He didn't want to spend the money on sweets.'

4 Reading task: *match sentences to gaps*

Let students finish the task individually, then work in pairs
to compare their answers. Finally, check answers as a class.

ANSWERS

4 D 'That day' refers to his 12th birthday. 'School began to
recede ...' links with 'postpone serious studying'. (line 43)

5 F 'As a result' links to the success mentioned in the
previous sentence. 'Also' in the following sentence needs
to be preceded by a first benefit.

6 C 'Two questions' links with 'One is ... . And the other: ...'

7 A Links with the topic of teachers and education.

Over to you

5 Discussion

You can do this as a class or in pairs. The expressions given
will be useful in the writing section of this unit, the informal
letter.

▶▶ *extra activity*

Students write a short letter to Tom advising him which
career path to follow and why.

Homework: ▶▶ *Exam Practice Workbook* page 24

Vocabulary (CB page 36)

This section focuses on those areas tested in the lexical
cloze task in Paper 3, Use of English. Encourage students to
use their dictionaries, as this will give them practice in using
a dictionary to research words.

1 Choosing the right word

Let students work in pairs.

ANSWERS

1 *teachers* (a '*professor*' is at the highest teaching level in a
university)

2 *practical*

3 *subjects*

4 *marks*

5 *grade* (in an exam A, B or C is a 'grade', a number or a
percentage is a 'mark')

6 *taking* ('*passing*' means being successful)

7 *grant* (a '*fee*' is paid by the student for tuition, a '*grant*' is
paid to the student to cover living expenses.)

8 *career* (a '*career*' is a job or series of jobs that describes
someone's working life; a '*profession*' is a job that
requires special education and training, e.g. medicine, law)

2 Words followed by prepositions

The aim of this exercise is to show students that their
dictionary gives them more information than just a
definition. Emphasise that noting down new words with the
prepositions they take is very useful preparation for
Paper 3, Use of English.

ANSWERS

Ex. 2.1

'accuse' and 'fond' are both followed by 'of'.

3 Verbs + prepositions

Remind them that the verb form after a preposition is
always the *-ing* form.

ANSWERS

1	from passing	4	for being
2	on playing	5	to starting
3	of going	6	to (me) telling

4 Adjectives + prepositions

Students could do this exercise individually and then
compare answers in pairs.

> **ANSWERS**
>
> **Ex. 4.1**
> 1 at ...; 2 at ...; 3 of ...; 4 in ...; 5 on ...; 6 about ...; 7 of ...;
> 8 of ...

5 Collocations: *do* or *make?*

Students should work in pairs. Encourage them to make a special note of any that they get wrong and make their own sentences using them.

> **ANSWERS**
>
> **Ex. 5.1**
>
> | *Do:* | *Make:* |
> |---|---|
> | a test | a mess |
> | some work | an attempt |
> | an experiment | a noise |
> | your homework | an effort |
> | some research | friends |
> | your best | progress |
> | a course (in something) | a mistake |
>
> **Ex. 5.2**
> 1 for making; 2 with doing; 3 about making; 4 on doing;
> 5 for making; 6 in making; 7 in making; 8 for making

Use of English 2: *lexical cloze*

(CB page 37)

If necessary, refer students back to the **exam strategy** in Unit 1 page 13.

1 Preparation

This exercise ensures that students read and understand the text before attempting the task.

> **ANSWERS**
>
> **Ex. 1.1**
> Life skills, e.g. how to send an e-mail, giving presentations, car maintenance, first aid, cooking, designing a webpage.
>
> **Ex. 1.2**
> Because many students cannot do these things; to encourage students to learn these things; to provide students with life skills.

2 Lexical cloze task

Students can do this exercise individually or in pairs. They should check their answers in pairs before you go over it as a whole class.

> **ANSWERS**
>
> 1A; 2D; 3B; 4A; 5B; 6C; 7D; 8A; 9C; 10B; 11D; 12C; 13B; 14A;
> 15D

Homework: ▶▶ *Exam Practice Workbook* page 25

Writing: *transactional letter*

(CB pages 38–39)

This is the second transactional letter that students have to tackle. In Unit 2, they focused on planning and organising the information which must be included in the letter. In this section, the focus is on expanding notes. Refer students to the **exam file** and the **exam strategy**.

1 Understand the task

1 Tell students to find the points to be included in the letter individually and then compare as a class.

2 Students can discuss these questions in pairs.

You could discuss how the points in the task should be organised and how many paragraphs there should be. Students can compare their ideas with the sample answer in Exercise 3.

> **ANSWERS**
>
> **Ex. 1.1**
> Points to be covered:
> *Registration* – dates, advice
> *Bookshop* – opening date and time, cost of books, suggest buying mine
> *First lesson* – date, advice to arrive early and why
> *Dance* – date, time, place, recommend it.
>
> **Ex. 1.2**
> 1 Informal and friendly.
> 2 Dear Paul, Best wishes/Regards/Love

Focus on expanding notes

2 Make notes into full sentences

In Paper 2, Part 1, students are given some of the information in note form. It is a common error for students to take language from these notes without converting it into full sentences. Elicit from students what kind of words are omitted when writing in note form, e.g. articles, prepositions, link words, the verb 'to be', 'it/there'.

Refer students to the **exam tip!** about using key words. Where there is no obvious and natural alternative for a key word from the text, they should use the word given. However, it is important to spell it correctly.

> **ANSWERS**
>
> **Note:** These answers are suggestions only.
> 1 There is a test at 10.00 on the first day so come prepared.
> 2 You will need a good dictionary. They are very expensive to buy from the school but you can buy them cheaper at a bookshop.
> 3 There is a welcome party at 7 p.m. on Friday. I recommend going/you to go as it's great fun.
> 4 There is a tour of the city on Wednesday at 3 p.m. It is very helpful so take notes. I suggest you buy a map as it's easy to get lost.
> 5 I recommend joining the sports club in the school because there is an excellent volleyball trainer.

3 Analyse a sample answer

Students can discuss these questions in pairs. The questions cover some of the criteria that the examiner is looking for. Students should be encouraged to evaluate their own work in the same way.

ANSWERS

Content
1 All the points are covered.
2 'Don't be late unless you want to get into trouble. The school is very strict about punctuality.' It is relevant but it means in this case that the letter has gone over the word limit.
3 Yes.
Style/register
4 The style is appropriate.
Accuracy
5 *The* course begins *on* Monday 22nd April ...
  The bookshop opens *at* 10.00 *on* Friday 19th.
  The first lesson is *on* Monday *at* 9.00.
  Finally, there's a Welcome Dance on Tuesday 23rd. It's in the College Hall and starts *at* 7.00 p.m.

Focus on grammar

4 Conditional sentences

Students work in pairs to find the examples of the conditionals and match their uses to those in the **grammar file**.

ANSWERS

There are six examples of conditional sentences in the letter:
'If I didn't have exams, I'd stay for another term myself.' – hypothetical situation in the present.
'If you go early, you'll miss the long queues.' – likely event in the future.
'If you buy your books there, they cost about £60.' – likely event in the future.
'If I were you, I'd get there early.' – advice.
'Don't be late unless you want to get into trouble.' – likely event in the future using the imperative.
'Let me know if you want to buy my books.' – likely event in the future using the imperative.

5 Practice: *gap fill*

Tell students to complete the exercise individually, then check their answers in pairs.

ANSWERS

1 wouldn't like, didn't speak
2 come, I'll show
3 could drive, would take
4 will really enjoy, don't mind
5 will not get, book
6 will meet, arrives
7 were you, would bring, rains

Over to you

6 Writing task

Set this task for homework.

CRITERIA FOR MARKING

Content: Make sure that the letter covers all the points required but does not add unnecessary information.
Organisation: Letter format, clear organisation of points, suitable opening and closing formulae.
Register: Informal or neutral.
Effect on target reader: Would have enough information to enjoy the language course.

Homework: ▶▶ *Exam Practice Workbook* pages 28–29

Unit 3 Test ▶▶ TB page 119

4 Places

Lead-in (CB page 40)

Books closed. Tell students they are going to read a text about New York. Find out what they know about New York. Has anyone been there? Would they like to go?

Books open. Focus attention on the photos of New York on pages 40–41. Get students to say what they can see in each photo and compare them. Encourage them to use the vocabulary items in the box by asking questions like:

In which pictures can you see skyscrapers?

Which pictures show people enjoying themselves and having a good time?

Students can discuss questions 2 and 3 in pairs or as a class.

PHOTOS

The photo at the top of page 40 shows Broadway at night. This is the theatre area of Manhattan. You can see a theatre in the photo. A New York yellow taxi is speeding past.
The photo below shows Washington Square. This is a favourite place for people to gather with their friends, sit by the pond, play music, watch street entertainers etc. There are always crowds of people in the Square.
The photo illustrating the text on page 41 is taken in Central Park, a very large park in the middle of Manhattan. The skyscrapers in the background are just outside the park. This is also a very popular place to spend free time and escape from the crowded streets full of traffic.
The background photo shows an aerial view of Manhattan, with all its skyscrapers.

Reading 1: *multiple matching*

(CB pages 40–41)

Use the **exam file** to introduce the task type. Elicit or point out that the text on page 41 consists of four sections, A–D, each with a separate heading.

Then refer students to the **exam strategy**, which tells them what reading technique to use for this task. Explain that scanning means running your eyes quickly over a text, looking ONLY for specific items of information which you want to find. Ask students to name some things they read to get specific information, e.g.:

• TV listings – to find out if there is a film on TV tonight.
• their dictionary – to find a specific word

1 Predict

Remind students of the value of getting a general idea of the task and text first. When discussing Question 3, encourage students to think about the needs of the different people.

ANSWERS

1   An article about living in New York, and what New Yorkers think of their city.
2   Four sections.
3   Answers will vary.

2 Strategy: *identify key words*

Lead students through these exercises, eliciting the answers as a class. The exercises are designed to encourage students to approach the task systematically. Emphasise that they will not be scanning for given words but for ideas.

ANSWERS

Ex. 2.1
1   Key words: <u>money</u>, <u>necessities</u>
2   Necessities: food, drink, clothes, somewhere to live, etc. Opposite of 'necessities': luxuries, extras
3   'She earns enough ... little left for luxuries' (lines 3–4)
Ex. 2.2
D   'free shower', 'they all give it away' (lines 74–76)
Ex. 2.3
'costs nothing' (lines 8–9). This refers to rollerblading, which is not a necessity.

3 Reading task: *multiple-matching questions*

Set the task up as a race to encourage students to scan the text, and discourage them from reading every word.

When discussing the answers, get students to read out the parts of the text where they found the answers.

ANSWERS

2C   'A few years ago ... considered moving out of New York.' (lines 44–45)
3A   'Rollerblading ... , which costs nothing' (lines 7–9)
4B   '... to invest so much in their education.' (lines 30–31)
5B   'New York is becoming more and more expensive' (line 41)
6A   'It's hard to get a good night's sleep' (line 17)
7D   'Financial support/food stamps/cans and bottles for recycling/I find stuff, like televisions and radios and sell them' (lines 67–72)
8C   'The clampdown on crime has improved the city tremendously' (lines 48–49)
9B   '... the diversity of people ... and are enriched by that' (lines 36–37)
10A   'She is paying her way through college' (line 11)
11C   'I hate that feeling of being closed in. We're trying to save up for a bigger home' (lines 57–59)
12A   'The aggressive nature of New Yorkers ...' (lines 17–19)
13D   '... doesn't display an ounce of self-pity.' (line 61)

Over to you

4 Discussion

Let students work in pairs. This exercise is good practice for Paper 5 (Speaking), Parts 3 and 4. Then compare answers as a class.

ANSWERS

Good aspects:
1 You can have a lot of fun (line 5)
2 The city has a lot of energy (line 14)
3 A rich cultural life (line 33)
4 Diversity: people from different cultures (line 36)
5 You can get whatever you want 24 hours a day (line 54)
Bad aspects:
1 Pollution and noise (line 15)
2 People are aggressive (line 18)
3 Children can't play in the streets (line 38)
4 It's expensive (lines 41, 51)
5 You can feel closed in – not enough space (line 58)

Homework: ▶▶ *Exam Practice Workbook* page 30

Grammar: *comparisons* (CB page 42)

Presentation

See **Introduction** page 7 for suggestions on how to use the **grammar file**. Below is a suggestion for presenting the comparative structures in this lesson.

Tell students to look at the **grammar file**. As you go through the examples, ask students if they agree or disagree with the statements/whether they think the statements are true or false. If they disagree, ask them to say what they think.

Tell them to think of two contrasting places in their own country and compare them using these structures.

1 – 2 Practice

Students can do these exercises individually or in pairs. Tell them to use the **grammar file** as a reference if necessary.

ANSWERS

Ex. 1
Mistakes:
1 one of **the** most dangerous cities in the world
2 the friendliest city I **have ever been** to
3 The longer I live here, **the happier I** feel.
4 Dublin is **like** most cities
5 life in Dublin is getting more and more **stressful**.
6 People don't have as much time to stop and talk **as** they did in the past.
7 the busier the city becomes, the **worse** the traffic problem gets.
8 the air is much **more** polluted than it used to be.
9 the countryside is just as exciting **as** the city.
10 living in the country must be the **worst** thing in the world!

ANSWERS

Ex. 2
1 the quietest
2 nearly as peaceful as
3 much more beautiful than
4 the most beautiful
5 slower
6 far friendlier/more friendly than
7 a lot safer
8 a great deal easier
9 far worse
10 the worst
11 lively enough
12 the longer ... the better

3 Discussion

Discuss this as a class.

Over to you

4 Discussion

This is good practice for Paper 5 (Speaking), Part 3. Students should work in pairs, and elect a spokesperson to summarise the ideas of the group at the end. They should:

• pay careful attention to the correct use of comparisons.
• use different expressions to express opinions, agree and disagree.

Homework: ▶▶ *Exam Practice Workbook* pages 30–31, Exercises 1–3

Use of English 1: *error correction*
(CB page 43)

Use the **exam file** to introduce the task type. Put some examples on the board of ways in which unnecessary words may be added. Ask students to identify the word types that have been added. E.g.:

*The countryside **it** can be great fun.*
*I learnt Spanish at **the** school.*
*We must **to** go home early.*
*I **did** lived in the capital city for ten years.*
*Take me to the village where he lives **in**.*

Exercises 1–4 show students how they should tackle this task type.

Before they start the task, refer students to the box:
! used to / would / use. Elicit the differences in meaning from the examples.

1 Read the instructions

It is important to train students always to put something on the line provided. If the sentence is correct, they must put a tick. Otherwise, they will not get a mark in the exam.

2 Read the title and text

As with all text-based tasks, students should always read through the text for general understanding before attempting the task. Use the questions to check their understanding before letting them do the task.

ANSWERS

1 He grew up in the countryside.
2 He enjoyed it.
3 He was lonely sometimes.
4 He developed a good imagination.

3 Error correction task

Refer students to the *exam tip!* Let them work in pairs, using the clues to help them.

ANSWERS

1	of (a preposition)	9	were
2	✔	10	the
3	am	11	in
4	✔	12	for
5	them	13	if
6	than	14	go
7	on	15	✔
8	✔		

Homework: ▶▶ *Exam Practice Workbook* pages 31–32, Exercises 4–5

4 Check answers

This is another important stage and students should get used to doing it.

Listening: *multiple-choice questions*

(CB page 44)

Tapescript: ▶▶ TB page 108

Refer students to the **exam file** to introduce them to the task type.

1 Read the instructions

Ask students to read the instructions for the task carefully. These will tell them the topic of the listening before they hear the recording. Point out that the instructions are also read out on the recording for them to follow.

Note: It is very important that students should read the instructions for Part 4 carefully as the format will vary in the exam. It could also be a true/false exercise (see Unit 5), saying which speaker said what (see Unit 12), or yes/no.

ANSWERS

1/2 They will hear two people, probably talking about an aspect of local history.
3 They have to choose the best answer from three choices.

2 🎵 Strategy: *listen for key ideas*

To tackle this task, students should first read the question, and identify what they must listen for. Underlining the key words in the question or sentence stem will help them focus on this. E.g.: for Question 1, the key words are: 'what has <u>changed most</u>?'

They should be aware that the words on the recording will paraphrase the words in the options. E.g.: for Question 1, the answer is option B, the size. The word 'size' summarises the words 'physically much, much larger' in the recording.

The first time they listen to the recording, students should listen for the answer to the question. They should mark the option that seems to answer the question most accurately. They can check during the second listening.

ANSWERS

1 In Question 1 the key words are 'changed most'. In Question 2 the key words are 'feel' and 'appearance'.
2 Phrase c) matches the answer B.
3 For Question 2, the section '... but it can't be helped. We just have to put up with it' matches the answer C.

3 🎵 Listening task

Give students time to read the remaining questions before playing the rest of the recording.

4 🎵 Task analysis

After the first hearing, ask students to compare their answers with a partner. If there are differences, they can check which is the correct answer during the second listening.

ANSWERS

1B 'It's physically much, <u>much larger</u>.'
2C 'But <u>it can't be helped</u>. We just have to <u>put up with it</u>.'
3B 'What's happening now is not so much the influence of one country, but that people want to adopt things <u>from all over the world</u>.'
4C 'All this has had a big effect on the choice of food you can buy in restaurants and shops – and <u>a very positive one</u>, I think.'
5A 'So I think the situation is more or less <u>under control</u>.'
6A 'People often complain about <u>the litter in the streets</u>, which is true.'
7C 'If you ask where the town centre is, people will direct you to the river. That's where <u>a lot of people congregate</u>.'

Over to you

5   Questionnaire

This exercise introduces useful vocabulary, and is good practice for Paper 5 (Speaking), Parts 3 and 4. Tell students to work in pairs and try to come to an agreement on the answers to the questions. They can then compare with the rest of the class.

Speaking: *three-way discussion*

(CB page 45)

Tapescript: ►► TB page 109

Part 4 of the Speaking test always develops out of the topic discussed in Part 3. In this lesson, students first do the Part 3 task. They then listen to a recorded model of two candidates doing the Part 4 follow-up questions, and finally discuss the questions themselves.

1 – 2 🔲 Part 3 Speaking task: *groupwork*

Play the first part of the recording, which contains the Part 3 task instructions. Elicit the task from the students. Draw their attention to the *exam tip!*.

Put students into groups of three. Remind them that:

- they should keep to the task they have been given.
- they should not spend too much time talking about each of the amenities in the pictures, otherwise they will not complete the task.
- when doing the task, they should encourage their partner to speak by asking their opinion.
- they should respond to their partner's point of view and not simply put forward their own.
- they must take turns to talk, but that they do not need to agree with each other.

Encourage students to use expressions from the **Functions file** on CB pages 200–201 during their discussion. Make sure they stop after three minutes.

PHOTOS

Clockwise from the top left the photos show a water fountain in a town square; a skateboarder in a skateboarding area; an indoor swimming pool with water slides at a leisure centre; a park with a children's playground; an outdoor theatre.

ANSWERS

Ex. 1
The task is to imagine that in the town where they live, there are plans to build two of the five amenities in the pictures and a) to discuss how useful each amenity would be b) decide which two they would choose and why.

Part 4 task

Refer students to the **exam file** and the *exam strategy*. The most important thing they must do is to give full answers, and take the opportunity to show the examiner how well they can express opinions and ideas. It is also important to involve the other candidate in the discussion.

3   Part 4 task: *questions*

Tell students to read the questions and think about their own answers before moving on to Exercise 4.

Note: The number of questions the examiner asks in the exam will vary.

4 🔲 Model interview: *content and functions*

1 Play the recording once all through, and let students answer the questions about the content.

2 Play the recording again. This time, the aim is to focus students' attention on functional language that they can use themselves for this type of task in the exam.

ANSWERS

Ex. 4.1
2   The examiner asked questions 2 and 4.

Ex. 4.2
(Numbers refer to the **Functions file** CB pages 200–201.)
13   Summarising and reporting a decision:
      Well, I chose ... ; So that was the conclusion we reached.
 7   Involving the other person:
      And what else?
      Which places do you think are (worse for noise, Rajmund)?
      Do you think there is a solution ... ?
      Do you agree?
      Don't you think ... ?

---

5   Part 4 Speaking task: *groupwork*

Encourage students to use expressions from the **Functions file** on CB pages 200–201. The 'examiner' should give feedback to the others after doing the activity. They can change roles if there is time.

Cultures and customs

Note: The reading text in this section of the unit is about different ethnic communities living within a city.

Lead-in (CB page 46)

1   Matching activity

Ensure that the students know the meaning of 'ethnic communities' (people from different countries and races). Tell them to look at the list of countries a)–f) and explain that communities of people from all these countries live in different parts of London. Ask them to compare with their own cities, if appropriate: what different ethnic groups live there?

Find out what students know about the different cultures of each country listed a)–f).

Where are these countries?
What kind of climate do they have?
What are they well known for?
etc.

Explain that the map shows the area of London and the places where the different community groups typically live. Each community is represented on the map by a building. Ask them if they can guess which community is represented by each building.

> **ANSWERS**
>
> 1f) The Polish community is represented by a typical Town Hall building.
> 2a) Japan. The arch is typical of Japanese architecture.
> 3b) Portugal. Portugal is represented by an ornate castle, typical of the country.
> 4c) Caribbean. The green vegetation represents the lush tropical vegetation that is found in the Caribbean islands.
> 5d) Lebanon. This community is represented by Greek columns, also found in Lebanon.
> 6e) India. Many Indians in London are Muslim, and the community is represented by a mosque.

2   Discussion

Do this as a class.

Reading 2: multiple matching

(CB pages 46–47)

Focus attention on the **exam file**. This explains how the multiple-matching task in Reading 2 is slightly different from Reading 1: there are more sections of text, and some questions have two answers. Elicit what they remember about the best way to tackle this type of task, then refer them to the **exam strategy** box to check.

1   Read the instructions/Predict

Explain or elicit the meaning of these words in the sub-heading:

treasure trove – valuable objects, coins, etc. that are found where they have been hidden or buried, which are not claimed by anyone

multiculturalism – the belief that it is important and good to include people or ideas from many different countries, races or religions

the world on your doorstep – a large number of different cultures in the area in which you live

Point out that the words 'multiculturalism, cafés, shops and markets' give clues to the content of the texts.

> **ANSWERS**
>
> **Ex. 1.1**
> 1   Six sections
> 2   Two

2   Reading task: *multiple matching*

Make sure students understand the questions. You could go through the questions, and the clues provided, with the whole class. Identify the key words together. Ask questions to get them thinking about the ideas they will need to scan for, e.g.:

Question 1: Ask: *What is another word for 'the main part of the country you come from'?* (elicit 'mainland'). *What do some countries have off the coast of the mainland?* (islands)

Question 3: Explain: *This question indicates that one of the communities does not live in one particular place like the others.*

Questions 4–5: Ask: *What sports could you scan for?*

Question 7: Ask: *What kind of social events take place every year in your community?* (e.g.: festivals)
etc.

If you set the reading task in class, allow no more than 15 minutes, to give students an idea of how much they can do in that time. Stop the class even if they have not finished, and check answers so far.

Draw attention to the **exam tip!** before they start. Tell them to tick off each question as they find the answer, so they know which ones to come back to if necessary.

> **ANSWERS**
>
> 1B 'The majority have come from the Island of Madeira rather than from the mainland of Portugal' (lines 34–37)
> 2A 'wearing the typical colourful sari, just as in India' (lines 23–24)
> 3F '... there isn't a geographically defined "Little Lebanon" (lines 136–138)
> 4B, 5D (in either order) B '... is mad about football' (lines 38–39); D 'The national affection for golf ...' (line 75)
> 6A 'The first Indians arrived in 1597' (lines 3–4), 'more came ... in the seventeenth century' (lines 5–8), 'Numbers increased ... in 1947' (lines 8–10), 'the community really took off in the 1950s and 1960s' (lines 10–12)

7B, 8C   (in either order) B '... holds its carnival every
February' (lines 40–41); C 'the Notting Hill Carnival'
(lines 56–57)
9D   'It isn't as permanent as other communities' (lines 85–87)
10A   '... is the second largest in London' (lines 2–3)
11E   '... full of advertisements in Polish' (line 113), '... There
is even a daily Polish-language newspaper'
(lines 118–120)
12F   'The community is getting stronger and bigger'
(lines 130–131)
13C   'prices are rising' (lines 70–71)
14E   'keeping up traditions isn't so easy' (lines 107–108)
15D   'The best restaurants tend to be in Central London,
where most of the community works' (lines 91–94)

Over to you

3 Discussion

1 Tell students to read the whole text again and make
notes. Then ask different students to talk about each point.

2 This could be done as a whole group discussion or in
pairs.

Homework: ▶▶ *Exam Practice Workbook* page 32

Vocabulary (CB page 48)

1 – 4 Practice

Students can work through these exercises in pairs, or you
can select the ones you want to do in class, and set the
others for homework. Encourage students to use their
dictionaries, as this will give them practice in using a
dictionary to research words. You can check as a class after
each exercise, or after students have completed all the
tasks.

ANSWERS

Ex. 1
1l department store; 2e leisure centre; 3i pedestrian precinct;
4h tourist office; 5f industrial estate; 6j skating rink;
7b shopping mall; 8d apartment block; 9k ring road;
10c public transport; 11g traffic jam; 12a bus station (where
many routes begin or end. Compare bus stop: a place at the
side of the road where buses pick up and/or drop off
passengers.)

Ex. 2
1 get away from; 2 wore off; 3 gave in; 4 moved in;
5 settled in; 6 pulled down, put up; 7 doing up;
8 gets run over

Ex. 3.1
Positive: unspoiled (also 'unspoilt'), welcoming, peaceful,
          stunning, well looked-after
Negative: shabby, polluted, ugly, unattractive, overdeveloped

Ex 3.2
1 historic; 2 stunning; 3 quaint; 4 unspoilt; 5 bustling;
6 hectic; 7 polluted; 8 shabby; 9 reserved

ANSWERS

Ex. 4.1
The last syllable may be dropped from the stem of the word,
e.g.: terror – terrify.
The last letter may be dropped, e.g.: simple – simplify.
There may be an internal change, e.g.: long – length.

Ex. 4.2
Mystify

Ex. 4.3
1 lengthen; 2 criticise; 3 horrified; 4 brighten; 5 enables;
6 strengthens

▶▶ *extra activity*

Ask the students to write two paragraphs about their own
towns – one with a positive description, the other more
negative, following the model of the description in
Exercise 3.3. This is useful preparation for the writing task on
CB page 51.

Homework: ▶▶ *Exam Practice Workbook* page 33,
Exercises 1.1–1.2

Use of English 2: *word formation*
(CB page 49)

Refer students to the **exam strategy**. Draw their attention to
the **exam tip!**.

1 Word-formation task

After students have read the text all the way through, ask
the following questions to establish general understanding:
Who organises the events in New York? (the ethnic
    communities)
When and where do they take place? (in the Spring, in Fifth
    Avenue)
Then let them continue individually or in pairs.

ANSWERS

1 variety; 2 attractions; 3 festivals; 4 seriously;
5 celebrations; 6 political; 7 generally; 8 enjoyment;
9 tendency; 10 meeting

2 Discussion

Students could discuss these questions in pairs or as a class.

▶▶ *extra activity*

Ask students to write a paragraph about the festival for a
tourist information sheet about their town.

Homework: ▶▶ *Exam Practice Workbook* page 33,
Exercise 2

Writing: *article* (CB pages 50–51)

Use the **exam file** to introduce the type of writing students will be doing in this section.

Discuss what kind of articles they like to read, and elicit the characteristics of an interesting article, e.g.:

an eye-catching title; an introduction that attracts the reader to read on; a lively style; interesting or amusing examples.

Then tell them to look at the **exam strategy** to check whether they have missed anything.

1 Understand the task

> **ANSWERS**
>
> 1 Points to include:
> A description of your town.
> A description of the people.
> What you like or don't like.
> 2 The article will be read by students. The style can be informal or semi-formal but should be consistent throughout.

2 Analyse a sample answer

Let students discuss the questions in pairs. The questions cover some of the criteria that the examiner is looking for.

During the class discussion, ask students how successful they think this article is. Ask, e.g.:

Is the style lively enough?
Do we know what the writer feels about her city?
Should the city have been named?

> **ANSWERS**
>
> Content
> 1 All the information is provided.
> 2 The title is a good one because it is relevant and makes the reader curious.
> Organisation
> 3 There are 5 paragraphs.
> 4 The paragraphs have separate topics. Each one deals with a different area of the city. The first and final paragraphs are the introduction and the conclusion.
> 5 The first sentence of each paragraph introduces the topic.
> 6 The introduction and conclusion are too short and do not develop the idea enough. They are not real paragraphs.

Focus on introductions and conclusions

3 Evaluate introductions and conclusions

This exercise gives students an opportunity to discuss what makes a good introduction and conclusion by comparing good and bad examples.

> **ANSWERS**
>
> **Ex. 3.1**
> Paragraph 2 is the best introduction because 1) it has a topic sentence; 2) the topic is developed in the rest of the paragraph; 3) it leaves the reader asking the question 'Why?'

> **ANSWERS**
>
> **Ex. 3.2**
> 2 Paragraph 3 is the best conclusion because it summarises the article, draws a conclusion and is well developed.

Focus on grammar

4 Relative clauses

Do the first two exercises as a class. Let students work individually or in pairs to do Exercise 4.3.

> **ANSWERS**
>
> **Ex 4.1–4.2**
> 1 ... , which means it's a bit like a concrete jungle (non-defining)
> 2 Shops and restaurants that open 24 hours a day (defining)
> 3 The area where the students live (defining)
> 4 The street cafes that you pass (defining)
> 5 You can do anything you like (defining)
> 6 The south of the city, which I don't often go to, ... (non-defining)
> 7 The district where the wealthy people live (defining)
> 8 Expensive houses, many of which have swimming pools and big gardens (non-defining)
> 9 The people who live here (defining)
>
> **Ex. 4.3**
> 2 ... , which is in the centre of the city, ...
> 3 which I bought as a souvenir
> 4 ... , who is an expert on Egyptian history, ...
> 5 (that/which) the teacher gave us to fill in
> 6 which/that are 9,000 years old
> 7 ... , which occupied one whole room, ...
> 8 who/that lived in Ancient Egypt
> 9 who had been to the special exhibition three times that week
> 10 where one of the Egyptian pharaohs was buried
> 11 whose school was also visiting the museum
> 12 in which we were allowed to spend a few minutes shopping

Over to you

5 Writing task

The article could be set for homework after preparation in class. Elicit some good suggestions for titles for an article about a museum. Students can individually make a list of ideas they would include and then discuss with their partner how they could best organise the ideas.

> **CRITERIA FOR MARKING**
>
> **Content:** The article should contain a description of a museum, reasons for liking or disliking it and reasons why it could be of interest.
> **Organisation and cohesion:** Introduction and conclusion. Clear development with appropriate paragraphing and linking of ideas.
> **Register:** Informal or neutral but must be consistent.
> **Effect on target reader:** Would have enough information to decide whether or not to visit the museum.

Homework: ▶▶ *Exam Practice Workbook* pages 36–37

Unit 4 Test ▶▶ TB page 120

Progress test 1 (CB pages 52–53)

Before you set **Progress test 1** on CB pages 52–53, tell students to do the **Progress check** in the *Exam Practice Workbook*, pages 38–39. This reviews the language tested in the *Coursebook*. (You will find the answers in the With Key edition of the *Workbook*.)

ANSWERS

Coursebook Progress test 1

1 Structural cloze

1 will; 2 onto; 3 of; 4 would; 5 that; 6 them; 7 about; 8 in; 9 the; 10 like; 11 been; 12 despite; 13 has; 14 to; 15 other

2 Key word transformations

1 been a member of the
2 was too ill to complete
3 whose name was
4 was the most interesting part
5 without having been/without being
6 let us take photos
7 isn't nearly as big
8 hadn't finished singing the song
9 no use waiting
10 never seen a more

3 Error correction

1 are; 2 the; 3 such; 4 it; 5 for; 6 ✔; 7 in; 8 has; 9 ✔; 10 time; 11 ✔; 12 across; 13 who; 14 yet; 15 too

4 Word formation

1 frozen; 2 explanation; 3 adaptable; 4 climatic; 5 beginning; 6 easily; 7 equipment; 8 originated; 9 highest; 10 naturally

---

After doing the test in the *Coursebook,* you could also use the photocopiable test:

Progress test 1 ▶▶ TB pages 121–123

(See TB page 139 for the answers.)

Lead-in (CB page 54)

Introduce the topic by asking students to name some places where people can go shopping, e.g.: small shops, supermarkets, department stores, chain stores, shopping malls, outdoor/indoor markets. Elicit the names of some well-known local chains and what they sell.

1 Tell students they are going to read about a new kind of shop, and ask what they think a 'supershop' is. Then tell them to look at the photographs. They should try to identify what is happening in the photos, and guess the answer to Questions 1 and 2. Ask:

What kind of shop would put in playstations/a dance club/ computers for its customers?
What other things would its customers enjoy?

2 Tell them to scan the text to check their answers. It will help if they look for the names of the shops. (These are: Levi's jeans store, Waterstone's booksellers, TopShop fashion store, Nike Town sports shop.)

PHOTOS

Clockwise from the left, the photos on page 54 show: Playstations at TopShop superstore; the dance club at the Levi's store; Internet stations at Waterstone's bookshop. The photo in the text shows Nike Town's projection equipment displaying sports from all over the world.

ANSWERS

According to the text, the shops offer the following attractions:
Levi's: 'an entertainment venue' (dance club) (line 7), computer stations, videos, a shop to buy music, an art gallery (lines 30–33)
Waterstone's: 'restaurant, juice bar, news café, Internet stations, gift shop, personal shopping suite' (i.e. where customers can find advice on what to buy), 'events arena, exhibition space, private meeting and dining rooms' (lines 23–27), 'guest authors' (lines 90–92)
TopShop: café, beauty salon, radio station, fashion shows, bands (lines 51–57)
Nike Town: information, running club, sports clinic, opportunities to meet sports personalities and get autographs (lines 68–71, 86–88)

Reading 1: *multiple matching*

(CB pages 54–55)

Refer students to the **exam file**. Tell students that the strategy required for matching summary sentences is similar to that for matching headings (Unit 1 ***exam strategy*** page 10).

1 Skim for gist

Set a time limit of 4–5 minutes for the first reading. Tell students that they are reading for general understanding and they should not worry about any words they do not know at this stage. Elicit the strategy for skimming (see Unit 1 page 4). Remind them not to look at the summary sentences for the moment.

ANSWERS

Paragraph:
0   It's also an entertainment venue in the evenings.
1   Waterstone's.
2   Customers can eat, drink, use the Internet, look at exhibitions, hold meetings, attend special events, watch videos.
3   Having to move from shop to shop.
4   Fashion shows, live music.
5   By giving the opportunity to find out about sports clubs, meet athletes, go to a sports clinic, watch sports videos.
6   It is made up of separate 'pavilions' with its own streets, signs, maps.
7   You can meet famous authors in Waterstone's and sportspeople in Nike Town.

2 Strategy: *identify key words*

1 Ensure that students do not look at the example answer until after they have worked out their own summary sentences.

2 Discuss the ways in which the students' sentences were different. Point out that their ideas may be just as valid as the summary sentence given.

ANSWERS

2   'After closing time' becomes 'at night'; 'a state-of-the-art entertainment venue' becomes 'a high-tech club'.

3 Reading task: *match summary sentences*

Students should do this task individually. Set a time limit of 10 minutes for this. They can then check their answers in pairs and discuss any differences.

ANSWERS

1C   'trend' > 'fashion'; 'first supershop' > 'was started by'
2E
3A   'nightmare' > ' problems'; 'changed'> 'solved'
4F
5B   'inspiration and opportunities' > 'information and ideas'
6H   'rival' > 'offer competition'
7D   'see face to face' > 'meet', 'famous/well-known/ popular' > 'celebrities'

Vocabulary: *prepositional phrases*

4 Vocabulary search

Tell students to find the answers for themselves from the text. Point out how important it is to be observant and to note down prepositional phrases even when the words themselves are not new to them.

> **ANSWERS**
>
> 1 in stock (line 23)
> 2 under one roof (line 45)
> 3 on offer (line 48)
> 4 on display (line 65)
> 5 face to face (line 87)

Over to you

5 Discussion

Students should work in pairs. When they report back to the class, encourage them to use the structures in the examples.

Homework: ▶▶ *Exam Practice Workbook* page 40

Grammar: *modals* (CB page 56)

Presentation

See **Introduction** page 7 for suggestions on how to use the **grammar file**.

! *could/was able to*

Draw attention to the information in the box. Emphasise that

a) the difference in meaning does not apply to the negative.

b) *was able to* can be used in all situations but *could* cannot be used for a particular situation which was completed successfully.

> **ANSWERS**
>
> 1 was able to OR could
> 2 managed to

1 Practice: *choose the correct verb*

> **ANSWERS**
>
> 1 was able to (a particular situation)
> 2 mustn't (it is forbidden/against the law)
> 3 needn't have spent (I did it but it wasn't necessary)
> 4 must (*need* is followed by *to*)
> 5 could (general ability)
> 6 don't have to (it isn't necessary)
> 7 are allowed (*may* is not followed by *to*)
> 8 have (an obligation imposed by someone else/*must* is not followed by *to*)
> 9 need (it wasn't necessary so I didn't do it/*must* never follows *didn't*)
> 10 will be able to (future form required)

2 Practice: *gap fill*

> **ANSWERS**
>
> 1 can't; 2 mustn't; 3 must (should/ought to);
> 4 won't be able to; 5 can't; 6 didn't need;
> 7 couldn't/wasn't able to; 8 had to; 9 couldn't; 10 can't;
> 11 don't have to; 12 can't; 13 will she be able

> ▶▶ **extra activity**
>
> Tell students to write down three or four pieces of advice for Clare (Exercise 2.1/2). OR Tell them to write a reply to Clare's friend, giving her some suggestions on what to do to help her friend.

Homework: ▶▶ *Exam Practice Workbook* pages 40–41, Exercises 1–3

Use of English 1: *structural cloze*
(CB page 57)

Remind students of the strategy for this task, by focusing attention on the **exam strategy** box.

1 Read the text

Check answers to the questions before students do the task.

> **ANSWERS**
>
> 1 Buying goods over the Internet.
> 2 Almost anything: the text mentions food and clothes.
> 3 Advantages: great choice, open 24 hours a day.
>   Disadvantages: delivery can be slow.

2 Structural cloze task

Refer students to the **exam tip!**. Point out that they do not need to fill in the gaps in order. Filling in the easier ones first will give them more context to help them with the more difficult ones.

> **ANSWERS**
>
> 1 but/except
> 2 to (a preposition after 'access')
> 3 could/would (a modal verb)
> 4 out/down (a phrasal verb)
> 5 what (this is not actually a question, though a question word is used)
> 6 anything
> 7 more (part of a linking expression)
> 8 can
> 9 on (a preposition: a fixed phrase)
> 10 than (a comparison)
> 11 allows
> 12 have/need
> 13 who (a relative pronoun)
> 14 when
> 15 may/might

Homework: ▶▶ *Exam Practice Workbook* page 41, Exercise 4

Listening: *true or false?* (CB page 58)

Tapescript: ▶▶ TB page 109

Refer students to the exam file. Remind them that they must always read the instructions very carefully as the tasks vary in Paper 4, Part 4.

1 Strategy: *identify key words*

1 This exercise is to help students predict what they are going to hear. For Question 3, elicit:

- different ways of buying clothes, e.g.: boutique, department store, mail order catalogue
- different words and expressions for describing clothes, e.g: good quality, cool, it suits you, designer labels, good value for money, cheap

2 Discuss as a class what students need to listen for. Get them to turn the statements into questions.

2 🔲 Listening task

Guide students through the task, answering as many questions as possible on the first listening. They then check their answers when they listen again, using the clues only if they have to.

> **ANSWERS**
>
> 1 False. ('she may have a point, actually')
> 2 False. ('she gets good value for money')
> 3 True. ('you actually sound more like me than my sister')
> 4 True. ('half the time I get home and realise that what I've bought is a mistake')
> 5 False. ('I think my mates are usually quite straight with me')
> 6 False. ('couldn't care less about designer labels')
> 7 True. ('and the other half worrying about what other people think of us')

3 Discussion

Students should work in pairs. This will give them the opportunity to practise the language they have heard on the recording.

Over to you

4 Questionnaire

The questionnaire provides useful vocabulary. Let students work in pairs, then compare results as a class.

Speaking: *individual long turn*

(CB pages 59/200–203/207)

1 Vocabulary presentation

The aim of this exercise is to ensure students know the meanings of the words and expressions in the vocabulary box. They will need to use some of the language to do the exam task in Exercise 3. For Exercise 1.2, ask questions such as:

Which of the teenagers are wearing more fashionable clothes?
Do you think any of them are wearing designer clothes?
What are the most popular designer labels now?
Why do people choose to wear the latest fashions? (They want to achieve an image/show they are fashion conscious.)
Are you fussy about what you wear?
etc.

> **PHOTOS**
>
> **Photo 1** shows a group of teenagers in the street. They are wearing casual clothes: baggy trousers, denims, sweatshirts, trainers. One seems to be wearing a tracksuit top.
> **Photo 2** shows another group of teenagers. They are wearing trendy 'smart casual' clothes, which look much smarter than those in Photo 1. The girls are wearing miniskirts or tight trousers, stretch tops or T-shirts, and the boy is wearing a short-sleeved shirt.

2 Strategy for the long turn

Refer students to the **exam strategy**. Remind them also that they should listen carefully to the task which the examiner sets, and not simply describe the photographs.

3 Speaking task 1: *groupwork*

Put students into groups of three, two candidates and an examiner. Ensure that the 'examiners' understand their role and know where to find the 'examiner's' instructions for the task (page 203). Emphasise that the 'examiner' should not show the instructions to the candidates, but should read them out. This is good practice in listening carefully to instructions. Remind candidates they can ask for repetition if necessary. Elicit ways of doing this, e.g.:

'Sorry, I don't understand very well what I have to do.'
'I didn't quite hear you. Could you repeat it, please?'

Draw attention to the **exam tip!** and tell the 'examiners' to be sure to stop the candidates after one minute. Encourage students to use expressions from the **Functions file** on CB pages 200–201.

Do the feedback as a class when the groups have completed the task.

4 Speaking task 2: *groupwork*

Students can stay in the same groups for this. The candidates should turn to the photos on CB page 203. The 'examiner's' instructions for this task are on CB page 207.

You could go through the vocabulary in the box on CB page 203 before students do the task. Get them to say which words/phrases describe which photo.

> **PHOTOS**
>
> **Photo 1** shows people shopping in a small shop. Two customers are standing at the counter, and the assistant is putting their goods into a paper bag. There is an electronic till on the counter.
> **Photo 2** shows customers shopping in a big supermarket. There are long queues at the checkout tills. Most customers are using trolleys.

Making choices

Lead-in (CB page 60)

The photographs provide further practice for the individual long turn (Part 2) in the Speaking test. They also introduce some of the vocabulary that students will meet in the text.

1 Vocabulary presentation

Do the matching task as a class and explain any words that students don't know.

> **POSSIBLE ANSWERS**
>
> **Photo 1** shows a room which could be described as: cluttered, personal, cosy, comfortable, homely, inviting. It looks lived-in.
> **Photo 2** shows a room which could be described as: bare, sparse, airy, functional, orderly (= tidy), impersonal, stylish, contemporary. It contains the basic necessities, but nothing unnecessary.

2 Compare and contrast

Let students work in pairs here and practise doing the task in one minute. Encourage them to use the words in Exercise 1 and expressions from the **Functions file** on page 200.

Reading 2: *multiple matching*

(CB pages 60–61)

1 Identify reading strategy

The aim of the exercise is to remind students what reading skills and techniques are appropriate for this type of task. Discuss the options as a class or let students work in pairs first.

> **ANSWERS**
>
> **Ex. 1.1**
> The text is about people's lifestyles. The task is to answer the questions by choosing from the people A–E. This is a multiple-matching task.
>
> **Ex. 1.2**
> The suggested strategy is:
> 1 b); 2 b); 3 b); 4 b)
> Reading the questions first tells you what information and ideas you need to scan for. Once you have found the part you think contains the information, you should read that part carefully to check it really does answer the question.

2 Reading task: *multiple-matching questions*

You could go through the questions and clues as a class, to prepare students for the task.

Set a time limit of 15 minutes for doing the reading task.

> **ANSWERS**
>
> Clues:
> 1   fashion statement (line 60), trend (line 63)
> 2   labels (line 27)
> 3   'I take ages choosing' (line 15)
> 4   'to throw it out' (line 44)
> 7   'I usually have a shopping spree <u>at the start</u> of each season' (lines 90–91)
> 9   'A few years ago, I would ...' (lines 29–30)
> 10 'fabrics' (line 94)
> 14/15   'it lasts so much longer' (line 86); 'rather than several inexpensive items which will soon wear out.' (lines 24–26)
>
> Reading task:
> 1D   'I did it because I like it, not because it's the current trend' (lines 62–63)
> 2B   'I've refined my wardrobe down to a couple of well-known labels' (lines 26–27)
> 3A   'I take ages choosing each piece of furniture or lamp ...' (lines 14–18)
> 4C   'But if I go off something, I won't hesitate to throw it out ...' (lines 43–44)
> 5E   'I buy a lot of cream-coloured and beige-coloured things' (lines 83–84)
> 6D   'I'm always having people round for dinner and they seem to like the informality of it.' (lines 70–73)
> 7E   'I usually have a shopping spree at the start of each season ...' (lines 90–91)
> 8C   'I'd like to work in a soothing, relaxing environment' (lines 48–49)
> 9B   'I am much more careful about clothes than I used to be' (lines 21–22)
> 10E 'I will only buy things in one or two quality fabrics' (lines 93–94)
> 11C 'I think if you keep your clothes and possessions tidy, it can improve your mood.' (lines 57–59)
> 12D 'very homely. It's also very functional.' (line 66)
> 13A 'As an architect, I work with drawings all day and I don't want to look at them in the evening.' (lines 11–13)
> 14, 15B, E (in either order)   'I take a lot of care whenever I buy something' (lines 27–28); 'But it lasts so much longer than cheaper clothes' (lines 86–87)

Over to you

3 Discussion

The statements are taken from the article students have just read. Let them work in pairs or small groups to compare and discuss their own answers to the questions.

Homework: ▶▶ *Exam Practice Workbook* page 42

Vocabulary (CB page 62/176)

1 Choosing the right word

ANSWERS

1 spend (How much did you *pay* for that CD?/Do you *buy* many CDs?)
2 charge (How much do cassettes *cost*?/They *are demanding* high prices for houses in this area.)
3 make (I got a good *mark* in my test./Those phones are much better – they're in another *class* altogether.)
4 stock (That shop has an *in-store* restaurant./There wasn't a single customer in the *shop*.)
5 queue (There is a taxi *rank* outside the station/The school keeps *files* on each student.)
6 cash (I did not have enough *money* to buy the dress./ I have notes, but no *coins*.)
7 receipt (I was given a book *voucher* for my birthday./That was a good meal. Who's going to pay the *bill*?)
8 refund (I got a good tax *rebate* this year./If it is too big, you can *return* it.); exchange/change (If your TV breaks down, the shop will *replace* it.)

2 Countable or uncountable?

Refer students to **grammar file 2** CB page 176 for notes on uncountable nouns.

ANSWERS

Ex. 2.1
1 money, change, cash
2 furniture
3 jewellery (**Note:** 'clothes' is a plural noun and is never used in the singular.)
4 cotton, silk, material
5 luggage, equipment, shopping
6 staff, advice, information

Ex. 2.2
1 some; 2 little; 3 much, some; 4 this; 5 the, some; 6 a, some

Ex. 2.3
1 countable; 2 uncountable

3 Describing objects: *order of adjectives*

Tell students to read the texts all the way through before underlining the adjectives. Discuss as a class what the order of adjectives is before they do Exercise 3.2.

ANSWERS

opinion – favourite, beautiful, ornate, amazing, great
dimensions/size – huge, wide, thick, full-length, small
age – old
shape – round
colour – purple, pale cream, black
origin – Japanese, Indian
material – clay, leather, silk

Draw students' attention to the information in the box
! made + preposition. The choice of preposition after *made* depends on the meaning and context.

Over to you

4 Describe a possession

This exercise could be set for homework. Students should use the paragraphs in Exercise 3 as models for text organisation; i.e.:
1 Name the object
2 Information about how/when it was acquired
3 A description of the object

Homework: ▶▶ *Exam Practice Workbook* pages 42–43, Exercises 1–2

Use of English 2: *lexical cloze*

(CB page 63)

1 Discussion

Do this either as a whole class or in pairs. Point out that there are no right or wrong answers. The aim is to prepare them for the ideas in the text 'Spoilt for choice'.

2 Read the text

Students should read the text only after they have thought about the questions in Exercise 1.

ANSWERS

1 a) Advantages: We can buy products which 'suit our needs'.
    b) Disadvantages: It is difficult to get enough information to make a choice; it makes people anxious and stressed
    c) Solutions: People can buy only well-known brands, or take advice from advertising.
2 The title is a reference to there being too much choice. It could be positive or negative, i.e. we are in a favoured position because we have so much choice, **or** our shopping is made worse by so much choice.

3 Lexical cloze task

Refer students to the **exam tip!**. Tell them to use the clues to help them complete the task. Remind them to check their work when they have finished.

ANSWERS

1B; 2C; 3B; 4C; 5A; 6D; 7A; 8B; 9C; 10D; 11C; 12A; 13A; 14B; 15D

Homework: ▶▶ *Exam Practice Workbook* page 43, Exercise 3

Writing: *letter of complaint*

(CB pages 64–65)

As a class, brainstorm situations in which people might write a letter of complaint, e.g. they have been sold defective goods. Elicit reasons for writing a letter of complaint; what people hope to achieve, e.g. an apology, a refund, etc.

Refer students to the **exam file** and *exam strategy*.

1 Understand the task

Remind students that it is essential that they include all the points that they are asked to include. Stress that the tone is very important. The letter must be firm but polite, otherwise it will not achieve its aim.

> **ANSWERS**
>
> **Ex. 1.1**
> Points to be included:
> 1 The game is childish
> 2 It was boring
> 3 It was not cheap
> 4 Unreadable instructions
> 5 Delivery was slow
> 6 No free computer magazine
> 7 Ask for refund or a better game
>
> **Ex. 1.2**
> The letter is to the manager of the company and should be formal.

Focus on paragraphing

2 Put paragraphs in order

Stress the importance of paragraphing and that students should give thought to the organisation of the points.

> **ANSWERS**
>
> **Ex. 2.1**
> The order of paragraphs:
> 1 I am writing to complain ...
> 2 To begin with, ...
> 3 My second complaint ...
> 4 While we are on the subject of advertising, ...
> 5 The problems do not stop here.
> 6 To sum up, ...
> 7 I look forward to hearing from you.
>
> **Ex. 2.2**
> In each case the topic sentence is the first one.

3 Register

> **ANSWERS**
>
> The sentences which are rude or too aggressive are:
> 'I could sue you!' It is better not to say anything here.
> '... but that was a lie.' It is better to say: 'but that was misleading.'
> '... otherwise there'll be trouble.' It is better to say: 'I will take matters further.'

Focus on grammar

4 Indirect speech

1–2 Ask students to find all the examples of reported speech in the sample letter. On the board, reconstruct the original sentences or questions in three separate columns; e.g.:

Statements	Questions	Original form
You said the game would arrive promptly.		→ 'The game will arrive promptly.'
	I ... asked where it was.	→ 'Where is it? it was.

Discuss the changes in tenses and word order. Then tell students to read the notes in the **grammar file**.

> **ANSWERS**
>
> **Ex. 4.1 and 4.2**
> Examples of indirect speech in the sample letter:
> 'You said the game would arrive promptly.' (para. 2)
> 'I rang and asked where it was.' (para. 2)
> 'They suggested I should be more patient.' (para. 2) (→ Please be patient.)
> 'You said it was "unbeatable".' (para. 3) (→ The price is unbeatable.)
> 'You said that it was for older teenagers.' (para. 4) (→ The game is for older teenagers.)
> 'You also said that the game was "action-packed".' (para. 4) (→ The game is action-packed.)
> 'The instructions you claimed were clear were actually unreadable.' (para. 5) (→ The instructions are clear.) (para. 5)

3 Students should refer to the **grammar file** and to **grammar files 12** and **13** on pages 180–181 when doing this exercise.

> **ANSWERS**
>
> 2 ... that the new video recorder didn't work properly.
> 3 ... asked where he/Alex had bought it.
> 4 ... suggested (that) he/Alex (should) take it back to the store the next day.
> 5 ... asked the assistant if he could have a refund on his video recorder.
> 6 ... claimed (that) they had never had any complaints before.
> 7 ... insisted that he would not leave the shop until the assistant gave him a refund.
> 8 ... said (that) he would refund the money but his manager would not be very happy with him.

4 This exercise is also good preparation for the writing task to follow.

ANSWERS

Suggested answers:
Your advertisement stated that you were the only company in this country licensed to sell this brand but in fact I've seen them in a local store.
Your advertisement claimed that the jeans were excellent quality but the zip was broken.
Your advertisement stated that a free T-shirt would be/was included with each purchase but mine was missing.
Your advertisement claimed that the price was unbeatable but in fact I've seen cheaper ones.

Over to you

5 Writing task

Set the writing for homework after preparation in class.

CRITERIA FOR MARKING

Content: jeans in a local shop, broken zip, wrong size, wrong colour, no free T-shirt, price, late delivery, request for a refund.
Organisation: Letter format, clear organisation of points, suitable opening and closing formulae.
Register: Formal.
Effect on target reader: Would consider giving a refund.

Homework: ▶▶ *Exam Practice Workbook* pages 46–47

Unit 5 Test ▶▶ TB page 124

O-17-S71-O3

ily life

pic of the text and
lary. During the
e words and
ew items.

to Question 3 as
this will be needed for the discussion in Reading Exercise 4.

Definitions

to nag – to keep asking somebody to do something so
often that it is annoying

to go on at someone – to keep repeating the same
complaint

to be a tip – to look like a place where rubbish is dumped

chores – unpleasant tasks that have to be done,
e.g. washing up.

PHOTOS

The photo shows a boy's bedroom. There is a PRIVATE KEEP
OUT sign on the door. The room is rather messy and untidy,
with clothes on the sofa, and magazines all over the bed. The
boy's mother is pointing at the mess on the bed. She is
probably telling her son off for not cleaning up after himself.
He is probably resentful, and thinks she is interfering with his
privacy. He probably thinks she is nagging.

Reading 1: *multiple-choice questions*

(CB pages 66–67)

1 Strategy

The aim of the exercise is to remind students what reading
skills and techniques are appropriate for this type of task.
Let students do the re-ordering task in pairs, then check
and discuss answers as a class.

ANSWERS

Suggested strategy:
1 Read the text quite quickly for general understanding.
2 Read the questions but not the options, and underline key
words.
3 Read the text carefully.
4 Find the parts of the text that you think answer the
questions, and underline key words there.
5 Read the options A–D and choose the one that best
matches the ideas in the text.

2 Skim for gist

Set students a time limit of 4–5 minutes for the skimming
task. Remind them not to worry about words they do not

know. They can discuss the answers to the questions in
pairs or as a class.

ANSWERS

1 The psychologist thinks that teenagers should be allowed
their privacy and parents should not interfere.
2 Because Tim's room was very untidy.
3 Tim likes the mess and will tidy up when he feels like it.
4 His mother did not like the mess and thought that an
untidy room meant an untidy mind.
5 His mother stopping interfering, and Tim started to clean
his room once a week.

3 Reading task: *multiple-choice questions*

Set a time limit of 15–20 minutes if you are doing this in
class. Encourage students to use the clues given.

ANSWERS

1C 'privacy should be respected' (line 5).
2B 'the problem is ... saying things like ...' (lines 28–30). The
answer is not A because he says 'as long as she knocks'.
3C 'I like the mess ... It's interesting watching it grow'
(lines 36–37).
4D 'Parents' anxiety' (lines 53–54).
5D 'I was very shocked by Tim's response' (lines 67–68). The
key word in the question is 'most'.
6A The word in the previous sentence is 'exploded' (line 69).
7A 'Tim ... has taken to cleaning his own room once a
week.' (lines 87–89)

Over to you

4 Discussion

Students can discuss these points in pairs or small groups.

▶▶ **extra activity**

Ask each group to produce a written set of guidelines for
parents of teenagers.

Vocabulary: *collocations*

5 Vocabulary search

Encourage students to use the text to find the answers;
it will help to train them to read observantly and learn
language from their reading.

ANSWERS

Ex. 5.1

Verb	Noun	Adjective	Noun
decide	*decision*	anxious	*anxiety*
agree	*agreement*	private	*privacy*
solve	*solution*		
insist	*insistence*		
argue	*argument*		

Ex. 5.2
1 to find a *solution*
2 to come to an *agreement*
3 to have an *argument*
4 to respect someone's *privacy*
5 to feel *anxious* about something
6 to *insist* on doing something
7 to make a *decision*

Homework: ▶▶ *Exam Practice Workbook* page 48

Grammar: *structures after reporting verbs*

(CB page 68)

See **Introduction** page 7 for suggestions on how to use the **grammar file**.

Presentation

Here is a possible approach.

Give students a short list of sentences on the board as follows:

I would ask your parents for permission if I were you.
I didn't tell him your secret.
Don't forget to visit your grandmother, Sue.
Why don't you ask someone for help?
Don't do that again!

Ask students to rewrite the sentences in reported speech using an appropriate verb from this list:

remind, suggest, advise, tell, deny

Then refer students to the **grammar file** on page 68 to check their answers.

ANSWERS

Suggested answers:
He advised me to ask my parents for permission.
She denied telling him my secret.
He reminded Sue to visit her grandmother.
He suggested that I should ask for help.
He told me not to do that again.

1 Practice: *spot the error*

Students can do this exercise in pairs. Tell them the sentences contain common errors made by candidates in the First Certificate exam. This will encourage them to check their own work.

ANSWERS

1 She **told** me I had to ...
2 She suggested I **spend**/(that) I (should) **spend** ...
3 She reminded **me** that ...
4 ... that I **would** not go out/**not to** go out
5 ... warned me **not** to invite ...
6 ... advised me **to** come in ...
7 ... persuade her **to let** me ... she refused **to let** me go
8 She forbade **me to** go ...

2 Practice: *choose the right verb*

1 Make sure students check the verb pattern following the gap so that they know which of the two verbs fits.

After checking the answers, you could ask students to rewrite sentences 1 and 4, using the alternative verb given.

ANSWERS

1 told him (OR explained **to** him)
2 warned
3 threatened
4 ordered (OR He demanded **that** I **(should)** apologise ...)

2 Elicit the original conversation orally or in writing. Discuss the changes students had to make as a class.

ANSWERS

Suggested answer:
Father: Why were you so late last night?
Ginia: I forgot the time and missed the last bus.
Father: Well, don't let it happen again. If it does, you won't be allowed out for a month. Now, (go and) apologise to your mother for worrying her.

3 Practice: *match and rewrite*

Make sure students understand that this exercise has two parts. Students have to match all the sentences 1–8 to an appropriate verb first, then they should rewrite the sentences as reported speech, beginning with the words given.

ANSWERS

1h) I promised to tidy my room OR I promised that I would tidy my room.
2e) My aunt advised me not to buy a motorbike.
3g) My best friend suggested (that) I (should) talk things over with my parents.
4d) My father asked me to tell my friends not to phone so late.
5a) I begged my mother to let me go out.
6f) My parents warned me not to come home late or there would be trouble.
7b) My friend tried to persuade me to go to the club with him/her.
8c) My uncle offered to pick me up after school.

Over to you

4 Pairwork

This exercise provides further practice of reporting verbs using a personal context.

Homework: ▶▶ *Exam Practice Workbook* pages 48–49, Exercises 1–2

Use of English 1: *error correction*
(CB page 69)

Tell students to read the instructions for the Use of English task to remind themselves what the task involves. Use the *exam strategy* box to remind them of the strategy for tackling this task type.

1 Read the title and text

Use the questions provided to ensure that students have understood the text thoroughly before doing any of the task. Encourage whole class discussion for Question 3.

> **ANSWERS**
>
> 1 The survey was about how much parents and teenagers talk to each other.
> 2 Adolescents talk less to their parents because they want to be independent of their parents.

2 Error correction task

Tell students to do the task individually and then to compare answers in pairs. Draw attention to the *exam tip!*. Remind them also that the clue to an extra word could be on a different line.

Point out the value of identifying the types of errors the task tests. This will help them to revise and be useful in the exam.

> **ANSWERS**
>
> Unnecessary word types:
> pronoun – lines 2, 4, 13; particle – line 9; adverb – line 1; verb form – lines 5, 7, 10, 14; preposition – line 0; *to*-infinitive – line 11; linking word – line 8
>
> 1 well; 2 it; 3 ✔
> 4 us (we can say EITHER 'explained that' OR 'explained to us that')
> 5 said ('is said to be a time' would be correct)
> 6 ✔
> 7 have (we can say EITHER 'are in need of' OR 'have need of')
> 8 but
> 9 up ('give up' is a phrasal verb; 'give the impression' is a collocation)
> 10 trying
> 11 to ('suggest' is never followed by 'to')
> 12 ✔;   13 them;   14 got;   15 ✔

▶▶ *extra activity*

Ask students to write a questionnaire about teenage relationships with their parents, using the ideas in the text as a basis. They can carry out their own survey based on the questionnaire.

Homework: ▶▶ *Exam Practice Workbook* page 49, Exercises 3–4

Speaking: *individual long turn*
(CB pages 70/204/207)

1 Strategy: *DOs and DON'Ts*

Ask students to complete the lists of DOs and DON'Ts in pairs. They can refer to the *exam strategy* recommended in Units 2 and 5 if they need to.

> **ANSWERS**
>
> See *exam strategy* Unit 2 page 21, Unit 5 page 59.

2 Speaking task 1

Before putting students into groups, ask them to look at the vocabulary in the box and decide which items describe which picture. Check understanding by asking questions about the photographs, e.g.:

Which photograph shows a wedding reception? (1)
What is the bride wearing? (a wedding dress)
Which man is the groom? (the man standing up)
Who do you think the woman in the blue suit is? (probably the bride's mother or mother-in-law)
What does the best man do? (he helps the bridegroom at the wedding ceremony)
What are they celebrating in the other photo? (probably a birthday party)
What usually happens at a children's birthday party? (the birthday boy or girl receives presents, the children play games, etc.)

Put students into groups of three and ensure that they understand the procedure. Make sure the 'examiner' reads the instructions for the task (page 204) aloud and does not let the other students read them. Encourage the 'candidates' to use expressions from the **Functions file** on CB pages 200–201.

Make sure the student playing the role of the examiner times the candidates. Encourage students to give feedback to each other on completion of the task.

> **PHOTOS**
>
> **Photo 1** shows a wedding reception. The bride is sitting down and the bridegroom is talking to an older woman, probably his mother or the bride's mother.
> **Photo 2** shows a children's birthday party. The children are dressed up and are eating. They are having a great time.

3 **Speaking task 2**

Students work in groups of three as before, using the photos on page 204. Students who are playing the role of the examiner should give the instructions on page 207. Again, encourage students to give each other feedback after they have finished.

PHOTOS

Photo 1 shows a group of schoolchildren posing for a class photo. Some of them are sitting and some are standing.
Photo 2 shows a group of friends in an informal setting. They are all standing and smiling at the camera.

Listening: *multiple matching*   (CB page 71)

Tapescript: ▶▶ TB page 110

1 **Understand the task/Predict**

Remind students that they should always read the instructions and the questions before listening. This will help them to identify the main topic of the extracts.

The questions in this exercise encourage students to use personal experience to aid understanding. For Question 2, elicit such words as:

presents, dancing, party, celebrate.

Make a list of these on the board.

2 🔲 **Listen for main ideas**

Play the recording once. Let students compare answers but don't confirm them. They can see who was correct and why after the second listening.

3 🔲 **Check answers**

Tell students to read Questions 1 and 2 before playing the recording a second time. The aim is to guide them to listen for words that confirm the answer they have chosen is really correct. The task instructions specify that the five speakers are talking about 'social events'. Therefore, for Option B, it is important to decide if the speaker is talking about **celebrating** a birthday as **a social event**, and not just mentioning a birthday in passing. The same applies to Option F.

If students have to make any changes to their answers on the second listening, discuss what misled them the first time they listened.

ANSWERS

1E   'a good start in a new place'
2C   'They won't actually be getting married for a while'
3A   'now we can relax until after the long holiday'
4D   'she'll have a new life in a new country'
5B   'it was nice to have it on the day itself'; 'I've still got some more presents to look forward to'

Over to you

4 **Discussion**

Do this as a class or pair discussion.

PHOTOS

Photo 1 at the bottom of the page shows May Day which is celebrated on 1 May. It celebrates the reappearance of flowers in the spring and is celebrated with dancing round a tall pole called a Maypole. It originates from Roman times.
Photo 2 shows Independence Day in the USA which celebrates the Declaration of Independence on July 4th 1776 in Philadelphia. It is celebrated with parades, public speeches and fireworks. Surprisingly, it was not declared a public holiday until 1941.

▶▶ **extra activity**

Set Exercise 4 for homework as an informal letter.

Like father, like daughter

Lead-in   (CB page 72)

Discuss the questions as a class.

▶▶ *alternative activity*

Ask one half of the class to write down three advantages of having a famous parent and the other half to write down three disadvantages. Make groups with one or two students from each half of the class and ask them to try and reach an agreement as to whether it is a good or a bad thing to have a famous parent.

PHOTOS

Clockwise from the left the photos show:
Sir Anthony Hopkins (famous for his role in *The Silence of the Lambs* and *Hannibal*) and his daughter.
The actor, Donald Sutherland, and his actor son, Kiefer Sutherland.
The singer, Madonna, and her baby, Lourdes.

Reading 2: *gapped text (sentences)*

(CB pages 72–73)

1 **Identify reading strategy**

To review the recommended strategy for this task type, have students do this exercise individually and then compare their answers with a partner before checking Unit 3 page 34.

Suggested strategy:
1   Read the whole of the base text including the sample answer.
2   Read the text around each gap carefully.
3   Read the extracted sentences and look for one that fits the meaning of each paragraph.
4   Check for language links before and after the sentence.
5   Read the whole text again.

2   Read the base text

Stress the importance of understanding the whole text before starting the task. Refer students to the **exam tip!**. Allow them about five minutes before discussing the answers to the questions, which check comprehension of key points in the text. (Students should be allowed longer to read the gapped text than the other task types as it requires more detailed study of the text.)

1   She remembers seeing her father on the stage in a red wig; going backstage after the performance.
2   She thought it would be boring to do the same thing as her parents.
3   Because it can be a very hard life.
4   You want to be just as successful as your parents.

3   Reading task: *match sentences to gaps*

Discuss the advice about language and topic links before students start the task. Point out that there are clues to help them. Set a time limit of 15 minutes for the reading task.

1F   'when I was a child', line 13, links with 'when I was about four'.
2B   'and so did the audience', line 19, links with 'at the centre of so much attention'; 'my father' is replaced by 'him'.
3C   'homely' and 'protected environment', lines 24 and 25–26, link with 'like a family'.
4E   'initially', line 28, suggests a different ambition, and this links with 'My first real aspiration'; 'That passed', line 30, refers to the whole idea of becoming an underwater explorer.
5A   'it' in the sentence before the gap, line 34, refers to 'the need to act'; 'But I realised that it ...' links the negative idea of the sentence before with the positive idea of the sentence after the gap.
6D   'It' in the sentence before the gap, line 45, refers to 'acting as a career'; 'but I already knew that' refers to 'what a hard life it can be', line 45.
7H   'high expectations', line 54 is replaced by 'those'; 'those feelings', line 55, in the sentence after the gap refers back to 'moments when you think ...'

Vocabulary: *synonyms*

4   Vocabulary search

The aim of the exercise is to focus on the writer's choice of vocabulary, and the effect it has on the style and tone of a text.

Note: The paragraph references are not the same as the question numbers in this exercise.

Ex. 4.1
1   really (line 8); hysterically (line 18); incredibly (extract I)
2   concept (extract I)
3   weep (line 21)
4   initially (line 28)
5   aspiration (extract E)
6   dissuade (line 44)

Ex. 4.2
The words in the text are less common and everyday, so they give the text more weight and seriousness.

Over to you

5   Discussion

This exercise is good practice for Part 4 of Paper 5 (Speaking). Let students work in pairs or small groups

Homework: ►► *Exam Practice Workbook* page 50

Vocabulary (CB page 74)

1   Adjectives describing personality

Ensure that students know the meanings of the words in the box before doing the exercise or tell them to use their dictionaries.

You could give pairs of students four or five words from the list and ask them to think of an example of behaviour for each characteristic, e.g.: *honest* – to admit you broke something.

Words with negative meanings:
argumentative, arrogant, bad-tempered, jealous, mean, rude, stubborn

2   Nouns for personal qualities

Ex. 2.1

–ence	–ity	others
intelligence	originality	honesty
patience	sensitivity	politeness
	sincerity	loyalty
	sociability	

3   Your ideal partner

Students fill in the form individually.

To prepare for the interviews, students could make up questions to find out who has the qualities they would like in their ideal partner. They could then move around the class asking these questions. E.g.:

Are you good at telling jokes? (a sense of humour)
Do you like going to parties? (sociability)
Do you always tell the truth? (sincerity)
etc.

4   Choosing the right word

ANSWERS

1   brought up ('raised' is American English and 'educated' refers to schooling)
2   grow up ('become' is not followed by 'to'; 'grow' implies only physical growth)
3   get to know (this is the only one that refers to a process)
4   character ('character reference' is a frequently used combination)
5   in common with (I am *very similar to* my mother. My mother and I are *very alike*.)
6   made ('make a success of' is a collocation)

5   Linking words

Students often confuse these groups of linking words. Ensure that they know how to use all the choices in each question. After doing the task, you could ask them to rewrite the examples using the other linking words and phrases, wherever appropriate.

ANSWERS

Note: Possible uses of the other linking words are suggested in brackets.
1   Afterwards, ... (this starts a sentence)
   (*After* leaving the party David walked Sonya home. They left the party at midnight. *After that* it took another hour to get home.)
2   Although (= a conjunction linking two clauses)
   (*However,* Sonya still needed a jacket. *In spite of* the warmth of the night, Sonya still needed a jacket.)
3   at first ('Firstly' is usually used when listing arguments. 'First of all' is used when listing things or actions.)
4   During
   (*While* they were walking ... . They walked home. *Meanwhile,* their friends continued the party at another house.)
5   at the beginning.
   (*In the beginning,* Sonya had felt a little shy.)
6   eventually
   (*At the end* of the evening, they walked home together.)
7   in the end ('lastly' is used when listing arguments)
8   At the end (*At last* he had found a girl he loved.)

Over to you

6   Pair/groupwork

Ask students to work in pairs or small groups. Encourage them to use appropriate link words for sequencing. This is useful preparation for the story writing to follow later in the unit. Remind them that the stories they tell do not have to be true.

7   Make up a story

You can set this for homework. Make sure the students know the meaning of the phrasal verbs.

Homework: ▶▶ *Exam Practice Workbook* page 51, Exercises 1–2

Use of English 2: *lexical cloze*
(CB page 75)

1 – 2   Predict/Read the text

The aim of these exercises is to help the students understand the content of the text.

ANSWERS

Ex. 2.1
According to the text, most teenagers want a loyal friend to share their secrets; the opportunity to experiment; a feeling of security.

3   Lexical cloze task

Discuss the advice given. Ask students to do the task using the clues given.

ANSWERS

1D; 2A; 3B
4D   A conjunction expressing a reason/result.
5A   The only word that makes sense in the context.
6A   A collocation with 'part'.
7B   The verb 'look' is the only one followed by the preposition 'for'; A and C would not be used in the continuous here.
8C
9D   This is the only word that does not need a preposition.
10A   'stand by someone' is a phrasal verb.
11B   A collocation.
12B   We tell a secret **to** someone.
13A   A and C are both followed by 'of' but C does not fit the meaning.
14C   The word 'also' in the next line shows that a linker of addition is needed.
15C   The only word that makes sense in the context.

4   Vocabulary search: *collocations*

Refer students to the *study tip!*. The aim of the exercise is to encourage students to get into the habit of noting down useful combinations of words. Point out to students that even if they know the individual words, they may not know all the ways in which they go together.

Homework: ▶▶ *Exam Practice Workbook* page 51, Exercise 3

Writing: *story (first line)* (CB pages 76–77)

Use the **exam file** to introduce the writing task type. Discuss what makes a good short story. What makes students want to read to the end of a story? Draw up a list of ideas for writing a good story.

Go through the *exam strategy*. Emphasise to students that:

- the given sentence **must** be at the very beginning or the very end according to the instruction. They should not add **anything** before or after it.
- they should include all the points in the given sentence, e.g. in the sample question: 'John', 'good friends'.
- they should write a new story specifically for this situation, not a previously written story.
- they do not have to write out the given sentence but it is a good idea to.

1   Understand the task

ANSWERS

Ex. 1.1
John must be the main character.
Two people must be involved, but there could be more.
Names/pronouns: 'John', 'he', 'Maria', 'she', 'they'.

Ex. 1.2
1   Students will read the story in a magazine.
2   It could be a love story or just a story about friendship.

Focus on working out a plot

2   Plan a story

Stress again the importance of planning. While doing this exercise, students should keep referring back to the sentence they have been given.

3   Compare a sample story

Compare the sample with the students' ideas drawn up at the beginning of the lesson. Allow a free discussion here.

Note: The sample includes an introduction about John and a flashback into the past.

Focus on grammar

4   *used to/would*

1   Refer students to the **grammar file**. Go through the difference between 'would' and 'used to', 'get/be used to'. Then tell them to correct the mistakes of form in the sample story.

2   Elicit examples and write them on the board in two columns: those that can be expressed with 'used to' or 'would' and those that can only be expressed with 'used to'. Ask students to tell you in which column to write them. E.g.:

used to/would	***used to***
sleep in the mornings	be able to stand on my head
my parents … read me stories	be in the football team

3–4 Pairwork
Students should work in pairs and then report back to the rest of the class to check accuracy. Students could then write some sentences of their own to keep as a record.

ANSWERS

Ex. 4.1
Errors in the sample story: *he would occasionally* see *her … he* was used to *being alone … he* used to sit *by himself*

5   Use of tenses

The aim of this exercise is to focus attention on the importance of using tenses accurately in stories. Draw attention to the information in the box first.

ANSWERS

Other tense errors:
Line 2: *Of course he'd seen her before* (past perfect for an action before another past action)
Line 10: *One evening John was walking home …* (past continuous for interrupted actions)
Line 15: *When Maria realised that the girls had gone …*

Over to you

6   Writing task

Ensure that students work out thorough plans for their stories in class. Then set the task itself for homework.

Students could work in pairs and work out one plan together or help each other develop their own ideas.

CRITERIA FOR MARKING

Content: Story must follow on from the first sentence.
Organisation: The story should reach a definite ending.
Register: Consistently neutral or informal.
Effect on target reader: Would be able to follow the storyline.

Homework: ▶▶ *Exam Practice Workbook* pages 54–55

Progress review 2 (Units 3–6) ▶▶ *Exam Practice Workbook* pages 56–57

Unit 6 Test ▶▶ TB page 125

7 Fitness

Lead-in (CB pages 78/199)

The exercises in the **Lead-in** introduce students to the topic of the text and will help them cope better with the content when they do the reading task.

Do Exercise 1 as a whole class. Let students work in pairs for Exercise 2, then discuss the results as a class. Find out if the results are different from the original survey by referring students to page 199.

Reading 1: *gapped text (sentences)*

(CB pages 78–79)

Refer students to the **exam file**. Explain that the gapped texts they read in Units 3 and 6 were narrative, and were organised according to chronological order. Discursive texts are about ideas rather than past events, so the linking expressions used will be different. It is even more important to read the base text thoroughly before doing the task, to get a good grasp of what the writer is saying.

1 Read the base text

Allow students about five minutes for the first reading of the base text. Then discuss the answers to the questions and any vocabulary queries related to the questions.

ANSWERS

1 Causes of stress: pressure to succeed, the need to have the right mobile phone or trainers, exams, large workloads, long days, wanting to be liked, family problems, boredom ('being stuck in a routine'), too many expectations to live up to (paras. 3–5)
2 Positive aspects of stress: 'the feeling of excitement you need to perform' (lines 61–63)
3 Ways of coping: playing loud music, kicking a ball around, chatting to a friend (lines 70–74)

2 Understand style

The aim here is to focus attention on a typical feature of magazine style: starting with a statement that is only explained later in the text.

ANSWERS

1 'It' must refer to something in the missing sentence, probably 'stress'.
2 'That anxious, gloomy feeling called stress'.
3 The first sentence is written in this way to attract the reader's attention and make him/her want to read on to find out what is being referred to.

3 Reading task: *match sentences to gaps*

You could go through the clues as a class to ensure students understand how they help them tackle the task. Then let them continue individually.

During the class check, refer back to the discussion about organisation of discursive texts at the beginning of the lesson. Elicit the way this text is organised:

- Description of the problem → how serious it is → ways of dealing with the problem.
- General comments → specific examples.

ANSWERS

1H The writer does think that stress should be taken seriously.
   'that ' = 'blowing problems out of proportion';
   'it' ='stress';
   'it' = 'blowing problems out of proportion'; 'it' = stress
2A The kind of pressure suggested is 'commercial' pressure: the pressure to buy certain goods.
   'In particular' introduces a specific example of 'pressures on young people'.
3B Other causes probably relate to the wider world.
   The linking expression 'On top of all that' introduces another example which is 'the bigger picture'.
4G The missing sentence probably adds another example.
   'despite the big pressures' links back to the examples of stress in the previous sentence; 'being tired' links with 'late nights' in the sentence after the gap.
5C Again, the missing sentence probably adds another example.
   The linker 'also' introduces another symptom of stress.
6E The missing sentence probably gives further explanation of the point.
   'Too little' contrasts with 'a small amount' in the previous sentence and 'not enough ... too much' in the sentence after the gap.
7F The missing sentence probably refers to further examples of things to do to beat stress.
   'Regular exercise ... .' = further examples of 'stress-busters'; 'stop you getting stressed in the first place' links back to 'things to beat stress'.

Vocabulary: *phrasal verbs*

4 Vocabulary search/Record phrasal verbs

Let students work in pairs to do the exercise. Encourage them to try and work out the meanings from the context.

Ensure that they have a system for recording vocabulary. It is a good idea to record phrasal verbs separately under the verb or the particle.

1   face up to – to accept and deal with (line 14)
2   give up – to stop trying (line 28)
3   live up to – to be as good as someone expects (sentence A)
4   end up – to find yourself in a certain situation (line 45)
5   come down to – to be caused by (sentence G)
6   put up with – tolerate (sentence H)

Over to you

5 Discussion

Students can work in pairs to complete the exercise.

> ▶▶ *extra activity*
> Students could write a letter giving a friend advice on what to do about stress.

Homework: ▶▶ *Exam Practice Workbook* page 58

Grammar: *the passive*   (CB page 80)

See **Introduction** page 7 for suggestions on how to use the **grammar file**.

Presentation

Tell students to look at the examples in Section **A** of the **grammar file (Form)**. Compare the examples of active versus passive sentences and discuss why it may be better to use the passive in these situations. Students should match the examples to the uses given in section **B (Use)**.

1 Practice: *active or passive?*

This exercise practises both the form and meaning of the passive. Students should focus on which is the subject and object of the verb.

1   suffer
2   have not always been recognised
3   were examined
4   will publish
5   are being researched

2 Practice: *rewrite sentences*

Elicit the occasions when it is not necessary to include the agent in a passive sentence:
• When the agent is unknown
• When the agent is obvious
• When the agent is not at all important

1   Teenagers are frequently worried by arguments with friends.
2   Many teenagers have been stressed out by pressure from parents.
3   Young people are always being pressurised (by advertisers) to spend money by advertisers.
4   New guidelines on coping with stress have recently been issued. OR New guidelines have recently been issued on coping with stress.
5   Students should be advised to do regular exercise.
6   Stress can be reduced by chatting to a friend.
7   Your performance will be improved by positive stress.
8   We were shown a video on yoga and head massage.

3 Practice: *transformations*

Before students start this exercise, refer them to the information in the box **! *make / let / allow***. Elicit that these verbs are followed by the *to*-infinitive in the passive, but the bare infinitive in the active.

1   is not allowed to
2   was advised not to
3   has been made to do
4   has been taken up by
5   she was accused of
6   deserve to be dropped

Over to you

4 Practice: *write sentences*

This is preparation for the report writing later in the unit.

Suggested answers:
1   The old building is being pulled down.
2   Plans for the sports hall are being drawn up.
3   The running track has not been finished yet.
4   The swimming pool has just been dug out.
5   The tennis courts will be/are going to be finished in one month.
6   The changing rooms will be opened soon after that.

Homework: ▶▶ *Exam Practice Workbook* pages 58–60, Exercises 1–4

Use of English 1: *structural cloze*

(CB page 81)

1 Strategy

Let students do the re-ordering task in pairs, then check and discuss answers as a class.

Suggested strategy:
1   Read the whole text for general understanding.
2   Read each sentence carefully.
3   Try to decide what type of word is missing.
4   Fill in the gaps.
5   Read the whole text again.

2   Read the text

Use the questions to check understanding before students do the task.

1   Methods of dealing with stress: laughing, telling a joke, eating chocolate, wearing the right colours.
2   Effective because laughter strengthens the immune system and improves performance, colours have different effects on your state of mind, chocolate protects from heart disease.

3   Structural cloze task

Point out the value of identifying the types of errors the task tests. This will help them to revise, and in the exam.

1   at – preposition (part of a phrasal verb)
2   or – linking word
3   for – preposition (after an adjective)
4   who – question word
5   it – pronoun
6   to – preposition (part of a fixed expression)
7   give – verb
8   in – preposition
9   is – auxiliary verb (part of a passive verb form)
10   other – adjective (part of a fixed phrase)
11   if/when – linking words
12   be – auxiliary verb (part of a passive verb form)
13   tells – part of a phrasal verb
14   against – preposition
15   all – quantifier (part of a fixed phrase)
Prepositions occur most often in this task.

Homework: ▶▶ *Exam Practice Workbook* page 60, Exercises 5–6

Speaking: *collaborative task and discussion*   (CB pages 82/207)

1   Vocabulary presentation

The vocabulary work helps prepare students for the Part 3 task.

Ex. 1.1
football pitch
basketball court
running track
sports hall
swimming pool
fitness centre
Ex 1.2
do gymnastics, aerobics
play basketball (tennis, volleyball)
go running, swimming (fishing, cycling)

2   Part 3 task

Put students into groups of three and ensure that they understand the procedure. The 'examiner' reads out the instructions for the task on page 207, making sure the 'candidates' do not see them. The 'candidates' should try to use vocabulary from the box on the page, and expressions from the **Functions file** on CB pages 200–201. The 'examiner' should time the 'candidates'. Remind them that they have three minutes.

Refer students to the *exam strategy* for Part 3 tasks before they start.

When they have finished, the 'examiner' can comment on how well the others have done the task. Did they

•   follow instructions?
•   encourage each other to speak?
•   respond to each other?

Clockwise from the top, the photos show young people involved in the following activities:
Running, weight-lifting, gymnastics, football, swimming, basketball.

3   Part 4 discussion

Students could change roles so that someone else is the examiner. Refer them to the *exam strategy* for Part 4 tasks before they start. Remind them that they have about four minutes for this part.

Listening: *multiple-choice questions*
(CB page 83)

Tapescript: ▶▶ TB page 110

Refer students to the *exam strategy* to remind them how to tackle the task.

1   Vocabulary

This exercise offers the chance to review or present some of the key vocabulary in the Listening script. Students should make sentences using the words and expressions in the box to show they know the meaning, as in the example supplied. Help them by referring to the photographs. Encourage discussion of some of the issues that come up. Ask questions like:

What is your favourite football <u>club</u>?

How do football clubs get new footballers? (often through 'transfer deals' – taking on someone from another club)

Look at the photo of three men. What is the man on the right doing? (tossing a coin) *Who is he?* (the referee) *Why is he tossing the coin?* (to see which team should kick off)

In which picture can you see someone <u>scoring a goal</u>? Which man is the goalkeeper? (the man in the yellow shirt)

Who are the people on the football pitch in the big picture? (fans running onto the pitch after a match)

Can you name some companies that sponsor particular sports? (Coca-Cola, Nike, Adidas, etc.) *Is sports <u>sponsorship</u> good or bad?*

Why can it be useful for sportspeople to have <u>a back-up career</u>? (= another career in addition to sport) (they might be injured)

2 **Strategy:** *predict*

Invite students to speculate, but don't confirm answers. Tell them they can find out if they are right when they listen to the recording.

3 📻 **Strategy:** *read the question carefully*

Play the first part of the recording and tell students to choose the best answer to Question 1. If any chose option C, discuss why it is wrong – it does not relate to the question asked.

ANSWERS

Question 1 asks 'what was <u>the first step</u> on the road to her present career' – being offered a job must be a later step, not the first one.

1A 'I discovered later that his wife was one of the people listening to me.'
    C is wrong: 'a bit later Julian challenged me to be his agent for a year.'
2C 'I try to point them in the right direction financially.'
3B 'I might work for a player for two years before asking them to pay me anything.'
4B 'I used to sneak off to football matches with the boys from school.'
5A 'The only problem ... was when I was banned from the annual dinner.'
6C 'women in football have to do that much more than their male colleagues.'
7A 'because they have a mother who knows the best footballers.'

---

4 📻 **Listening task**

Play the rest of the recording. Then play it again all the way through so that students can check their answers.

Over to you

5 **Discussion**

These questions are similar to the type of questions asked in Part 4 of the Paper 5, Speaking.

Olympic sports

Lead-in (CB page 84)

The aim of the **Lead-in** is to prepare students for the topic of the text.

You could ask students to put the words in the vocabulary box into three groups before they discuss the questions.

equipment/facilities	physical skills	mental skills

goggles
net
whistle
trainers
flippers
rowing machine
running machine
helmet
weight-lifting equipment
cycling machine
racquet
gloves
stick
punchbag
	speed
	fast reflexes
	stamina
	a good sense of
	  balance
	hand-eye
	  coordination
		determination
		motivation
		dedication
		courage

Reading 2: *multiple matching*

(CB pages 84–85)

1 – **2** **Reading task:** *multiple matching*

Remind students of the recommended **exam strategy** if necessary. Then ask them to do the task individually before comparing their answers with other students. Set a time limit of 15 minutes.

ANSWERS

1A 'I can't run ... and I'm not keen on it.'
2A, 3E (in either order)
    A 'my diet is pretty much what I like';
    E 'I eat ... whatever they put in front of me.'
4C 'They're developed over very long periods.'
5B 'I've got to keep my weight below 57 kilograms.'
6D 'When you look back over the record ...'
7B, 8E (in either order)
    B 'whatever my coach says';
    E 'My coach warned me ...'
9D 'I've got a static bicycle in my garage.'
10B 'many boxers are keen on ballet.'
11C, 12D (in either order)
    C 'not too much high-protein food';
    D 'I steer clear of fatty food.'
13E 'I never do more than two hours a day.'
14C 'On long training runs ... But in a race, it's very different.'
15D 'I don't stick to traditional mealtimes.'

Vocabulary: *using context*

3 Meaning from context

Do not allow students to use dictionaries for this exercise. They should think about the situation and what fits logically. Point out that the clue to the meaning of a word is not always in the same sentence: it could be in the sentence before or the one after.

ANSWERS

1 momentum = the force that makes something move.
  Clue: 'strength'.
2 bulky = big.
  Clue: 'most swimmers have <u>very big</u> shoulders. Chest muscles are <u>less important</u>. My arm muscles are <u>not</u> bulky <u>either</u>'.
3 lean = thin.
  Clue: the opposite of 'bulky'.
4 agility = the ability to move quickly and easily.
  Clue: 'to make my footwork <u>faster</u>'; the reference to ballet.
5 replenish = to replace used reserves.
  Clue: 'because I'm burning up a lot of calories'.
6 methodical = always done in the same way.
  Clue: 'I try and do a fraction more each time.'
7 static = not moving.
  Clue: What kind of bicycle is he likely to use in his garage?
8 a fraction = a small amount.
  Clue: you can only see the difference 'over a long period of time'.

Over to you

4 Discussion

Let students discuss these questions in pairs. Ask them to try to reach an agreement.

Homework: ▶▶ *Exam Practice Workbook* page 60

Vocabulary (CB page 86)

1 Healthy eating

1–2 Students should work in pairs. Check answers as a class.

3 There are several possibilities here. If students come from different countries, they could tell each other about the most common cooking method in their own countries.

4 In order to get a more varied discussion, students should work in groups of 3 or 4.

ANSWERS

Ex. 1–2
Note: Items in italics are in the text on CB pages 84/85.
Carbohydrates
pasta, toast, bread, cereal, rice, potatoes, crisps, chocolate, French fries (chips), root vegetables.
Proteins
eggs, fish, white meat, nuts, lentils, cheese, milk, shellfish.
Vitamins
orange juice, fruit, salad vegetables, green vegetables.
Fat
cream, chocolate, cheese, milk, French fries, butter, crisps.
Fibre
porridge, rice, fruit, lentils, green vegetables.
Salt
crisps
Ex. 1.3
Suggested answers:
fish – baked, grilled, steamed, barbecued
meat/steak/beef – roast, barbecued, grilled, stewed
sausages – grilled
vegetables – roast, boiled, steamed
snacks – microwaved
potatoes – boiled, roast, baked

2 Parts of the body

1–2 If necessary, use the photo to revise the parts of the body in the box before students do Exercise 2.1.

Point out the difference between 'break' and 'sprain': 'break' involves the bone and 'sprain' the muscle, usually in a joint.

3 As a class elicit other situations that can make parts of the body 'ache', 'hurt' or 'be sore'.

4 Focus attention on the labelled illustration, which provides some useful vocabulary for discussing treatments. Check understanding by asking questions like:

What do you do if you cut your finger? (put a plaster, or Band-Aid, on the cut)
What does the doctor do to treat a broken leg? (he puts it in plaster – this is a different meaning of 'plaster')
What do you need to help you walk if you break your leg? (crutches)
Why has the girl in the picture got her arm in a sling? (she has broken it)

Then allow students to talk about their own experiences in pairs or as a class.

ANSWERS

Ex. 2.1
1 a) inside the body – heart, muscle, vein, lung, tongue, stomach
  b) limbs – leg, arm
  c) joints – wrist, ankle, elbow, knee, hip, shoulder
  d) other – thumb, toe, forehead, thigh, calf, finger, chest
2 You could break your wrist, thumb, leg, ankle, arm, finger, hip, toe.
  You could sprain your wrist, ankle, knee.

Ex. 2.2
1 forehead; 2 shoulder; 3 muscle; 4 hip; 5 thigh; 6 calf;
7 ankle; 8 knee; 9 finger; 10 thumb; 11 wrist; 12 elbow;
13 chest

Ex. 2.3
ache – head, ear, back, stomach, teeth, arms, feet
hurt – you can use this for any part of the body
be sore – throat

3 Choosing the right word

Let students do the first task in pairs. You can do the
second task as a class after checking answers.

1 symptoms; 'symptom' is a medical term, 'sign' is a more
general term for evidence that something is happening
2 temperature; 'fever' is an illness in which you have a
very high temperature
3 injured; 'wound' is used to mean injure or hurt someone
else
4 pain; 'ache' refers to a dull pain, not a sharp one
5 injury; 'wound' is used to describe an injury made by a
knife or bullet
6 infection
7 cure
8 recover; 'cure' is not followed by 'from'
9 treated; 'operate' is not followed by 'with'
10 sick

Use of English 2: *word formation*

(CB page 87)

1 Read the text

Use the questions to check students' understanding of the
text.

1 Functional foods are foods that do more than satisfy
hunger.
2 They are popular because people believe they can prevent
illness.

2 Word-formation task

3 Check and analyse answers

The aim of this exercise is to remind students how
important it is to look at the whole meaning in order to
decide what form of the word is needed in the gap.

Ex. 2/3
1 simply (suffix)
2 hunger
3 pleasure (suffix)
4 achievements (suffix + plural form)
5 capable
6 healthy (suffix)
7 popularity (suffix)
8 natural (suffix)
9 illness(es) (suffix + plural form)
10 unnecessary (negative prefix)

Homework: ▶▶ *Exam Practice Workbook* page 61

Writing: *report (evaluating)*

(CB pages 88–89)

Use the **exam file** to introduce the task type. Ask students if
they have ever read or written a report. What kind of
information might be included in a report about a facility
such as a sports centre? Who might want the information
and why?

Go through the *exam strategy*. Explain that they will
practise each of the points in this lesson.

1 Understand the task

Ask students to read the task and then answer the questions
in pairs.

1 Points to be included: a description of the sports centre,
plus its good points and its bad points.
2 1 The report is for the club secretary. A neutral style, as
you are a member of the club, and the secretary is a
fellow student.
2 b)

2 Analyse a sample answer

Ask students to read the sample report and compare it with
the advice in the *exam strategy*. Point out that there are
some things wrong with the sample answer. Elicit what
these are: there are no headings; the introduction is too
short, so it is not clear.

1 The writer has covered all the points asked for although
the section on bad points is rather short.
2 The style is appropriate.
3 The writer could use sub-headings. See Exercise 3.2.

Focus on format

3 Improve the sample answer

Point out that there is a standard format for reports. Using headings will help them to organise their ideas. The wording of introductions and conclusions is very similar in most reports.

> **ANSWERS**
>
> **Ex. 3.1**
> Format 1 (memo) is more appropriate.
>
> **Ex. 3.2**
> The order of the paragraph headings:
> Introduction
> General information
> Prices
> Good points
> Bad points
> Conclusion
>
> **Ex. 3.3**
> 1 The style is inappropriate and it contains no information.
> 2 b) It informs the reader of the content of the article.
>   a) is too short.   c) is too informal.
>
> **Ex. 3.4**
> 1 The conclusion makes a general comment, summarising the report.
> 2 It is suitable for this task.

Focus on grammar

4 Expressing purpose

Students match the examples in the report with the appropriate section of the **grammar file**.

> **ANSWERS**
>
> **Ex. 4.1**
> 'A booking scheme is being introduced <u>in order to</u> limit numbers.'
> 'there are secure lockers <u>for</u> belongings'. (= to store belongings)
> 'patrols the rooms regularly <u>so as to</u> discourage thieves'.
>
> **Ex 4.2**
> 1 to see (same subject)
> 2 so that he could (different subject)
> 3 in order to (same subject)
> 4 so as not to (same subject)
> 5 so that I wouldn't (different subject)
> 6 so as to (same subject)

Over to you

5 Writing task

Go through the task. Ask the students to underline the points to be included:

- types of facilities
- good points of each
- bad points of each
- opening times
- prices

Ask them to identify the intended reader (the group leader). As a class, draw up a list of the sub-headings that could be used.

Tell students to write the report for homework.

> **CRITERIA FOR MARKING**
>
> **Content:** The report should describe the facilities, mention good and bad points, give details of opening times and/or prices.
> **Organisation:** Report format with sub-headings.
> **Register:** Consistently neutral or formal.
> **Effect on target reader:** Would be fully informed.

Homework: ▶▶ *Exam Practice Workbook* pages 64–65

Unit 7 Test ▶▶ TB page 126

8 Travel

Lead-in (CB page 90)

The **Lead-in** is designed to introduce the topic of holidays and travel and encourage students to relate it to their own experiences and opinions. Begin by asking students:

What kinds of holiday can you think of? (e.g. beach holiday, etc.)
What is the purpose of a holiday for you?

1 – 2 Discussion

Ensure that students know the meaning of the following words:

package tour operator – a company that sells inclusive holidays, i.e. travel, accommodation and sometimes food and/or activities.
Blind date – a game based on a TV show where people are chosen for a date on the basis of answers to questions, without being seen by their proposed partner.
Karaoke – singing to recorded music

Let students complete the tasks in pairs. This is good practice for the Paper 5 (Speaking) Parts 3 and 4. Then compare as a class.

Reading 1: *multiple matching*

(CB pages 90–91)

Check that students remember the **exam strategy** for this task.

1 Predict

For Exercise 1.2, tell students to skim the text to get a general impression of what type of holiday each text describes. Point out that one holiday could come under more than one type.

ANSWERS

Suggested answers:
A – beach holiday
B – educational, activity holiday
C – walking holiday
D – educational, activity holiday
E – educational, cultural holiday
F – sightseeing, cultural holiday

---

2 Reading task: *multiple-matching questions*

Tell students to underline the sentence(s) that gave them the answer as they do the task. If you are doing this in class, set a time limit of 15 minutes.

3 Compare answers

Encourage students to compare their answers. If they have got different answers, they should try and justify their own answers and then reach an agreement.

ANSWERS

1F   'you'll find places that are much cheaper …'
    (lines 103–104)
2A   'year-round good weather' (line 6)
3D   'if you're ever going to write, it will happen here …
    a beautiful, tranquil setting' (lines 59–61)
4E, 5F   (in either order)
    E   'gain an insight into the local way of life'
        (lines 84–85);
    F   'all the background to the sights and the local
        customs' (lines 107–109)
6A, 7B   (in either order)
    A   'local dolphin population' (line 17);
    B   'photos to identify individual animals' (lines 36–37)
8B   'collecting skin samples for analysis and monitoring
    their movements' (lines 37–39)
9C, 10D   (in either order)
    C   'The walks are divided into easy, average and
        difficult … select wisely' (line 49–51);
    D   'The centre offers dozens of other self-improvement
        courses' (lines 64–66)
11A   'it only takes four days to pick up the basics of scuba
    diving' (lines 10–11)
12C, 13E   (in either order)
    C   'Could there be a better way to make new friends?'
        (lines 55–56);
    E   'an ideal environment for getting to know your
        fellow guests' (lines 81–83)
14E   'to try your new-found expertise out on all your
    friends on your return' (lines 92–95)

Vocabulary: *adjectives*

4 Vocabulary search

1 Students could work in pairs to find the words in the text.

2 Elicit from the whole class other words that can be described by the adjectives in Exercise 4.1. Draw up a list on the board.

ANSWERS

Ex. 4.1/2
Note: Other possibilities are in brackets.
1   break (line 3) (job)
2   beach resort (lines 5–6) (holiday, evening)
3   hotels (line 46) (restaurant)
4   walks (lines 49–52) (job, climb, situation)
5   setting (line 61) (scene, atmosphere)
6   holiday (line 72) (performance, news)
7   food (lines 88–89) (meal)
8   shops and restaurants (line 100) (view, setting, food, etc.)

Over to you

5 Describe a holiday

Students should work in pairs. Encourage them to use as many of the adjectives in Exercise 4.1 as possible.

Homework: ▶▶ *Exam Practice Workbook* page 66

Grammar: *determiners and quantifiers*

(CB pages 92–93)

See **Introduction** page 7 for suggestions on how to use the **grammar file**.

Presentation

Here is a possible approach.

Refer students to the **grammar file**. Elicit differences between the examples in each group.

Draw up a table on the board to show determiners and quantifiers used with uncountable and countable nouns:

	Positive	Negative/Questions
Countable	some several a lot of (a) few	many any
Uncountable	some plenty of a lot of a great deal of (a) little	much any

1 Practice

Students can do the exercises in pairs and refer to the **grammar file** if they are in doubt. Ensure that they read the text through before they begin.

> **ANSWERS**
>
> The numbers in brackets refer to the sections of the Grammar file
> 1 a lot of (C2)   7   a little (D5)
> 2 many (D7)   8   a lot of (C2)
> 3 want (B2)   9   any (A3)
> 4 little (D6)   10 so many (D1)
> 5 every (E2)   11 much of (D2)
> 6 most (D9)   12 either (F3)

2 Practice: *complete a survey*

Ensure that students understand how to do the task. Tell them to look at the survey table on page 92, then read the text at the top of page 93 all the way through. Do the first few gaps with them if necessary to show them where to find the information from the survey table:

The information for gap (1) is given at the top of the table: 'Number of people interviewed: 300+', so the answer is

'over <u>three</u> hundred'. For the remaining gaps, students have to interpret the results. For example, out of the people interviewed, 280 said they like going abroad for their holidays, and only 26 said they didn't, so the answer to gap 2 must be 'Nearly <u>all</u>', etc.

Then let students continue in pairs.

> **ANSWERS**
>
> 1 three; 2 all; 3 a few; 4 Most; 5 any; 6 some; 7 many;
> 8 a lot of; 9 both; 10 all; 11 either; 12 little; 13 every/each;
> 14 some; 15 any; 16 any

Over to you

3 Conduct a survey

This should be set for homework.

Homework: ▶▶ *Exam Practice Workbook* pages 66–67, Exercises 1–4

Use of English 1: *error correction*

(CB page 93)

1 Exam strategy

Students should work in pairs to remind themselves of the exam strategy used for this task.

> **ANSWERS**
>
> **Recommended strategy:**
> 1   Read the whole text to find out what it's about.
> 2   Read each whole sentence, not just the numbered line.
> 3   Underline the words you think should not be there.
> 4   Read the sentence again without the word.
> 5   Read the whole text again to check your answers.

2 Read the text

Tell the students to read the whole text quite quickly and use the questions to check understanding. Students should back up their answers to Question 2 with reasons relating to the text, e.g. they like/don't like spending holidays in the country, etc.

> **ANSWERS**
>
> 1   A young person writing to a friend.
> 2   Answers will vary.

3 Error correction task

To help students identify the error types, you can refer them back to the **exam file** in Unit 4 page 43, which gives a list of typical errors.

1 lots (quantifier – this would need to be followed by 'of')
2 a (article – not used in front of uncountable nouns like 'work')
3 up (particle after a verb – a person 'grows up')
4 of (preposition – not used before an adjective)
5 too (adverb – this word cannot be used in this position, but would have to go at the end of the sentence)
6 ✔
7 that (conjunction – not used with 'in case')
8 as (conjunction)
9 ✔
10 the (definite article – not used in the phrase 'after dark')
11 ✔
12 it (pronoun – not needed in a relative clause as 'which' replaces 'it')
13 of (preposition)
14 through (preposition – we say either 'all through the summer' or 'the whole summer')
15 so (this is used to avoid repeating something that came before, e.g. 'You would be welcome to stay here. My parents say so'.)

Homework: ▶▶ *Exam Practice Workbook* pages 67–68, Exercises 5–6

Listening: *note-taking* (CB pages 94–95)

Tapescript: ▶▶ TB page 111

Refer students to the **exam file** and the **exam strategy**. Emphasise that:

• they should always read the instructions carefully
• they should use the time given on the recording in the exam to read the questions and try to predict the content of the text.

1 Predict

Ask students to read the instructions and the notes and ask them for their ideas about 21st-century holidays. Write a list of their ideas on the board.

2 🔲 Listening task

Draw students' attention to the **exam tip!** before playing the recording twice. After the first play through, ask students to check exactly what they need to listen for during the second hearing.

While checking answers, compare the facts with the students' predictions on the board. You could develop this into a discussion about students' own predictions.

1 4.1%; 2 information technology; 3 beach; 4 self-catering; 5 food/music (in either order); 6 hire(d) car; 7 country; 8 scuba diving; 9 working; 10 the Internet.

Speaking: *collaborative task and discussion* (CB pages 94–95)

Follow the procedure recommended in Unit 7, TB page 66.

1 Part 3 task

Before you put students into groups for the Part 3 task, you could discuss the map on CB page 95. Explain that the photos illustrate types of holidays. Ask students to identify what these are.

2 Part 4 discussion

Make sure students understand the vocabulary supplied for the Part 4 task, before they move on to the discussion.

The photos show the following:
United Kingdom: the Houses of Parliament in London, with the clock tower. The bell in the tower is known as Big Ben; the Lake District a popular holiday area in the North of England.
Europe: skiers in a winter ski resort in the Alps; a Club Med holiday resort in Spain.
Middle East: the Pyramids with a camel in front.
Africa: holidaymakers on safari in Zimbabwe, photographing elephants.
Australia: a scuba diver.
New Zealand: swimming with dolphins.
USA: horse-riding cowboy style in Texas.
South America: a parrot in the rainforest.

Ecotourism

Lead-in (CB page 96)

The discussion is useful practice for Paper 5 and can be done either in pairs or as a whole class. Use the photographs and the vocabulary in the box to elicit answers to the questions.

Definitions

ecotourism – short for 'ecological tourism', i.e. holidays that do not destroy, and may even protect, the environment, e.g. by providing a financial incentive to protect wildlife, which tourists pay to see
revenue – income
habitats – places where wild animals live

Photo 1 shows tourists on a wildlife safari in Africa. They are watching a zebra from two vans.
Photo 2 shows tourists 'whale watching'. They are taking photos of the whale which can be seen to the left of their boat.

Reading 2: *multiple-choice questions*

(CB pages 96–97)

1 Strategy

1 Refer students to the photograph to ensure they know what a lizard is. Ask them to predict how they think this animal will behave.

2 Review the recommended strategy for multiple-choice questions.

2 Skim for gist

Set a time limit of three or four minutes for the first reading of the text.

> **ANSWERS**
>
> 1 It eats quite large animals.
> 2 By feeding them with a goat.
> 3 The writer is making the point that tourists provide income for the islanders but as a result the dragons do not lead a natural life and the goats are sacrificed. The question is, is this worth it?

3 Reading task: *multiple-choice questions*

Set a time limit of about 15 minutes for the task.

> **ANSWERS**
>
> 1C 'After watching documentaries ...' (lines 21–24)
> 2D 'Having spent the previous night in luxury ...' (lines 25–28)
> 3C 'The zoologist filled me in ...' (lines 39–40)
> 4A
> 5D
> 6B 'Although the Komodo dragon can live quite happily on a single pig or deer a week ... this group was getting perhaps three goats a day.' (lines 76–79)
> 7C 'no one I met had ever seen one on Flores' (lines 95–96)
> 8B 'Is the goat's death worth an hour's entertainment?' (lines 100–101)

Vocabulary: -ing *adjectives and nouns*

4 Identify word class

The aim of this task is to show that words that look similar because they all end in -ing can nevertheless have different functions. Let students do the exercise in pairs.

> **ANSWERS**
>
> 1 adjective (line 46)
> 2 adjective (line 61)
> 3 part of a compound noun – 'viewing platform' (lines 67–68)
> 4 adjective (line 74)
> 5 adjective (line 85)
> 6 adjective (line 85)
> 7 noun – countable (line 94)
> 8 part of a compound noun – 'feeding area' (line 97)
> 9 noun – uncountable (line 103)
> 10 adjective (line 106)

Over to you

5 Discussion

You can do this in pairs or small groups. Tell students to keep their list of pros and cons as this will help with the writing task at the end of the unit.

Homework: ▶▶ *Exam Practice Workbook* page 68

Vocabulary (CB page 98)

1 Past participles + prepositions

1 Tell students to read through the text 'ENJOY ... a weekend break in Scotland' and answer the following questions:

a) *In what ways is Scotland separate from England?* (It has its own Assembly, flags and legal system.)

b) *What does Scotland have to offer tourists?* (history, shopping, scenery, wildlife)

Students then work in pairs to complete the text. They should first fill in the phrases that they know and then use the context to fill in the remainder. Ask them to then check those that they are not sure of in a dictionary.

> **ANSWERS**
>
> 1 linked to; 2 blessed with; 3 surrounded by; 4 Twinned with; 5 visited by; 6 Set on; 7 crowded with; 8 lined with; 9 located off; 10 situated in; 11 included in

2 If students are from the same country, they should work out the answer to these questions in pairs. If they are from different countries, they could ask and answer the questions in pairs.

2 Choosing the right word

Ask students to do the exercise individually and then check their answers in pairs. If they disagree, they should check in a dictionary.

Ask them then to make their own sentences with the other word in each pair.

> **ANSWERS**
>
> 1 coast (We walked along the rocky *shore.*)
> 2 vacancies ('vacancy' is usually used for accommodation; you might find 'spaces' in e.g. a car park)
> 3 excursions (a 'journey' is often over a long distance and is from A to B.)
> 4 trip ('voyage' is on the sea)
> 5 rare ('strange' or 'odd' would imply that something is not normal)
> 6 waited ('I *attended* evening classes in English for a year.')
> 7 take (to *make* a mistake)

3   Phrasal verbs

Students should first read the whole of each dialogue for context before attempting the exercise.

ANSWERS

1A	slow down
1B	get to; take off; set out
2A	check in
2B	make for
3B	turn back; hold us up
4B	has broken down; drop him/her off
5B	speed up
6B	get off; pick us up

Over to you

4   Ask and answer

Tell students to do this exercise in pairs and make a note of any new vocabulary connected with airports in their Vocabulary notebooks.

> ▶▶ *extra activity*
>
> Students could write a letter to a friend telling him/her about their holiday mishaps.

Homework: ▶▶ *Exam Practice Workbook* page 69, Exercises 1–3

Use of English 2: *lexical cloze*

(CB page 99)

1   Predict/Read the text

Begin by eliciting what the good or bad effects of tourism can be. Ask students to consider how far their own lives are affected by tourism. This discussion gives students a reason for reading the text.

ANSWERS

Ex. 1.2
According to the text:
good effects of tourism: it provides work for the local inhabitants, it brings money into the country.
bad effects of tourism: damage to the natural environment, endangers the country's wildlife.

2   Lexical cloze task

Students complete the task using the clues given. Discuss students' answers as a class.

ANSWERS

1B		
2C	Clue: the following preposition 'on'.	
3B	The only word that makes sense in the context.	
4D	A collocation.	
5D	Clue: the negative introduction 'Not all ...' shows that a linker of contrast is needed.	
6C		
7B	A collocation.	
8C		
9A	The only word followed by 'of'.	
10A	Part of a fixed phrase with 'of'.	
11B		
12A	A linking expression that includes 'that'.	
13C		
14C	A collocation.	
15D	Clue: in + *-ing*.	

3   Word + preposition combinations

Encourage students to get into the habit of noting the use of prepositions after verbs/nouns/adjectives in their general reading.

ANSWERS

Combinations in the text:
bring (advantages) to
to spend (money) on
to provide (someone) with
to have a (bad) effect on
associated with
to make aware of
as a result of
a (good) market for
to adapt to something

Homework: ▶▶ *Exam Practice Workbook* page 69, Exercise 4

Writing: *discursive composition*

(CB pages 100–101)

Use the **exam file** to introduce the task type. Go through the *exam strategy*. Explain to students that they will practise each of the points in this lesson. Emphasise that:

- it is essential to stick to the question.
- it is very important to plan carefully.
- it is essential to use paragraphs.
- the composition is much more interesting to the reader if the arguments are supported by examples.
- it is better to have a few well-developed arguments than to try to fit in too many ideas.
- the correct use of link words is very important to convey the writer's point of view.

1 Understand the task

1 Points to be covered are:
   The good and/or bad points of mass tourism; whether you agree with mass tourism or not.
2 Your teacher is going to read the composition. The style could be neutral or formal, but must be consistent.

Focus on brainstorming and planning

2 Develop a paragraph plan

You can work through these tasks as a whole class or let students work in pairs.

1 You could refer students to the discussion for and against mass tourism which they had before doing the lexical cloze on CB page 99 and put up their points on the board.

2 Students select which points to include in their composition. Remind them that it is better to have a few well-developed arguments with supporting details than to try to fit in too many ideas.

3 Build up a paragraph plan on the board and compare it with Plans A and B.

ANSWERS

Ex. 2.3
In Plan A the points are not well organised – positive and negative aspects of tourism are mixed up and related points are not put together.

3 Analyse a sample answer

Ask students to discuss the sample composition in pairs.

ANSWERS

Ex. 3.1
1 The first sentence in each paragraph is the topic sentence. The sample composition is organised as in Plan B.
2 Linking words that list points: 'First', 'Also', 'Another point is that ...' , 'A second problem is that ...'
3 '... tourists don't like dirty places, <u>for example</u>, oil on beaches.' (para 2); '<u>For example</u>, they take coral from the sea ...' (para 3)

Ex. 3.2
A suggested introduction:
Tourism is an important industry in many countries and it has a great effect on all aspects of life in those countries. It can bring a lot of benefits if it is managed well, but in many cases it is not.

Focus on grammar

4 Modal verbs

1 Ensure that the students understand 'modal verbs' so they know what they are looking for in the sample composition: 'can', 'ought to', 'should', 'must'.

2 When doing the transformation exercise, students should pay particular attention to whether the sentences refer to the past or the present. Ask them to match each answer to the appropriate function in the **grammar file**.

ANSWERS

Ex. 4.1
Modal verbs in the sample composition:
'can force', 'can benefit' (= ability)
'ought never to have allowed this' (= criticism of past actions)
'should have left it alone' (= criticism of past actions)
'should be taught' (= obligation)
'We must be careful' (= obligation)

Ex. 4.2
1 could have visited (= missed opportunity)
2 should be kept (= obligation)
3 must close down (=obligation)
4 shouldn't have kept (= criticism of past action)
5 have to keep some zoos (= obligation)
6 needn't have taken (= criticism of past action)

Over to you

5 Writing task

Help students to plan this composition in class before asking them to write it for homework. Refer them back to the points they thought of for and against zoos after Reading 2 on CB pages 96–97. They should:

- decide what their opinion is.
- make a short list of points to include.
- make a paragraph plan.

CRITERIA FOR MARKING

Content: Statement of opinion of whether zoos are unnecessary.
Organisation: Clear development of argument with appropriate paragraphing and linking of ideas.
Register: Formal or neutral. <u>Must </u>be consistent.
Effect on target reader: Would be able to understand the writer's viewpoint.

Homework: ▶▶ *Exam Practice Workbook* pages 72–73

Unit 8 Test ▶▶ TB page 127

Progress test 2 (CB pages 102–103)

Before you set **Progress test 2** on CB pages 102–103, tell students to do the **Progress check** in the *Exam Practice Workbook*, pages 74–75. This reviews the language tested in the *Coursebook*. (You will find the answers in the With Key edition of the *Workbook*.)

ANSWERS

Coursebook Progress test 2

1 Structural cloze

1B; 2C; 3A; 4B; 5B; 6C; 7D; 8B; 9D; 10A; 11A; 12D; 13C; 14A; 15D

2 Key word transformations

1 were you, I would take
2 used to forget to do
3 he shouldn't have asked
4 have been living in my
5 wasn't able to play
6 once she had eaten
7 had fewer friends when
8 told him not to open
9 to avoid disturbing
10 offered to get me some

3 Error correction

1 have; 2 to; 3 me; 4 where; 5 ✔; 6 all; 7 reach; 8 ✔; 9 for; 10 ✔; 11 is; 12 an; 13 it; 14 ever; 15 them

4 Word formation

1 especially; 2 replacement; 3 competitions; 4 excessive; 5 products; 6 impossible; 7 importance; 8 supervision; 9 friendly; 10 attractive

---

After doing the test in the *Coursebook*, you could also use the photocopiable test:

Progress test 2 ▶▶ TB pages 128–130

(See TB page 140 for the answers.)

9 | Discoveries

Lead-in (CB page 104)

The **Lead-in** introduces the topic of the reading text, and allows students to activate their knowledge of the subject before reading. It also pre-teaches some key vocabulary.

1 Compare and contrast photos

Explain that the photos show different images of space exploration and extra-terrestrial or alien life forms. The main pictures are film stills. Ask students to match the vocabulary in the box to the images. Then ask questions to encourage discussion, e.g.:

Can you identify the three films?
Have you seen any of them?
What films have you seen about extra-terrestrials?
What would be the advantages of building space colonies?
etc.

Definitions

extra-terrestrial – from outside planet Earth
alien creature – (in this context) from another planet
galaxy – a large group of stars
to orbit (the earth) – to go around the earth in a spacecraft

---

PHOTOS

The photos show:
Darth Vader, from the film *Star Wars* - he represents a hostile alien group that poses a threat to Earth.
The alien, ET, from the film *ET* - he represents a friendly alien.
A still from the film *Mission to Mars*, in which a human search party travels to Mars, to find out what happened to an earlier expedition to the planet. The still shows the rescuers approaching the original spacecraft. They are wearing space suits and helmets.
The photo at the bottom of page 104 is of a radio telescope.
The background photo on page 105 shows the night sky, with some of the planets in Earth's solar system.

---

2 Discussion

This exercise provides a reason for students to skim read the text in Exercise 3.

Elicit students' opinions as a whole class. Then take a poll to find out how many students agree, and how many disagree with the statement. Put the results on the board. When students have read the text, you can find out how many students have changed their minds based on the facts in the text.

3 Skim for gist

Allow three or four minutes for students to skim the text to find any information that supports the statement in Exercise 2.

ANSWERS

At first, it seems that the article is suggesting that intelligent life on another planet is unlikely:
- it has been proved that there is no life on Mars or Venus. (lines 9–12)
- it is the very special position of the Earth that makes it able to sustain life (lines 13–16), and it is unlikely that this situation can happen very often.
- UFOs have been discredited. (paras. 2–3)

However, the enormous size of the universe makes it highly probable that there is intelligent life somewhere. (lines 66–79)

Reading 1: *multiple matching*
(CB pages 104–105)

1 Strategy

Use the questions and the *exam tip!* to review how to tackle this task type.

ANSWERS

1　b)
2　Students do not need to understand every word, because the task tests understanding of general meaning not detail. (See *exam tip!*)

---

2 Reading task: *match headings*

1 Tell students to find the headings in the exam task which are questions. Use the example given (I) to show how to identify answers to the questions.

2 Students then complete the task using the clues given. Set a time limit of 15 minutes.

ANSWERS

1E	'The Earth's position ... makes it the only planet in our solar system' (lines 13–15)
2D	'Many people claim to have seen ...' (line 31), 'the formation of crop circles' (lines 36–37)
3A	'Recently, more information has been released ...' (line 59)
4B	'... has worked out an equation ...' (lines 67–69)
5C	'But unless they visit us, this won't happen' (lines 83–84)
6G	'So scientists are pinning their hopes on exchanging messages ...' (lines 94–95)
7F	'... you can be named as a co-discoverer' (lines 125–126)

Over to you

3 Read for detailed information

The aim of this task is to get students to read the text again carefully and learn as much as they can from it. Let them work on this activity in pairs or small groups to encourage discussion.

ANSWERS

Suggested answers:
Life was able to develop on Earth because it is just the right distance from the sun.
Signs which were thought to show alien activity include sightings of UFOs and the formation of crop circles.
Scientists are trying to identify radio signals from alien civilisations. Frank Drake's Institute has invited people with personal computers around the world to join in the search.
The size of the universe suggests that there must be intelligent life on other planets. However, although we might like the idea of meeting aliens, it is unlikely to happen.

Homework: ▶▶ *Exam Practice Workbook* page 76

Grammar: *modals* (CB pages 106–107)

See **Introduction** page 7 for suggestions on how to use the **grammar file**.

Presentation

Go through the statements in the **grammar file** and ask students to say which they agree or disagree with and why.

1 Practice: *match the sentences*

Do the first two or three items as a class, and ensure that students understand the context and the vocabulary. Then let them continue in pairs.

ANSWERS

1d); 2g); 3a); 4h); 5f); 6b); 7e); 8c)

2 Speculate about photos

PHOTOS

The photos show:
• pyramids in Egypt; the death mask of the Pharaoh Tutankhamun
• the skull of a large (wild) cat; a panther-like creature on a wall near a field of sheep, believed to be a big cat

Do this as a class. The topic leads into Exercise 3. Explain that many people in Cornwall (in south-west England) claim to have seen a big black cat like a panther. This animal has been called 'the beast of Bodmin Moor' but has never been caught. The photo at the bottom of the page on the right is supposedly a picture of the animal. Elicit possible

explanations for these sightings, and the skull, which is of a big cat with fangs.

ANSWERS

Possible answers:
Wild cats may have escaped from a zoo.
Someone may have owned a big cat as a pet and it escaped.
The photo must/may be a fake.
The skull could belong to a prehistoric animal.

3 Practice: *gap fill*

Students should read the whole dialogue first before filling in the gaps. Discuss the questions in 3.2 after doing the class check.

ANSWERS

1	can't have seen	5	must weigh
2	must have been	6	must have killed
3	may not have been	7	Could (it) have escaped
4	can have gone	8	must have imagined

Over to you

4 Discussion

Do this as a class discussion.

BACKGROUND INFORMATION

Loch Ness is a long, narrow lake in Scotland. It stretches from Fort William to near Inverness. The **Loch Ness monster** is believed to be a huge snake-like creature that lives in the lake. There have been many photos taken of the monster but these are all thought to be fakes.
The **yeti** is a large animal like a human which is supposed to live in the Himalayan mountains of Tibet. Most people do not believe that it exists.

Homework: ▶▶ *Exam Practice Workbook* pages 76–77, Exercises 1–3

Use of English 1: *structural cloze*
(CB page 107)

1 Read the text

1/2 After reading the text, ask students to close their books while one student retells the story and the others comment on accuracy.

ANSWERS

The title refers to finding the answer to a secret message or clue.

3 Encourage the use of modals here. Answers will vary.

! substituting words

Focus on the grammar point in the box before students do the cloze task.

> **ANSWERS**
>
> 1 built (them); 2 sent a spacecaft to Mars

2 Structural cloze task

Students should complete the task individually and compare their answers in pairs. Remind them that it helps to identify the word types required when doing this task.

> **ANSWERS**
>
> 1   before/previously (adverb)
> 2   never (adverb)
> 3   which (relative pronoun)
> 4   no (determiner)
> 5   someone (pronoun)
> 6   whose (relative pronoun)
> 7   on (preposition)
> 8   its/the (possessive adjective/article)
> 9   at (preposition)
> 10 are (auxiliary verb, part of a passive)
> 11 Anyone/Anybody (pronoun)
> 12 were (auxiliary verb, part of a passive)
> 13 Since (linking word)
> 14 despite (linking word)
> 15 does (substituting verb)
>
> Pronouns occur most often in this task.

Homework: ▶▶ *Exam Practice Workbook* pages 77–78, Exercises 4–5

Listening: *sentence completion*

(CB page 108)

Tapescript: ▶▶ TB page 112

Refer students to the **exam strategy**. The exercises that follow take them step by step through the strategy.

1 – 2 Predict content

Students may know nothing about the Bermuda Triangle. The purpose of the map is to arouse interest in the topic and to help them understand the location of the Bermuda Triangle. Encourage them to work out as much about it as they can from the map and from the incomplete sentences in the exam task. Tell them they will find out more when they listen to the recording.

> **BACKGROUND INFORMATION**
>
> See tapescript TB page 112.
> The Bermuda Triangle is an area of sea in the Atlantic Ocean near Bermuda where many ships and planes, together with their crews, have mysteriously disappeared over the past 500 years.

3 Predict missing information

Remind students that they should think about what kind of information they need to listen for in the time allowed before the recording is played.

> **ANSWERS**
>
> Type of information that is missing:
> 2   some kind of publication
> 3   some method of flying – a noun or adjective is needed here
> 4   a job/position
> 5   some equipment
> 6   a place/building
> 7   a form of transport
> 8   something that is needed to fly a plane
> 9   something that can cause a plane to crash
> 10 another factor that can cause a plane to crash

4 📼 Listening task

Play the recording once all the way through. Then play it again all the way through so that students can check their answers and fill in any gaps.

> **ANSWERS**
>
> 1   one thousand/a thousand/1,000
> 2   magazine (article)
> 3   low-level
> 4   senior instructor
> 5   compass/instruments
> 6   control tower
> 7   flying boat
> 8   fuel
> 9   human error
> 10 bad luck

5 📼 Identify paraphrase

The aim of this exercise is to show students that they need to listen for different ways of expressing the information on their question papers in order to pinpoint the answers.

> **ANSWERS**
>
> Question:
> 5   'ceased to function'
> 8   'Shortly after this, it was calculated, the planes must have run out of fuel'
> 9   'The US Navy's original report put the disappearance down to human error'
> 10 'was ... the result of'

Over to you

6 Discussion

This is a further opportunity to practise the use of modals.

Speaking: *individual long turn*

(CB pages 109/205/207)

Follow the procedure recommended in Unit 6, TB pages 59–60. Students should change roles for the second speaking task (the photographs on page 205).

Before students start, check understanding of the vocabulary provided for the photos by asking questions. For the photos on page 109, you could ask, e.g.:

Where do you think the people in the first photo are? (It looks like a hot country, the columns in the background are ancient, the people are wearing Arab clothing, so it must be somewhere like Egypt.)
What have the people in the hole found? (It looks like a statue.)
What do you think their job is? (They must be archaeologists.)
What have the men in the second photo found? (Coins)
How did they find them? (The man on the left is holding a metal detector, so they must have found the coins using this.)

Refer them to the **exam tip!**. Suggest that they spend the first 30 seconds or so comparing and contrasting the photographs and the remaining 30 seconds talking about the theme according to the instructions the examiner gives them.

During the groupwork, encourage them to speculate about the content of the photographs using modals.

PHOTOS

Speaking task 1:
Both photos show people who have found something under the ground.
The first photo shows an archaeological dig somewhere in Egypt.
The second photo shows three men who have found some old coins buried in a field. There is a tractor in the background, so one of the men is a farmer.

Speaking task 2:
Both photos show strange phenomena.
The first photo shows a saucer-shaped Unidentified Flying Object hovering or flying over a desert area in the United States.
The second photo shows a ghost holding a candlestick at the foot of an old-fashioned flight of stairs.
Both photos are in fact fakes.

Discovering the past

Lead-in   (CB page 110)

Discuss what the illustrations show about the lives of our prehistoric ancestors. Ask, e.g.:

Where did they live? (In caves)
What were their clothes made of? (From the skins of animals they killed)
What kind of food did they eat? (Meat and probably things like berries from the trees; the people in the illustrations probably hadn't started to farm the land yet.)
How did they get their food? (They hunted wild animals, and also herded sheep and gathered plants.)
How did they cook their food? (They probably roasted meat over an open fire of wood.)
How did they travel? (On foot or maybe on horseback)
etc.

Then encourage students to use modals to speculate about their way of life compared with ours, e.g.:

It must have been hard to keep warm. They didn't have heated houses.
They probably didn't do a lot of travelling.
They can't have lived as long as we do today.
etc.

Reading 2: *gapped text (paragraphs)*

(CB pages 110–111)

Refer students to the **exam file** to introduce this new task type. Point out that the strategy remains the same for inserting paragraphs as for inserting sentences. Elicit the recommended strategy.

1   Predict

The aim of the exercise is to activate students' knowledge of the topic, and start them thinking about the content of the text. These questions should be done with the whole class as a brainstorming activity. Put the questions students come up with on the board.

ANSWERS

Suggested answers:
1   The discovery of an ancient man
2   (students should share information here)
3   Possible questions that the text may answer:
   • When did the man live?
   • Who discovered him?
   • When and how was he discovered?
   • What does the discovery tell us about life in ancient times?

2 Read the base text

Students should read the text individually to find how many of the group's questions they can answer. Point out that they may not find the answers to all of the questions.

3 – 4 Strategy: *identify main ideas/predict development of ideas*

These exercises aim to encourage students to think about meaning and to actively engage in following the ideas in the text. Lead students through the tasks step by step, discussing answers after each stage. Point out that the clues to the contents of the missing paragraphs could be either in the paragraphs before or after the gap, or both.

ANSWERS

Ex. 3
1 Paragraph H explains **why** the find was important.
2 Parallel words and expressions:

Para. 1	Extract H
three modern-day hunters	the trio
Arctic wilderness	a melting glacier/most unforgiving terrains
our most ancient predecessors	5,000 years old

Ex. 4
Suggested answers:
The paragraph before Gap 1 describes where the body was found.
Gap 1 a)
The paragraph before Gap 2 gives more specific details about where the body was found and begins to describe what was with him.
Gap 2 b)
The paragraph before Gap 3 compares the find in the Yukon with another find in Europe.
Gap 3 a)
The paragraph before Gap 4 describes how valuable the Yukon find is.
Gap 4 a)
The paragraph before Gap 5 tells us more details about how the body was found by the three hunters.
Gap 5 The missing paragraph will probably tell us more about what the hunters saw.
The paragraph after Gap 5 introduces the Indian tribe that lives in that area.
Gap 6 The missing paragraph will probably tell us about the Indians' reaction.

5 Reading task: *match paragraphs to gaps*

Allow up to 20 minutes for the task. Discuss the links that helped students identify the answers when checking as a class.

ANSWERS

1D; 2F; 3G; 4A; 5E; 6C

Vocabulary: *using context*

6 Meaning from context

Discourage students from using a dictionary for this exercise. Remind them that they do not have a dictionary in the exam and they may need to work out the meaning of unknown words from the context. Remind students also to look at prefixes and suffixes. Encourage them to record the words with an example sentence.

ANSWERS

1 predecessors = people who lived before us (pre = before)
2 remote = a long way from civilisation
3 heated = intense, excited
4 potential = possibility
5 artefacts = objects that were made and used a long time ago
6 time immemorial = for a very long time
7 ailments = illnesses
8 inhospitable = unwelcoming, hostile to man
9 tattered = torn
10 pouch = small bag
11 edible = can be eaten
12 succumbed to = gave in to/was killed by
13 terrains = areas of land

Over to you

7 Read for detailed information

The aim of this task is to get students to read the text again carefully and learn as much as they can from it. Let them work on this activity in pairs or small groups to encourage discussion. By doing this they will reinforce any new language they have learned while reading the text.

Homework: ▶▶ *Exam Practice Workbook page 78*

Vocabulary (CB page 112)

1 Choosing the right word

Students have to decide which word fits in each sentence according to the meaning. Let them do the exercise in pairs.

ANSWERS

1 a discovery; b invention
2 a rumour; b legend
3 a hoax; b fake
4 a refuse; b has ... denied
5 a to prove; b try

2 Expressions with *bring/make/take/come*

Check students' comprehension of the text by asking questions before they do the gap-fill task.

Ask students to do the gap-fill exercise as far as they can based on their existing knowledge. Then for the remaining gaps ask them to think about the meaning of the expression and say which word seems to make sense in each case. They should make a note of any expressions that are new to them in their Vocabulary notebooks.

ANSWERS

1 take – 'take anything for granted'
2 make – 'make a discovery'
3 brought – 'brought to light some amazing facts'
4 came – 'came across the fossil'
5 taking – 'taking part in some geological research'
6 taken – 'it must have taken his breath away'
7 take – 'it didn't take long to see' (compare: to take a long time)
8 make – 'What did scientists make of this find …'
9 come – 'They have come to the conclusion that …'

3 – 5 Spelling

These exercises will help students with the word formation task in the Use of English Paper, where correct spelling is required. Encourage students to use a dictionary to check spellings so that they will do this for themselves when preparing homework.

▶▶ extra activity

Ask students to make up their own sentences using the words they have formed. This will help them to check that they are aware of how to use the different word types.

ANSWERS

Ex. 3
1 arrival, famous, advertising, advertisement, careful
2 Rule: … _drop_ the -e if the suffix starts with a vowel and _keep_ the -e if it begins with a consonant.
3 exploration, behaviour, starvation, agreement
4 Rule: … _keep_ the second -e.

Ex. 4
1 laziness, lazily
   happiness, happily
   nastiness, nastily
2 mysterious, historical, glorious
3 Rule: … you must replace the -y with i

Ex. 5
receipt	poverty
failure	warmth
knowledge	height
flight	breadth
loss	beauty
laughter	pride

Homework: ▶▶ _Exam Practice Workbook_ page 79

Use of English: _word formation_
(CB page 113)

1 Read the text

Tell students that the photos show Hadrian's Wall, the subject of the text. Use the questions to check their understanding.

ANSWERS

1 It was a defensive or protective barrier between England and Scotland.
2 It runs along the old border between England and Scotland.
3 It was built by the Romans 2,000 years ago to defend England from the Scots.

BACKGROUND INFORMATION

Hadrian was Emperor of Rome from 117–138. He declared an end to the expansion of the Roman Empire. He was one of the most cultured of the Emperors and surrounded himself with poets, philosophers and scholars. He ordered the building of a huge defensive wall across the north of England to protect the inhabitants of his Empire from invading tribes. It is 119 kilometres long, 6 metres high and was built between 121 and 126 AD.

2 Word-formation task

Refer students to the **exam strategy** in CB Unit 2, page 25, if necessary. Remind students always to check their spelling carefully when they have completed the task.

ANSWERS

1 formerly (adverb)
2 incredible (negative prefix needed – clue: the context and the article 'an', which indicates the next word begins with a vowel)
3 easily (adverb)
4 sight (noun)
5 existence (noun)
6 mysterious (adjective)
7 historians (plural noun – it must be plural because there is no article)
8 impression (noun)
9 wonderfully (adverb describing 'lonely')
10 imagination (noun)

3 Discussion

Students could discuss these questions in pairs or as a class.

▶▶ extra activity

Students could write an article for an international tourist magazine to encourage tourists to visit a historical monument that they know.

Writing: *story (last line)* (CB pages 114–115)

Use the **exam file** to introduce the task type and then go through the *exam strategy*. Review students' ideas of the characteristics of a good story.

1 Understand the task

ANSWERS

1 Target readers: students; the story will be published in a student magazine
2 With the sentence: 'It was the strangest experience of my life.'
3 First person ('my life').
4 It could be either of those suggested or a mystery, an unusual event, science fiction, etc.
5 b) narrative tenses.

2 Read a sample answer

1/2 Ask students to cover up the ending in Exercise 3 while they write their own ending to the story. They could work in groups for this.

3 Compare endings

Ask different students to read out their own endings. Ask the rest of the class to choose the best.

Then discuss students' reactions to the sample story. Ask them to think about interest, originality, style, organisation, range of vocabulary as well as content. Can they suggest any improvements?

Focus on vivid vocabulary

4 Vocabulary search

Students could work on these activities in pairs.

In Exercise 4.2 students could write their sentence ending on different cards, and exchange cards with other groups to match with the sentence openings. They should then discuss any differences. Encourage them to use their imaginations.

ANSWERS

Ex. 4.1
In the first part of the story:
1 isolated   4 scruffy
2 desperate   5 furiously
3 wonderful   6 raced
In the second part of the story:
7 hunted
8 vanished
9 My blood ran cold

Ex. 4.2
Possible answers:
2 ... she read the note.
3 ... he heard footsteps approaching.
4 ... she saw the flames.
5 ... she saw her long-lost brother enter the room.

Focus on grammar

5 Participle clauses

1 Refer students to the **grammar file** and ask them to look for examples in the sample story. Ask them to match each example with an example in the **grammar file**. Elicit why it is a good idea to use participle clauses (it allows you to vary the sentence structure).

2 When doing the practice exercise students should think about a) which verb they will need to make into a participle and b) whether this will be at the beginning of the sentence or in the middle.

ANSWERS

Ex. 5.1
Examples in story:	Examples in **grammar file**:
'Being city kids, ...'	1
'Sitting on my bed ...'	4
'while resting ...'	7
'Looking up, ...'	5
'... , looking back anxiously ...'	4
'having fallen from a tree.'	6

Ex. 5.2
1 After climbing/Having climbed through a window, he ...
2 Shining a torch into a large room, he ...
3 Then he heard a noise coming from ...
4 Shaking with fear, he hid ...
5 Looking up, he saw a man standing in the doorway./When he looked up, he saw a man standing in the doorway.
6 Not wanting the man to see him, John held his breath ...
7 Pointing a finger towards John, the stranger gave a ...

Over to you

6 Writing task

Tell students to look back at the questions in Exercise 1 while reading the task and try to answer them. Check their answers:

1 Students will read the story in a magazine.
2 It must end with the given sentence.
3 It must be told in the third person (about John).
4 They could write any of the types of story listed in Exercise 1.
5 They will need narrative tenses.

Students should plan their stories in pairs in class as in Unit 6 (see TB page 63). Set the writing itself for homework.

CRITERIA FOR MARKING

Content: Story must lead up to and end with the given sentence. It must involve John.
Organisation: The story should reach a definite ending.
Register: Informal or neutral. Must be consistent.
Effect on target reader: Would be able to follow the storyline.

Homework: ▶▶ *Exam Practice Workbook* pages 83–84

Unit 9 Test ▶▶ TB page 131

10 Technology

Lead-in (CB page 116)

The **Lead-in** introduces or reviews some useful vocabulary related to computers, and gets students thinking about the importance of computer technology in our lives.

1 Label photos

First find out how many of the numbered items students can identify without looking at the items in the vocabulary box. Then tell them to look at the box and finish the labelling task in pairs. This is good practice for Paper 5 (Speaking) Parts 3 and 4. Then compare as a class.

> **ANSWERS**
>
> 1 hand-held positioning device
> 2 printer
> 3 floppy disk
> 4 lap-top computer
> 5 CD drive
> 6 disk drive
> 7 desktop computer
> 8 monitor
> 9 screen
> 10 keyboard
> 11 mouse on mousepad

2 Discussion

You can brainstorm these questions as a class or in small groups. Write up useful vocabulary on the board. The second task provides useful revision of conditional forms.

> **ANSWERS**
>
> Possible answers:
> Computers are used:
> - by students to write assignments or use the Internet.
> - in schools to help students learn languages.
> - to play computer games.
> - to help pilots fly planes.
> - to control lifts in buildings.
> - to control traffic lights.
> - to control cash tills in shops.
> - to help air traffic controllers land aeroplanes safely.
> - to help weather forecasters tell what the weather will be like.

Reading 1: *multiple-choice questions*

(CB pages 116–117)

1 Predict/Skim for gist

Do Exercise 1.1 as a class, then tell students to continue individually. Give them about five minutes for this first quick reading.

> **ANSWERS**
>
> **Ex. 1.1**
> 1 'Smart stuff' refers to electronic gadgets.
> 2 Examples of 'new products that promise to change our lives'.
>
> **Ex 1.2**
> 1 **Products mentioned:**
> body sensors in the 'frown headband', in watches, rings or shoes – give the user feedback about stress and offer advice. (lines 34–37)
> special glasses – for viewing the Internet or gaining instant access to other useful information. (lines 47–48, 52–58, 74–75)
> a microchip that gives off scents if hidden inside a ring. (lines 81–83)
>
> **Ex 1.3**
> The text was written for a popular science magazine.

2 Reading task: *multiple-choice questions*

Elicit the exam strategy for this task type. Draw attention to the **exam tip!**. Set a time limit of 15 minutes.

> **ANSWERS**
>
> 1B 'It came as a shock to Rosalind to realise just how often she frowned. Stuck in a traffic jam recently, ... Rosalind kept hearing the sounds of the tiny sensor ...' (lines 17–22)
> 2C
> 3B 'your glasses will immediately become windows to the Internet' (lines 46–48)
> 4D 'the glasses will flash your notes in front of your eyes' (lines 52–53)
> 5C 'looks more like a pair of ski goggles ...' (line 59) 'Students who don't mind being stared at ...' (lines 64–65)
> 6D 'That, of course, may or may not appeal to you' (lines 83–84)
> 7A '... they will pop up in all sorts of easily-wearable accessories' (lines 97–98)

3 Analyse the task

This task gives students the opportunity to discuss and reflect on how well they tackled the task. Give students time to record any useful new vocabulary in their notebooks.

> **ANSWERS**
>
> **Ex. 3.1**
> **Question types:**
> a) detailed comprehension: Q1, 4, 5
> b) meaning in context: Q3
> c) understanding grammatical links: Q2
> d) identifying writer's point of view: Q6, 7

Over to you

4 Discussion

This exercise allows students to respond to the content of the text, and express their own ideas.

After groups have thought of their own device, they should describe it to the class and let the others choose the best idea.

Homework: ▶▶ *Exam Practice Workbook* page 84

Grammar: *future forms*

(CB pages 118–199/199)

Note: The photo is a still from the science fiction film, *Back to the Future* starring Michael J. Fox.

See **Introduction** page 7 for suggestions on how to use the **grammar file**.

Presentation

Tell students to read the examples in the **grammar file**, section by section, and ask them to give you further examples about themselves. Ask questions to encourage them, e.g.:

A
What do you think you'll buy your (mother) for her birthday?
What will change in your life in the next few years?

B
What do you think you will be doing in 20 years' time?
What will you be studying next year?

etc.

1 Practice: *choose the correct tense*

When students have chosen the correct tense, ask them to comment on the content of the sentences. *Do they agree? What kind of problems can they foresee when we are all living longer?*

> **ANSWERS**
> 1 have been discovered
> 2 be living
> 3 will have to

2 Practice: *a survey*

1–2 Let students read the explanation of the survey result in the back of the *Coursebook* page 199 before moving on to Exercise 2.2.

3 You can do the survey as a class by asking students to raise their hands, and putting the results on the board. Students can then summarise the results for homework. This is good revision of quantifiers.

> **ANSWERS**
> **Ex. 2.1**
> 1 Will; 2 Will ... have; 3 Will ... been; 4 Will ... be;
> 5 ... have been

> **ANSWERS**
> **Ex 2.2**
> 6 Will we have managed to ... ?
> 7 Will we still be driving ... ?
> 8 Will scientists have discovered ... ?
> 9 Will people be living ... ?
> 10 Will time travel already have become ... ?
> 11 ... will robots be doing ... ?
> 12 Will we ever learn ... ?

Over to you

3 Practice: *question and answer*

This exercise allows students to use the language in a personal context.

Homework: ▶▶ *Exam Practice Workbook* pages 84–85, Exercises 1–2

Use of English 1: *error correction*

(CB page 119)

1 – 2 Predict/Read the text

Use the questions to ensure students have read and understood the text before starting the Use of English task.

Ask students to comment on the photo, which shows two teenagers in a pizza bar. They are talking, not to each other, but to their mobile phones!

3 Error correction task

Students should work individually, then compare answers in pairs, and add to the list of error types. Remind them to read the whole sentence, including the line before or after if necessary.

> **ANSWERS**
> 1 even (adverb – doesn't make sense in the context)
> 2 them (object pronoun)
> 3 are (verb)
> 4 the (definite article)
> 5 ✔
> 6 up ('take up' is a phrasal verb, but here the fixed phrase is 'take the trouble')
> 7 it (unnecessary object pronoun)
> 8 ✔
> 9 there (adverb)
> 10 ✔
> 11 of ('a few' must be followed by a noun not the preposition 'of')
> 12 to (make someone do something – 'make' is not followed by *to*-infinitive in the active)
> 13 ✔
> 14 rather (adverb – doesn't make sense in the context)
> 15 that (link word introducing a 'that' clause – but there is no 'that' clause)

Homework: ▶▶ *Exam Practice Workbook* pages 85–86, Exercises 3–4

Listening: *multiple matching* (CB page 120)

Tapescript: ▶▶ TB pages 112–113

1 Vocabulary

The aim of these exercises is to prepare students for the ideas in the recording.

For Exercise 1.2, students could take it in turns to describe how a piece of equipment works without naming it, using the vocabulary supplied. The others guess which item he/she is talking about.

ANSWERS

Ex. 1.1
1 A A lap-top computer can be used for typing reports and for accessing the Internet when you are travelling/away from the office. You can send or receive e-mail messages on a lap-top.
   B A pocket calculator is useful for doing calculations, such as adding up, subtracting, calculating percentages, etc.
   C A mobile phone helps you to keep in touch.
   D E-mail can be used for sending text messages to another computer, and is cheaper than the telephone.
   E A CD player is used for playing music.
   F Voice mail can be used for leaving messages for someone who is not there when you phone.

Ex 1.2
Possible answers:
A It can run on electricity or batteries. If you are using electricity, plug it in first. Then switch it on. The button is usually at the back. (lap-top computer)
B You tap the right numbers and press the 'Plus' key to add up, the 'Minus' key to subtract, etc. (pocket calculator)
C It runs on batteries. You tap in the right number and you speak after the tone. (mobile phone)
D You need to have a modem, which you plug into the telephone line. You tap in the right number, then you press the 'send' button. You check your message box to see if you have any incoming messages. (e-mail)
E You switch on the player, put in a CD and press the Play button.
F You listen to the message and then you speak after the tone and leave your message. (voice mail)

2 – 3 📼 Listening task

Draw students' attention to the **exam tip!** before playing the recording.

ANSWERS

Exs. 2/3
1D (e-mail) 'At the end of each day, I send a quick report to my bosses ... that's when I check my message box'.
2E (CD player) 'so that's what I listen to a lot of the time'.
3C (mobile phone) 'I know that they're annoying if they go off at the wrong moment, but on the whole ...'
4A (lap-top) 'I can even print stuff out, and ... I can get the details of the meeting down before I forget'.
5F (voice mail) 'I make sure they've got my home number ... At least with this I can always be reached but it lets me decide who to get back to immediately'.

Speaking: *collaborative task and discussion* (CB pages 121/207)

Follow the procedure recommended in Unit 7, TB page 66.

1 Part 3 task

Before you put students into groups for the Part 3 task, make sure they understand the vocabulary necessary. Ask them to identify the items in the photos, then elicit which of the items:

• are labour-saving devices, i.e. inventions which make household chores easier. (vacuum cleaner, washing machine)
• are means of transport. (car, plane)
• are forms of entertainment. (TV, video recorder)
• are means of communication. (phone, computer if it has e-mail)
• require electricity to work. (vacuum cleaner, light bulb, computer, TV, video recorder, washing machine)

Ask questions like:

Which ones are likely to make people lazy?
Have we become dependent on technology?
Has the pace of life become faster as a result?

PHOTOS

Clockwise from top left, the photos show the following: a vacuum cleaner, a ball-point pen, a light bulb, a Porsche sports car, a desktop computer, a plane, a television and video recorder, a telephone set, a washing machine

Crime prevention

Lead-in (CB page 122)

Explain any new vocabulary in the box with the help of the photos. Then use the photos to discuss ways in which policing has changed due to technology.

Definitions

closed circuit television (CCTV) – a camera or series of cameras linked to a viewing screen
a network of cameras – a series of cameras linked together
to monitor the public – to watch the behaviour of the public
to scan a crowd – to move (a camera) over a crowd of people
to improve security – to make a place safer for people to be in
officers on the beat – police officers walking around an area
to patrol an area – to walk (or drive) around an area checking for security/crime
patrol car – a car used by the police for patrolling
better communications – improved ways of police officers staying in touch with each other

basic/sophisticated equipment – 'basic' equipment would be phones so that police officers can remain in contact. 'Sophisticated' equipment includes 'infra-red' scanning devices to find criminals at night and computers to find criminals from evidence.

to respond quickly – to answer a call for help from the public in as short a time as possible

PHOTOS

Photo 1 shows a 'bobby' or policeman on the beat in the 1950s. He is making a call from a police phone box on the street. Communications have become much better today.
Photo 2 shows a police patrol car, which is equipped with police radio equipment. Police cars have largely replaced police officers on the beat – some say this is a bad thing.
Photo 3 shows the main control room of a police CCTV system - the police are monitoring the public by looking at the CCTV screens in the control room.
Photo 4 shows the old 'Information Room' of Scotland Yard, the Police Headquarters in London. This has now been replaced by a sophisticated computer system.

Reading 2: *gapped text (paragraphs)*

(CB pages 122–123)

Refer students to the **exam strategy**.

1 Predict

This exercise activates students' knowledge of the topic, and starts them thinking about the content of the text. These questions should be done with the whole class as a brainstorming activity.

2 Read the base text

Set a time limit of about 5–8 minutes for the first reading. Then elicit the main points that students have understood in the class discussion. Deal with any content and vocabulary queries students may have.

3 Strategy: *understand the development*

This exercise focuses students' attention on the development of ideas, and encourages them to actively engage in following the ideas in the text while doing the exam task.

ANSWERS

Para. 3 describes how the new system works – by using computers linked to video cameras.
Words that refer to the new technology:
Para. 1: 'more advanced technology'
Extract H: '... (VIP), a highly sophisticated system'
Para. 3: 'The new system'

4 Reading task: *match paragraphs to gaps*

Give students 15–20 minutes to do the exam task. They should use the clues provided to help them.

ANSWERS

1F 'Although such facial recognition systems are highly reliable' in F links back to the description of the new system in the previous paragraph; 'their results are not yet acceptable in a trial' links forward to the next paragraph: 'Prototype systems are being used ...'
2A 'His team' refers back to Barry Irving.
3G 'The system' in G links back to 'a huge database' and 'Linking private systems and police records'. Extract G gives more details about what the system 'will make it possible' to do.
4E 'the question of freedom' links back to 'people concerned about their civil rights'.
5B 'Another use' introduces an example of 'Future possibilities' in the previous paragraph; 'video camera' links forward to 'The greater use of video' in the next paragraph.
6D Extract D introduces another example of 'the areas police are investigating'. The final paragraph refers to 'all these different systems', i.e. video, PNC links and PDAs.

Over to you

5 Read for detail/Make notes

The note-taking task gives students practice in extracting the main points from a text. The tasks could be set for homework: ask students to summarise the main points in writing using the headings supplied in Exercise 5.1.

Homework: ▶▶ *Exam Practice Workbook* pages 86–87

Vocabulary (CB page 124)

1 Crimes and criminals

1 Brainstorm on the board all the types of crime students can think of. Then compare the list with the one in Exercise 1.1. If necessary, let students use dictionaries to complete the definitions.

ANSWERS

A 2 mugging = robbing (someone) using violence, usually in a public place
3 pickpocketing = stealing something from someone's pocket, especially in a crowd
B 2 fraud = (an act of) deceitful behaviour for the purpose of making money
3 forgery = a copy of something which is intended to be taken for the original
C joyriding = stealing a car and driving it, for pleasure and, often, dangerously
speeding = driving too fast, breaking the speed limit
D burglary = the crime of breaking into a house by force with the intention of stealing
hijacking = taking control of (usually) an aeroplane by force, and usually with the intention of making political demands

2 Again, let students use dictionaries. This will encourage them to use their dictionary to check word formation when they do their own writing.

ANSWERS

Person
pickpocket, smuggler, (no noun for person), forger, drink-driver, joyrider, speed merchant, arsonist, burglar, hijacker
Verb
to mug, to pickpocket, to smuggle, to defraud, to forge, to drive while drunk, to joyride/go joyriding, to speed/to be a speed merchant, to commit arson, to burgle, to hijack

3 This exercise practises commonly confused collocations. Ask students to give their opinions during the class check.

ANSWERS

1d); 2c); 3e); 4b); 5f); 6a)

4 Students could discuss this in pairs, then report their views to the class.

5 Ask students to explain the sequence of events in their country when a person commits a crime before they do this task. This will allow you to explain key vocabulary before they focus on individual items.

ANSWERS

1   John Brown was suspected of committing a crime.
2   He was arrested.
3   He was handcuffed and taken into custody.
4   He was questioned and his fingerprints were taken.
5   He was charged.
6   He was sent for trial.
7   He was found guilty by the jury.
8   He was sentenced.
9   He was imprisoned.
10 He appealed.
11 He was pardoned.
12 He was set free.

2   Choosing the right word

You could discuss the answers to the questions during the class check.

ANSWERS

1 court; 2 fine; 3 burgles; 4 commit; 5 tried; 6 cell; 7 witness; 8 hostages; 9 guilty; 10 penalty

3   Phrasal verbs

ANSWERS

1	made off with	5	break into
2	let her off	6	getting up to
3	gave themselves up	7	get away
4	gave himself away	8	got off with

Homework: ▶▶ *Exam Practice Workbook* page 87, Exercise 1

Use of English 2: *lexical cloze*

(CB page 125)

1   Predict/Read the text

Ask questions to elicit the information in the text, e.g.:

How did a police officer call for help in the 19th century? (he used a whistle)
How did police officers still travel around in the early 20th century? (by bicycle)
How long did it take to match a criminal's fingerprints to the ones in the police collection in the past? (days or even weeks)
What did the police have to do in the past if they wanted to check a car registration number? (phone up Police HQ in London, etc.)

ANSWERS

1   The first paragraph tells us that the text will describe how the police used to work in the past without scientific and technological aids.

2   Lexical cloze task

Students complete the task using the clues given. Discuss students' answers as a class.

ANSWERS

1B   The only word that makes sense in the context.
2C   'to be the case' is a fixed phrase.
3C
4D   'get into difficulty' is a collocation.
5B   The only word that makes sense in the context. 'begin' is followed by *to*-infinitive.
6B
7A   'take advantage of' is a collocation.
8A   The rest of the sentence shows that a linker introducing a contrast is needed here.
9D
10C   'take (time)' is a collocation.
11D
12B
13A
14D
15B   'go through' means 'search'.

3   Vocabulary: *noun + of*

This exercise encourages students to pay attention to word combinations. It could be set for homework.

ANSWERS

'all kinds of'
'way of (doing something)'
'to take advantage of'
'one of'
'a search of'
'the owner of'

Homework: ▶▶ *Exam Practice Workbook* page 87, Exercise 2

Writing: *report (recommending)*

(CB pages 126–127)

Use the **exam file** to introduce the task type. Ask students if they remember the features of a report and how it is different from a composition. (See CB Unit 7, page 88.)

Then go through the **exam strategy**.

1 Understand the task

Ask students to read the task and elicit the answers to the questions.

ANSWERS

1 The community police officer will read the report so the style should be formal.
2 The aim of the report is to suggest reasons for local youth crime and make suggestions for dealing with it. The report should give at least two reasons and recommendations.

2 Develop a paragraph plan

You can work through these tasks as a whole class or let students work in pairs.

ANSWERS

Possible answers:
Not enough for young people to do.
Youth unemployment.
Drugs.

3 Analyse a sample answer

Let students work in pairs to discuss the sample report.

ANSWERS

1 The writer gives three reasons (see numbered points in report).
2 The recommendations seem to be very appropriate.
3 The report is clearly set out. It uses numbered headings, and each reason for crime is followed by a recommendation for tackling it.
4 The report should not begin 'Dear Sir' as this is used for letters not reports.

Focus on style and register

4 Identify inappropriate expressions

ANSWERS

Too informal:	Formal equivalent:
'give you some tips'	make some recommendations
'pricey'	expensive
'You wouldn't believe the state of the lights in the area!'	The lighting in the area is in a very poor condition.
'You've really got to fix ...'	The broken lights really must be fixed.
'Some young people don't have a clue about the effect ...'	... do not appreciate the effect ...

Focus on grammar

5 *have something done*

1 Go through the **grammar file**, and discuss the difference between doing something yourself and 'having it done' by someone else. Ask students to say what things they or their family pay someone else to do for them, e.g.:

Do you decorate your house yourself or have it decorated for you?

Do you cut your hair yourself or have it cut at the hairdresser's?

Then get students to find more examples in the sample report.

2 Let students work in pairs to do the gap-fill exercise.

ANSWERS

1 have had their cars broken into
2 had his wallet stolen
3 have a youth centre built
4 have alarms installed
5 have a closed circuit television installed
6 have notices put up

Over to you

6 Writing task

Set the task for homework after preparation in class. Elicit what has to be included in the report. Brainstorm a list of ideas on the board. Ask students which ideas they think they will include, and what headings they can use.

CRITERIA FOR MARKING

Content: Reasons why criminals target the area, some measures that should be taken to protect houses and shops from criminal attacks.
Range: Language of explanation and recommendation.
Organisation and cohesion: Report should be clearly organised; the use of headings will be an advantage.
Register and format: Formal register; format as for a report.
Target reader: Would understand the reasons for crime in the area and know what steps to take against it.

Homework: ▶▶ *Exam Practice Workbook* pages 90–91

Progress review 3 (Units 7–10) ▶▶ *Exam Practice Workbook* pages 92–93

Unit 10 Test ▶▶ TB page 132

11 The environment

Lead-in (CB page 128)

The discussion point in the **Lead-in** is animal intelligence and the differences between humans and animals. The photos illustrate different animals solving problems that require an intelligent response of some sort.

The questions could be answered as a whole class activity or in pairs. Encourage students to use the vocabulary in the box. Elicit the theme of the photos – animal intelligence – rather than telling students.

Make a list on the board of things that make humans different from animals. This will be useful preparation for the text on page 129. Get students to focus on mental rather than physical differences.

ANSWERS

1/2 See PHOTOS box.
3 **The common theme of the photos:** they all show animals using intelligence to perform an activity.
4 **Some things that make humans different from animals:** humans use language to communicate; they can read and write and therefore pass on information to later generations through books; they can appreciate music and literature.

Reading 1: *gapped text (paragraphs)*

(CB pages 128–129)

Elicit or remind students of the **exam strategy** for this task type. (See CB page 122.)

1 Predict

Do this exercise as a class to encourage students to think about the topic of the text and what they already know.

ANSWERS

1 The article is about research into the behaviour of chimpanzees.
2 People usually think 'culture' is related to music, literature, etc. and therefore they do not associate animals with culture.
3 'What have thirty years of research uncovered about the intellectual and social life of chimpanzees?'
4 **Possible answer:** the photo of the chimp shows that these animals are able to use tools, so research has probably indicated that they are quite intelligent.

2 Read the base text

Ask students to underline key words in each paragraph or note down the main points so that they can summarise these in the class discussion. Make sure students have fully understood the key ideas before doing the exam task.

ANSWERS

Ex. 2.1
Key points:
Paragraph after Gap 0: the paragraph makes clear that 'the report' omits a lot of things.
Paragraph after Gap 1: an example of something chimps can do – 'ant dipping'.
Paragraph after Gap 2: the point is that we should not measure animal intelligence in the same way as human intelligence.
Paragraph after Gap 3: an example of chimps imitating each other – washing vegetables in water.
Paragraph after Gap 4: the results of research with captive animals have shown chimps are more intelligent than was previously thought.
Paragraph after Gap 5: another example of intelligence – self-awareness.
Paragraph after Gap 6: the problem of how to treat chimps.

Ex. 2.2
a) **Examples that show that chimpanzees are intelligent:** They have developed techniques for catching ants; they can count up to nine; they can recognise themselves in a mirror or photos.
b) **Examples that show that they can learn from each other:** the habit of washing vegetables.

3 Reading task: *match paragraphs to gaps*

Go through the advice and draw attention to the **exam tip!** before students start the task. Allow about 15 minutes for the task. Ask students to justify their answers during the class check.

ANSWERS

Ex. 3

1D 'the project' links back to 'a recently published study' in H, and forward to 'the international team' in D; 'there was too little evidence' is followed by a contrasting point: 'But the international team did find thirty-nine examples ...'

2A 'One example' in the previous paragraph links to 'Another such activity' in A; 'These things are regarded as "culture"' in A is followed by a contrasting question in the next paragraph: 'But is this like human culture?'

3G 'what if we look at them in a different way' in the previous paragraph links to 'The first scientist to propose such a change in how we regard animals' in G.

4B the paragraph after gap 3 describes the 'spread of potato washing' mentioned in G; 'Kinja Imanishi in Japan' referred to in G links to 'Western scientists didn't agree with Imanishi's idea' in B

5F 'Chimpanzees cannot imitate human speech' in the paragraph before gap 5 links to 'Chimpanzees kept in captivity can be taught simple sign language, however.' in F

6E 'self-awareness' in the paragraph before the gap links to 'The discovery that chimpanzees may possess "culture" raises an urgent conservation issue' in E, which links to the following paragraph: 'Another problem is ...'

Vocabulary: *using context*

4 Meaning from context

Encourage students to do this exercise without using a dictionary. Remind them that they will not have a dictionary in the exam. Encourage them to record the words with an example sentence.

ANSWERS

1 diversity = variety, differences
2 sweeping = taking them with a quick movement of the hand
3 nowhere in sight = (other animals) have not achieved nearly as much
4 spread = was copied by other chimpanzees
5 fieldwork = research involving studying animals in the wild
6 controversial = open to discussion/disagreement
7 self-awareness = ability to recognise oneself
8 instinct = behaviour and skills that animals are born with
9 distinct = clearly different from each other
10 absent = not there
11 extensive = a great deal of

Over to you

5 Read for specific information/Discussion

Tell students to work in pairs to note down all the examples of cultural behaviour mentioned in the text.

Remind them about the question they discussed in Exercise 1: 'Why might people laugh at the idea of animals having "culture"?' Point out the definition of 'culture' in extract A: 'things that are learned from others rather than things that are done by instinct'.

Finally, discuss as a class if students agree that chimps have culture or not.

ANSWERS

More examples to add to those found in Ex. 2.2: the ability to use sign language; rain dancing; use of tools; ability to form relationships; keeping clean

6 Discussion

Do this as a class or in pairs. It is useful practice for Paper 5.

Homework: ▶▶ *Exam Practice Workbook* page 94

Use of English 1: *structural cloze*

(CB page 130)

Note: In this unit, the Use of English task introduces in context the grammatical point in the Grammar section: *conditionals*.

1 – **2** Read the text

Get students to retell the story to each other before filling in the gaps. Ask them how the story relates to the pictures.

ANSWERS

Ex. 1
1 Tom and his friends.
2 Off the coast of Australia.
3 They were tourists.
4 Tom was rescued from a shark attack by some dolphins.
5 Dolphins feel closely linked to humans.

3 – **4** Structural cloze task

Students should compare their answers in pairs and try to agree on the correct answers. During the class check, elicit the types of word class they used to fill the gaps.

ANSWERS

1 his/the (possessive adjective/article)
2 had (auxiliary verb, part of past perfect tense form)
3 what (short for 'that which')
4 nothing (noun)
5 have (auxiliary verb, part of a conditional verb form)
6 and (linking word)
7 at (preposition)
8 by (preposition)
9 it (pronoun)
10 same (adjective, part of the phrase 'in the same way')
11 are (auxiliary verb, part of a passive verb form)
12 until/and (linking word)
13 was (auxiliary verb, part of a passive verb form)
14 who (relative pronoun)
15 as (preposition after the verb 'regard')

Over to you

5 Discussion

This could be done in pairs or as a brainstorming exercise with the whole class.

Grammar: *conditionals* (CB page 131)

See **Introduction** page 7 for suggestions on how to use the **grammar file**.

Presentation

Here is a possible approach.

Refer back to the cloze text on CB page 130. Elicit some sentences of cause and effect, e.g:

Why was Tom saved?
Because the dolphins came to help him.
Why was the shark scared off?
Because the dolphins slapped the water with their fins.
Why did the dolphins help him? What had he been doing with them?
They may have helped because he had been playing with them.

Now ask students to rephrase these ideas beginning 'If …'
Ask:

What would have happened if the dolphins hadn't come to help Tom?
If the dolphins hadn't come to help Tom, he would have been killed.
What would have happened if the dolphins hadn't slapped the water with their fins?
If … , the shark wouldn't have been scared off.
What would have happened if he hadn't been playing with the dolphins?
If … , they may not have helped him.

1 Practice: *gap fill*

Now tell students to complete the sentences in C and D in the **grammar file**.

For revision of the other conditional structures, ask students to complete the sentences in A and B of the **grammar file**.

> **ANSWERS**
>
> **A**
> 1 go, may; 2 don't
> **B**
> 1 might; 2 were, would
> **C**
> 1 had, have; 2 been, not have
> **D**
> If the dolphins had not protected Tom, anything could have happened.
> **E**
> 3 didn't, would/might not have

2 Practice: *combine sentences*

Let students do the exercises in pairs.

> **ANSWERS**
>
> 1 If Hans hadn't quarrelled with his friends, they wouldn't have gone off for the day without him.
> 2 If Hans hadn't been feeling bored, he wouldn't have decided to go up the mountain, snowboarding.
> 3 Had he heard the weather warning, he would have known there was a danger of an avalanche in that area.
> 4 If he hadn't ignored the rumbling noise above him, he wouldn't have continued snowboarding.
> 5 Had he taken shelter, he wouldn't have been caught in the avalanche
> 6 If his dog hadn't sensed that something was wrong, he wouldn't have set off to search for Hans.
> 7 If the dog hadn't found Hans's body buried in the snow and dug out a hole, Hans wouldn't have had enough air to breathe.
> 8 If the dog hadn't run off and returned with help, Hans wouldn't have been rescued.
> 9 Had the dog not acted intelligently, Hans would have died.

3 Discussion

This task could be set for homework after a brief brainstorming discussion in class.

4 Practice: *gap fill*

Tell students to read all the sentences before they fill in the gaps, and check comprehension of the text.

> **ANSWERS**
>
> 1 compare
> 2 had suggested, would have thought
> 3 look, will discover
> 4 would not be able, did not have
> 5 wants, dives
> 6 would not be able, had learnt OR were able to learn
> 7 will find, were not, would not have used

Homework: ▶▶ *Exam Practice Workbook* pages 94–96

Listening: *sentence completion*
(CB page 132)

Tapescript: ▶▶ TB page 113

1 Predict

Remind students of the importance of reading through the task before listening, to predict content and decide what type of information they need to listen for.

2 🔲 Listening task

Play the recording once all the way through. Then play it again all the way through so that students can check their answers and fill in any gaps.

Over to you

3 Discussion

Discuss these questions as a class. They provide an opportunity to discuss the content of the recording.

4 Prepare a speech

Students could work in pairs to discuss and prepare the speech. Or you could set the task for homework.

Speaking: *collaborative task and discussion* (CB pages 132–133/207)

1 Vocabulary presentation

Explain that the leaflet on page 133 suggests various ways in which we can stop damaging the environment and do something to help it instead. Ask students to read the leaflet quickly and tell you how many suggestions it makes. (eight)

Elicit the problems and the suggested ways of dealing with them. Bring in some of the vocabulary in the leaflet. For example, ask questions and elicit answers like this:

What is the problem about water?
We waste it.
How can we conserve water?
We can collect rainwater.
How? What is that in the photo? (a barrel)
How can we protect wildlife?
By supporting local wildlife reserves.
What do you think a 'walking bus' is? (See PHOTOS box.)
Why are pesticides dangerous for people and animals?
They leave chemical residues in food.

Then ask students to prepare answers to Question 2 in pairs, using the examples as a guide. If time is short, allocate different suggestions to different pairs. Then discuss as a class.

PHOTOS

Clockwise from top left:
a barrel for collecting rainwater
a packet of environmentally friendly washing powder
a sign outside a wildlife reserve
schoolchildren in a 'walking bus' – this is a scheme where parents take turns to take a group of children to school on foot, aimed at reducing the number of cars around schools in the mornings and afternoons.
cyclists, one wearing a mask to protect himself against air pollution
organically grown vegetables
various cuts of meat
a recycling area with containers for various types of waste that can be recycled

2 – 3 Speaking tasks

Follow the procedure recommended in Unit 7, TB page 66 for the Part 3 and Part 4 tasks.

The weather

Lead-in (CB page 134)

The aim of the **Lead-in** is to introduce the topic and weather vocabulary in a way that links it to students' own experience.

Ensure that students know the meaning of all the types of weather conditions in the box before they do Exercise 1.2.

PHOTOS

The photos on page 134 show:
lightning
a tornado
waves crashing against a pier in a seaside town in southern England
cars in foggy conditions on the motorway
The background photo on page 135 is of the Earth seen from space.

Reading 2: *multiple matching*

(CB pages 134–135)

Elicit or remind students of the *exam strategy* for this task type. (See CB page 10.)

1 Predict/Skim for gist

This exercise is designed to encourage students to predict the content of the text and give them a reason for reading it once all through. Set a time limit of five minutes for the first reading of the text.

Ex. 1.1
Answers may vary.

Ex. 1.2
1   Hurricanes, also called cyclones.
2   Scientists are not sure.
3   By using satellites, radar and aircraft.
4   At the moment, their predictions are not very accurate.
5   For the reason given in paragraph 3: the formation of a hurricane involves so many unknown factors.
6   A lot more than 12 hours is needed.
7   To prevent loss of life, they should abandon their homes in time.
8   Not stated in the text.

2 – 3   Reading task: *match headings*

Before they start the matching task, remind students that they should look for words in the headings that paraphrase the text. Also, draw students' attention to the **exam tip!**.

Ask students to justify their answers in pairs, then check as a class.

1E   'each one is given the name of a person' (line 17)
2H   'involves so many unknown factors' (line 21); 'for reasons that are unclear' (line 30)
3A   'pilots fly bravely into the turbulent clouds of the hurricane' (lines 34–35)
4C   'the question ... is a tricky one' (lines 40–41)
5G   'residents should follow the example of the Seminole Indians' (lines 49–50); 'The Seminoles were correct both times' (line 59)
6F   'low-lying coastal communities ... are always prepared for the worst' (lines 67–69)
7B   'they can give rise to tornadoes' (lines 71–72)

Vocabulary: *word formation*

4   Word search

Let students do the exercises in pairs. When they have finished, suggest that they record useful items in their Vocabulary notebooks under the topic heading 'Weather'. They could do this for homework.

Ex 4.1

Verb	Noun	Adjective
threaten	threat	threatening
warn	warning	–
terrify	terror	terrifying
rotate	rotation	rotating
predict	prediction	(un)predictable
evacuate	evacuation	–
deceive	deceit	deceptive
trick	trick	tricky
–	catastrophe	catastrophic
–	turbulence	turbulent
–	disaster	disastrous

Ex. 4.2
threatening weather conditions (line 5)/storm clouds
rotating storm (line 12)
unpredictable winds
deceptive calm (line 25)
turbulent clouds (line 35)
catastrophic damage (line 75)/floods
disastrous floods/storms

Over to you

5   Discussion

Students should work individually, then compare their ideas as a class.

Homework: ▶▶ *Exam Practice Workbook* page 96

Vocabulary   (CB page 136)

The vocabulary in this section will be useful for the Writing section on pages 138–139.

1   What is the greenhouse effect?

Ask students what they know about 'the greenhouse effect'. Focus attention on the illustration and elicit what they can see. Label the diagram as a class. Students match the descriptions in Box A to the parts of the picture, and write numbers 1–4 in the boxes provided. Then let students work in pairs to complete the text, which explains the greenhouse effect.

A
1   Tree stumps illustrate 'cutting down trees'.
2   Cars and lorries illustrate 'vehicle exhausts'.
3   Smoke rising from the chimneys of homes illustrates 'burning of fossil fuels'.
4   Fumes rising from large chimneys illustrate 'power stations'.
B
2 balance; 3 coal; 4 traps; 5 forests; 6 give off

2   Phrasal verbs

1 face up to; 2 run out of; 3 used up; 4 cut down on;
5 give up

3   Choosing the right word

You could discuss the answers to the questions during the class check.

1 species; 2 extinct; 3 grown; 4 soil; 5 coast; 6 dump;
7 catastrophes

Use of English 2: *lexical cloze*

(CB page 137)

1 Read the text

> ### ANSWERS
>
> 1 **Causes:** use of oil and coal, use of private cars.
>   **Effects:** extreme weather, rising sea levels.
> 2 Temperatures will rise by 0.2% per decade.

2 Lexical cloze task

Tell students to read the advice given before doing the task.

> ### ANSWERS
>
> 1C Clue: what causes pollution?
> 2D Clue: private cars are another cause.
> 3A Clue: what is the result of climate changes? which verb
>   can be followed by 'to'?
> 4B Clue: part of a collocation.
> 5D Clue: part of a collocation.
> 6C Clue: only one word can be followed by a *to*-infinitive.
> 7A
> 8C Clue: read the whole sentence.
> 9D Clue: only one word can be followed by 'with'.
> 10A
> 11C Clue: which word means the same as 'becoming'?
> 12B
> 13A Clue: only one word makes sense. Read the next
>   sentence too.
> 14B Clue: part of a collocation.
> 15B

3 Vocabulary

This exercise encourages students to pay attention to word combinations and to continue adding to their Vocabulary notebooks.

> ### ANSWERS
>
> 1 results from, cope with, lead to, prevent from
> 2 take place, take action
> 3 have an effect

Homework: ▶▶ *Exam Practice Workbook* page 97

Writing: *discursive composition*

(CB pages 138–139)

Use the **exam file** to introduce the task type. Point out that this is different from the composition type they met in Unit 8, in which they had to argue a point of view, but not suggest solutions. Go through the **exam strategy**. Explain that they will practise each of the points in this lesson.

1 Understand the task

> ### ANSWERS
>
> 1 The key words are 'What should we <u>do</u>?' The composition
>   should include at least one suggestion (but probably
>   several) for reducing global warming.
> 2 The style should be formal or neutral.

2 Plan your answer

You can work through these tasks as a whole class or let students work in pairs.

3 Choose the best introduction to a sample answer

Students should work individually to read the introductions and the sample answer. They can then discuss in pairs which is the best introduction.

> ### ANSWERS
>
> Introduction 2 is best. It introduces the problem. There is a
> topic sentence which is developed and explained in the rest
> of the paragraph.
> Introduction 1 does not contain enough information and only
> has one sentence.
> Introduction 3 is about pollution and not global warming.

Focus on organisation

4 Analyse the sample answer

> ### ANSWERS
>
> Ex. 4.1
>
> | Main points | Solutions |
> | --- | --- |
> | Use of fossil fuels | use alternative energy sources, e.g. solar power |
> | Traffic pollution | use public transport more |
> | Packaging | stop buying things with a lot of packaging; dispose of old fridges safely |
> | Cutting down trees | plant trees |

ANSWERS

Ex. 4.2/4.3
Corrected sample answer:

(Introduction 2)
There are many ways we can help. <u>First of all</u> (1C), the use of fossil fuels is said to be one of the main factors affecting the atmosphere. We should persuade our governments to use alternative sources of energy, like solar power.

<u>Secondly</u> (2A), traffic pollution adds to global warming so we should use public transport more. If bus and train services aren't good, we should make our governments improve them.

<u>Thirdly</u> (3B), we should stop buying things with a lot of packaging because it contains materials that damage the atmosphere. Moreover, old refrigerators that still contain CFC coolants should be disposed of safely and not left in the streets.

<u>Finally</u> (4A), we must stop cutting down trees. They are said to be the 'lungs of the Earth' because they absorb carbon dioxide and produce oxygen, so we should think about planting trees wherever and whenever we can.

<u>To sum up</u> (5B), I believe we can all do something about global warming, and we must. If we ignore the problem, the consequences will be disastrous.

Focus on grammar

5 Impersonal passive constructions

1 Go through the **grammar file** with the class. When students have found the examples of the impersonal passive patterns in the sample composition, get them to rewrite them in the active forms. Discuss the differences in style.

2 Students could do the exercise in pairs. Encourage them to refer to the **grammar file** if necessary. Tell them they will have to change the tense in some of the sentences.

ANSWERS

Ex. 5.1
Examples in the text:
'It is feared that ...' (introduction 2)
'The use of fossil fuels is said to be ...'
'They are said to be "the lungs of the Earth"'
(Active forms:
People/Scientists fear that ...
People/Scientists say that the use of fossil fuels is one of ...
People/Scientists say that they are 'the lungs ...')

Ex. 5.2
1 Pollution from factories and cars is claimed to be poisoning our planet.
2 A third of the world's rainforests are thought to have been destroyed.
3 We are expected to have run out of oil by the end of the century.
4 It is believed that cutting down trees has caused the recent severe floods in many parts of the world.
5 It is expected that temperatures will continue to rise by about 0.2% per decade.

Over to you

6 Writing task

Help students to plan this composition in class before asking them to write it for homework. Elicit what has to be included in the composition. Brainstorm a list of ideas. Ask students to make a paragraph plan based on some of the ideas on the board.

CRITERIA FOR MARKING

Content: At least one suggestion for saving endangered animals.
Organisation: Clear organisation of points with appropriate paragraphing and linking of ideas.
Register: Formal or neutral but must be consistent.
Effect on target reader: Would be aware of what can be done to save endangered animals.

Homework: ▶▶ *Exam Practice Workbook* pages 100–101
Unit 11 Test ▶▶ TB page 133

12 Careers

Lead-in (CB pages 140–141)

Ask students to identify the jobs in the photos on pages 140 and 141. They could discuss the questions as a class or in pairs. Ensure they know the meanings of the words in the box before they do Question 3. Ask them to think of other jobs that require each quality.

Definitions

drive – determination and energy that make you successfully achieve something

commitment – the hard work and loyalty that someone gives to a company, activity, etc.

initiative – the ability to make decisions and take action without waiting for someone to tell you what to do

maturity – the quality of behaving in a sensible way like an adult

resourcefulness – the quality of being good at finding ways of dealing with practical problems

> ▶▶ *extra activity*
>
> When students have discussed all the questions, they could practise the one minute long turn (Paper 5), each student spending one minute comparing and contrasting two of the photos and answering one of the questions: 1, 2, or 3.

> **PHOTOS**
>
> On page 140, clockwise from the left, the photos show: a doctor wearing a white coat with a stethoscope round her neck; a chef in a tall chef's hat, holding a plate of food; a ballet dancer in a white tutu doing an arabesque; a sailing instructor in a sailing boat.
>
> On page 141, in the order of the text: a disc jockey wearing headphones; two Army officers in camouflage jackets; a teacher in a classroom; a model wearing a pink coat; a group of young people, members of a conservation organisation, involved in fieldwork by the coast.

Reading 1: *multiple matching*

(CB pages 140–141)

1 Strategy

The aim of this exercise is to remind students of the recommended strategy for this task type. (See CB page 46.)

> **ANSWERS**
>
> 1 Choose from the people A–E to answer the questions.
> 2 c)
> 3 It is advisable to read the questions first.
> 4 No, because you are looking for certain information only.

2 – 3 Reading task: *multiple matching*

Allow students 15 minutes to do the task.

When they compare their answers with the class, focus on the way the questions paraphrase the text, as in the example given.

> **ANSWERS**
>
> 1E 'I started doing voluntary work' (lines 87–88)
> 2A 'I'm now in charge of signing new bands' (lines 14–15)
> 3C 'The advantage is that you build up a teaching style quite quickly, but you do miss out a bit on the educational theory behind it' (lines 55–57)
> 4A 'No two days are ever the same ... and an average day can change in an instant ... The thrill of that ...' (lines 17–20)
> 5D 'Anyone who says ... is totally wrong.' (lines 65–68)
> 6E 'setting up courses for people who want to come and study ...' (lines 93–94)
> 7D 'I'm building up the experience necessary to start my own agency' (lines 76–77)
> 8B 'I hope to have been promoted ... in two years' time.' (lines 41–44)
> 9A, 10B (in either order)
>   A '... assistant to the marketing manager' (line 13);
>   B '... shadowed another officer for two months' (lines 35–36)
> 11D 'It is often exhausting.' (lines 74–75)
> 12E 'I also have to ... try to get sponsorship for our schemes.' (lines 94–96)
> 13B, 14C (in either order)
>   B 'after a year I ... swapped to a Geography degree' (lines 27–30);
>   C 'after two years switched to Biology and returned to my original plan.' (lines 52–53)
> 15C 'the rather troublesome pupils' (line 59)

Over to you

4 – 5 Discussion/Vocabulary

The aim of these exercises is to encourage students to read the text again and focus on useful topic vocabulary. Encourage them to use the vocabulary from the text when discussing the questions, and to record any new vocabulary and useful word combinations in their Vocabulary notebooks.

Homework: ▶▶ *Exam Practice Workbook* page 102

Grammar: *hypothetical meaning*

(CB page 142)

See **Introduction** page 7 for suggestions on how to use the **grammar file**.

Presentation (1): *wish/if only*

Here is a possible approach.

Books closed. Write three examples on the board, one from each section of the grammar file, **A–C**, e.g.:

I wish I could find a job.
I wish I hadn't given up my university course.
I wish the train would come.

Ask students about the meaning of each example:

Can you find a job? (No)
Did you give up your course? (Yes)
Is the train late? (Yes)
What time does each example refer to, present, past or future?

Then ask about form:

What forms follow 'wish' in each case?

Ask students to re-express each example using 'If only'. Ask:

What's the difference? (No difference in form, but 'if only' is more emphatic.)

Now tell students to open their books at page 142, and read **grammar file 20**, and find one more use of 'wish' (Section C, example 2, for complaints)

1   Practice: *choose the correct verb*

Let students do the exercise in pairs, referring to the **grammar file** if necessary.

> **ANSWERS**
>
> 1 had stayed (regret about the past)
> 2 could ('would' is not possible with the first person 'I')
> 3 would give (complaint)
> 4 was (wish about the present: his workplace **isn't** nearer home)
> 5 didn't need (wish about the present: I **do** need to work)
> 6 earned (wish about the present: we **don't** earn more money)
> 7 had paid (regret about the past)
> 8 were ('would' is not possible with the first person 'I')

Presentation (2): *It's time/would rather*

Write the following examples on the board, underlining the differences in verb form. Elicit the difference in meaning:

It's time <u>to stop</u> work. (= a statement of fact – we always stop work at this time)
It's time <u>you stopped</u> work. (= you should stop work now, you have been working too long)

Contrast these examples in the same way:

I'<u>d rather be</u> a doctor than a soldier. (= a personal preference for myself)

I'<u>d rather you didn't go</u> into the army. (= a preference for someone else)

Tell students to read the second **grammar file** and find out what other tenses can follow 'would rather'.

2   Practice: *sentence completion*

This exercise practises all the structures presented. Point out that students should use their imagination: there is not one right answer.

> **ANSWERS**
>
> **Sample answers:**
> 1 went home
> 2 lived in the city
> 3 didn't do your hair
> 4 had seen
> 5 learnt to drive?
> 6 would ring me
> 7 wouldn't
> 8 didn't go out

Over to you

3   Practice: *pairwork*

This exercise provides a chance for students to use the structures in a personal context.

You could ask students to write their answers down before they talk about them in pairs. You could do a class check by asking one student to tell the class what his/her partner said (giving practice in the use of third person), then finding out if any other students had similar wishes or regrets.

Homework: ▶▶ *Exam Practice Workbook* pages 102–103, Exercises 1–3

Use of English 1: *error correction*

(CB page 143)

Remind students of the **exam strategy** for this task. (See CB page 69.)

1   Discussion

Set the context by discussing the questions as a whole class.

2   Read the text

Students read the text through and answer the questions before they do the error correction task.

> **ANSWERS**
>
> 1 Strawberry picking
> 2 No

3 – 4 Error correction task

Students should work individually, then compare answers in pairs.

Elicit the grammar areas tested by the task during the class check, in preparation for Exercise 5.

ANSWERS

1. have (past simple not present perfect is needed with 'Last year')
2. on (the phrasal verb 'go on' = 'continue')
3. ✔
4. it ('myself' is the object of the 'let … in for' so another object 'it' is unnecessary)
5. ✔
6. and ('have picked' is the present perfect tense)
7. what ('which' would be correct, but 'what' is the wrong relative pronoun, and a relative pronoun is not needed when it is the object of the clause)
8. been (this is not a passive verb, so 'been' is not needed)
9. ✔
10. all (we don't use two quantifiers together)
11. both (the use of 'both' would require another item in addition to 'insect repellent')
12. only
13. ✔
14. as ('think' introduces a clause here; the conjunction 'that' has been omitted; 'as' cannot be used in this situation)
15. much (you can say either 'so boring' or 'very boring' but you can't say 'so much boring')

5 Revision

Refer students to the **Contents map** at the front of the *Coursebook* to find the Unit numbers, and the **Grammar file** section beginning on CB page 176 to find the file numbers. You could give students time to make a grid themselves, then put it up on the board.

ANSWERS

	Extra word	Grammatical area	Unit	Grammar file
1	have	present perfect/ past simple	1,2	6, 8
6	and	present perfect	1, 2	8
7	what	relative clauses	4	23
8	been	the passive	7, 11	21
10	all	quantifiers	8	2
11	both	quantifiers	8	2
14	as	indirect speech	2, 5	13, 14, 15
15	much	comparison, clauses of reason/result	4	3, 26

Homework: ▶▶ *Exam Practice Workbook* pages 103–104, Exercises 4–5

Listening: yes/no *answers* (CB page 144)

Tapescript: ▶▶ TB pages 113–114

Refer students to the **exam file** to introduce the task type. This task is very similar to the true/false exercise.

1 – 2 Understand the task/Predict

Set the context by talking about the questions as a whole class. Refer students to the photographs, which show young gap-year volunteers at a summer camp in the USA. Point out that the meaning of 'gap year' is given in the instructions.

3 – 4 ▭ Listening task

Refer students to the **exam tip!**. Play the recording once all the way through. Then play it again all the way through so that students can check their answers.

ANSWERS

1. YES 'as long as you can convince them [universities and colleges] you've spent your time wisely'
2. NO 'My parents … didn't mind me going'
3. YES 'There was no one to fall back on but myself. It was great in terms of building my self-confidence'
4. NO 'it was sad leaving the school … But I didn't feel too guilty'
5. NO 'I realised it would be a mistake to go and do something I didn't want to do, just to be with them.'
6. YES 'I found the information they gave me very helpful. It really got me started. … I don't think I'd have gone otherwise.'
7. YES 'And the best thing was … I'm really fluent in the language now.'

Over to you

5 Discussion

Students could discuss these questions as a class or in pairs.

> ▶▶ *extra activity*
>
> Set a composition for homework:
> Your class has had a discussion on the advantages of taking a gap year. Your teacher has asked you to write a composition saying whether you agree or disagree with the following statement:
> 'Every student should take a gap year before going to university.'
> Write your composition in 120–180 words in an appropriate style.

Speaking: *individual long turn*

(CB pages 145/206–207)

Follow the procedure recommended in Unit 6, TB pages 59–60. Students should change roles for the second speaking task (the photographs on page 206). Remind students of the **exam strategy** for this task (see CB pages 21/59).

PHOTOS

Speaking task 1:
Both photos show young people doing work experience.
Photo 1 shows a girl working as a classroom assistant with young children in primary school. They are working in a small group and seem to be making something.
Photo 2 shows a group of young people digging a well in Africa. There are two people in the well, and someone else is handing one of them a bucket of water.
Speaking task 2:
Photo 1 shows an open-plan office. Several workstations can be seen, each one equipped with a computer and filing cabinet. In the foreground, a small group of people are discussing something at a table.
Photo 2 shows a man working from home using a lap-top computer. He may be freelance or self-employed. The child sitting next to him playing must be his daughter.

Working in the arts

Lead-in (CB pages 146–147)

The **Lead-in** tasks could be done in pairs or as a whole class. The first activity is further useful practice for Paper 5, the long turn. Ask students to identify the instruments in the pictures before they start.

PHOTOS

Photo 1 shows young schoolchildren playing in a steel band.
Photo 2 shows a group of girls practising ballet positions.
Photo 3 shows schoolchildren practising for the school play. As well as actors, there is a school orchestra which will provide musical accompaniment.

Reading 2: *multiple-choice questions*

(CB pages 146–147)

Elicit the recommended exam strategy for multiple-choice questions. (See CB page 22.)

1 – 2 Reading task: *multiple-choice questions*
Allow students to do the exam task individually. Set a time limit of 15–20 minutes. Students then compare their answers with the whole class.

ANSWERS

1A 'She quickly gained an understanding of her own progress.' (line 8)
2D 'neither could have anticipated the outcome of Hilary's brilliant playing' (lines 17–18)
3C David Zinman ... first heard Hilary when she was rehearsing for a competition' (lines 22–23)
4B
5C 'Some kids focus on ... and I'm the same' (line 33)
6B
7A 'I want to continue doing the same ... there is so much that I have yet to do.' (lines 46–47)

Over to you

3 Discussion
This is another opportunity for students to read the text and think about the content. Give them time to think about their answers before discussing as a class.

Homework: ▶▶ *Exam Practice Workbook* pages 104–105

Vocabulary (CB page 148)

1 Choosing the right word

ANSWERS

1 filled in; 2 flexitime; 3 earn; 4 promotion; 5 reference; 6 out of work; 7 experience; 8 retire

2 Prepositions and prepositional phrases
Encourage students to check the prepositions in a dictionary if they are not sure.

ANSWERS

1 for; 2 in; 3 with; 4 of; 5 in; 6 at; 7 in, about, for; 8 from; 9 on; 10 out of

3 What's important in a job?
Check that students understand the expressions in the list. Then let them discuss their opinions in pairs.

4 Word formation/Discussion
1 Tell students to decide first what part of speech they are going to form.

ANSWERS

1 worried; 2 technological; 3 skilled; 4 imagination; 5 flexibility; 6 employee; 7 obliged; 8 absolutely

2 Discuss as a class.

Use of English 2: *word formation*
(CB page 149)

Remind students of the **exam strategy** (CB page 49).

1 Word-formation task

> **ANSWERS**
>
> 1 solution; 2 unbelievable; 3 comical; 4 global;
> 5 achievements; 6 millionaire; 7 poverty; 8 creator;
> 9 memorise; 10 proud

2 Revision: *forming adjectives*

Students can complete the chart individually or in pairs.

> **ANSWERS**
>
> -able: achievable/(un)suitable/(un)memorable/(un)predictable
> -al: (un)musical/(un)professional/traditional/(un)critical
> -ful: (un)successful/(un)helpful/hopeful
> -ic: optimistic/photographic
> -ive: (un)competitive/creative/(un)imaginative/(un)productive
> -y: (un)lucky/funny/sleepy

Over to you

3 Groupwork

Students work in small groups to come up with ideas for a small business. Compare answers with the class.

Homework: ▶▶ *Exam Practice Workbook* page 105

Writing: *transactional letter*
(CB pages 150–151)

Use the **exam file** to introduce the task type. Remind students that it is very important to read the task carefully and include all the points asked for. But refer them to the **exam strategy**, which points out that it is necessary to select relevant information only and not include unnecessary information.

1 Understand the task

Let students read the task and think about the questions individually before discussing as a class.

> **ANSWERS**
>
> **Ex. 1.1**
> 1 Two English-speaking friends.
> 2 They are in your country, you are in London.
> 3 They are coming next month, to visit you. You are planning to go to Glasgow.
> 4 They need information about trains, flights and car travel; a recommendation with reasons.
>
> **Ex 1.2**
> Informal because it is a letter to friends.

2 Plan your answer

> **ANSWERS**
>
> **2.1**
> 1 Variable times but plane is always faster. Car is slowest way to travel.
> 2 a) plane   c) car
> 3 Train (Sunday → Thursday)

2.2
Students could work in pairs to plan the letter. They could then compare their plan with another pair of students and discuss the advantages and disadvantages of each one. Alternatively, students could work through these tasks as a whole class.

Put up an agreed plan on the board. Students can then compare this with the sample answer in Exercise 4.

Focus on linking words

3 Combine sentences

Tell students to try Exercise 3.2 without looking at the list of linking words and expressions in the information box. Ask them to think of a different way of combining the ideas each time. When doing the sentence combining exercise, students should first identify whether the link word should compare or contrast.

Then tell them to check their answers by referring to the information box and examples.

> **ANSWERS**
>
> 1 **Although/While** the plane is comfortable, it costs more.
> 2 **Even though** the train is fast, it isn't as fast as the plane.
> 3 **Both** the weekday **and** the weekend flights are quite expensive.
> 4 The train is expensive. **Nevertheless**, I think ... OR **Although** the train is expensive, I think ...
> 5 **Although/While** I would like to take you in my car, I'm afraid I won't be able to.
> 6 **Neither** the motorway **nor** the smaller roads are very good.

Focus on editing

4 Improve a sample answer

Students should consider each area individually. Alternatively divide the class into groups and ask each group to focus on one area.

> **ANSWERS**
>
> Corrected sample answer + added linking words (see Exercises 4.1 and 4.2).
>
> Dear Daniel and Susana,
>
> I'm so pleased you're coming to see me in London. I have planned a fantastic day sightseeing for you. More later!
>
> There are three ways for us to get to Glasgow. The first option is we could travel by car. However, it's 641 kilometres and car hire costs £40 per day plus petrol. The second option is to take the train. There are regular services each morning and the journey takes about five and a half hours. It's £75.25 on Fridays and Saturdays or £66.25 on all other days. The last possibility is to take a plane. There are flights every hour and it costs £123.20 on weekdays or £95.00 at weekends.
>
> On the whole, I suggest going by plane. Although it may seem expensive, there are advantages. The train journey would be quite tiring as you will already have been travelling. The plane would get us there in just over an hour and would cost us only £20 more than the train if we go at the weekend. While the car is not a bad option, the plane would get us there more quickly and comfortably.
>
> Anyway, let me know what you think and I'll book the tickets.
>
> Best wishes
> Ana

Over to you

5 Writing task

Encourage students to make a different recommendation from that made by Ana in the sample answer.

> **CRITERIA FOR MARKING**
>
> **Content:** The letter must include information about travel by train, by plane and by car. A suggestion of the best way with at least one reason why.
> **Organisation and cohesion:** Letter format, clear organisation of points, suitable opening and closing formulae.
> **Register:** Informal.
> **Target reader:** Would have enough information to agree or disagree with the recommendation.

Homework: ▶▶ *Exam Practice Workbook* pages 108–109

Unit 12 Test ▶▶ TB page 134

Progress test 3 (CB pages 152–153)

Before you set **Progress test 3** on CB pages 152–153, tell students to do the **Progress check** in the *Exam Practice Workbook*, pages 110–111. This reviews the language tested in the *Coursebook*. (You will find the answers in the With Key edition of the *Worbook*.)

> **ANSWERS**
>
> ## Coursebook Progress test 3
>
> ### 1 Structural cloze
>
> 1 that; 2 of; 3 lead; 4 On; 5 result; 6 who; 7 one; 8 is; 9 a; 10 have; 11 So; 12 much; 13 least; 14 all; 15 will
>
> ### 2 Key word transformations
>
> 1 is due to leave at
> 2 wishes he had kept up
> 3 you were able to stay
> 4 enjoy having her portrait
> 5 their holiday despite the wet
> 6 might have left her
> 7 is said to have signed
> 8 must have been lying
> 9 would have bought the dress
> 10 to have my hair cut
>
> ### 3 Error correction
>
> 1 am; 2 ✔; 3 so; 4 have; 5 ✔; 6 it; 7 gets; 8 ✔; 9 that, 10 to; 11 such; 12 up; 13 ✔; 14 your; 15 for
>
> ### 4 Word formation
>
> 1 previously; 2 famous; 3 unexpected; 4 understandably; 5 Information; 6 latest; 7 updated; 8 majority; 9 fascinating; 10 solutions

After doing the test in the *Coursebook*, you could also use the photocopiable test:

Progress test 3 ▶▶ TB pages 135–137

(See TB page 141 for the answers.)

Practice exam • Answers

(CB pages 154–175)

Paper 1 Reading

Part 1
1E; 2C; 3G; 4A; 5B; 6F

Part 2
7A; 8B; 9B; 10C; 11A; 12C; 13D; 14A

Part 3
15G; 16 E; 17B; 18A; 19C; 20D; 21F

Part 4
22B; 23D; 24C; 25A; 26D; 27E; 28B; 29E; 30C; 31C; 32C;
33A; 34/35A/E

Paper 3 Use of English

Part 1
1B; 2A; 3D; 4D; 5C; 6B; 7A; 8B; 9D; 10C; 11C; 12A; 13B; 14B;
15A

Part 2
16 not; 17 by; 18 be; 19 a; 20 on; 21 the; 22 have; 23 or;
24 what; 25 made; 26 in; 27 go; 28 but; 29 so; 30 into

Part 3
31 brother's bicycle without asking
32 take any notice of
33 apologised for his late
34 gets on very well with
35 wish I had bought
36 are being investigated by
37 Unless we hurry we will
38 isn't deep enough
39 has been a steady improvement
40 did not intend to miss

Part 4
41 they; 42 and; 43 one; 44 have; 45 often; 46 ✔; 47 make;
48 ✔; 49 so; 50 ✔; 51 in; 52 if; 53 of; 54 ✔; 55 it

Part 5
56 scientists
57 influential
58 impossibility
59 heavier
60 announcement
61 unconvinced
62 photographers
63 flights
64 invention
65 seriously

Paper 4 Listening

Part 1
1A; 2C; 3B; 4C; 5C; 6B; 7A; 8B

Part 2
9   A Strange Case
10   detective
11   Italy
12   mother
13   romantic fiction
14   short story
15   great fun
16   an older man
17   science fiction
18   next October

Part 3
19E; 20B; 21F; 22D; 23A

Part 4
24C; 25B; 26A; 27C; 28C; 29A; 30B

Paper 5 Speaking

Part 2
The photos for candidate A are on page 173 of the
Coursebook.
Photo 1 shows a schoolboy sitting at a desk or table in his
home with a text book and his notebook. He is dressed
casually. He is probably doing his homework.
Photo 2 shows another boy in school uniform in a classroom
at school. He is painting and there is another pupil in the
background also working. There is a display of artwork on the
wall.

Candidate B's photos are on page 174 of the *Coursebook*.
Photo 3 shows two boys and a woman (probably their
mother). They are sitting on a sofa, wearing football kit. One
is holding a football. There is a TV remote control on the table
together with crisps and drink cans. They are excited and are
probably watching a football match.
Photo 4 shows three people sitting at a kitchen table. They
are probably members of a family eating dinner. An old
woman, probably the grandmother, is pointing at something,
and a younger woman is looking in the same direction and
smiling. They could be looking at someone who has just come
in, or they could also be watching something on TV.

Part 3
From the top left, the photos on page 175 of the *Coursebook*
show:
a windsurfer; someone watering their garden with a hosepipe;
someone taking a shower; a bottle and a glass of, probably,
fizzy water; someone taking washing out of the washing
machine; a family with young children in the sea; a girl
catching a fish.

Tapescripts

Unit 1

Page 8. Listening Part 1: extracts. Exercises 1, 2 and 3

One.

Have you got a ticket yet? No? I'm not surprised. John went on Tuesday, but all the seats were sold out. You know, there's a ticket agency near the railway station that sells tickets in advance – why don't you try them? It's called 'Concorde Tickets', I think. You can book over the phone and pay by credit card, and they post the tickets to you. They charge a bit extra, but they're very reliable – and they do everything! You can even book a flight or a train ticket through them if you want to. Anyway, you'd better hurry if you want to go – Friday is the last night.

Page 8. Exercise 2.

Two.

So I said to them: Look, the team is together. We're ready to start. And we were. Of course, all the technical stuff was second-hand but it worked OK, most of the time. And some of the advice they were giving us wasn't so good but we could deal with that. But in the end they wouldn't give us the funding. We put in five thousand from our own pockets but it wasn't enough and we couldn't get any more, so we had to stop before we got into debt.

Three.

Interviewer: So when did you actually start?
Man: When I was about eight but I didn't take it seriously then. I wanted to be a footballer.
Interviewer: In fact you became one, didn't you?
Man: Well, yes. I got an offer from Chelsea Football Club when I was 15, I mean I was a pretty good player. But when I won the competition, when I was 16, I had to give everything else up. I began to make records, perform in public. Someone even wrote a book about me called *The New Mozart*, although I was much older than Mozart was when I became successful.

Four.

I just happened to look up and there sitting opposite me was this really familiar face and I thought 'Do I know this person?' and I began thinking of old friends I hadn't seen for years. Then I realised who it was. Of course, I've seen him so many times but he seemed shorter than I expected. I couldn't see any bodyguards. I know he's not the President or Prime Minister or anything like that but I still wouldn't have expected him to travel on a train by himself. As soon as I got home I watched him on my favourite video. I should've asked for his autograph.

Five.

… Plus you get a free book – the original novel that it's based on – and a separate CD with the soundtrack of the film. And remember, this version isn't available in the shops. You can only buy it by telephoning the number that you'll hear at the end of this message. Don't miss this opportunity to have your own copy of the Director's Cut, a special version including twenty minutes of extra material which has never been seen before. And now – the number to phone is 0800 …

Six.

I can see them, just about, but I can't actually hear anything from where I'm standing. I tried to move forward before, but there are just too many people. There are a lot of police about too, I don't know why. Actually, I've just realised that the reason I can't hear them is they haven't started playing yet! … But with all these planes flying over it's hard to tell! It's going to be pretty difficult even when they do start up. Really not a good idea to hold it so near to the airport. I think you did the right thing staying at home.

Seven.

It's amazing to have something like that in the street where I live. It looks just like an ordinary house from the outside. There is no sign or anything but there are always Rolls-Royces parked outside and you should see the people who get out of them! There are always people waiting to see them, so the shops round here do good business selling things to the fans, takeaway food and so on. You can't hear them performing – it's completely soundproof – but you can often smell cooking, which is rather strange.

Eight.

Well, I'm very sorry this has happened too, and I do appreciate your apologies. But I paid in advance so I'd be sure to get the tickets, and you gave me a receipt – which I have here – I showed it to you and I mean, I understand the problems you describe, but you know, I really think you have to give me what I paid for. I don't actually want my money back, I want to have the tickets that I paid for, because after all, what good is the money to me?

Page 9. Speaking Part 1. Exercises 1 and 2.

Examiner: Good morning. Could I have your marksheets, please? Thank you. My name is John. So, you are Maria and Carlos? Right. First of all, I'd like to know something about you, so I'm going to ask you some questions about yourselves. To start with, I'd like to ask you a few questions about your home town – the place where you live in your country. Can you tell me something about your home town, Maria?

Maria: I'm from the capital city of my country, so it's quite big.

Examiner: What do you like most about your home town?

Maria: I enjoy everything really, it is very good.

Examiner: And what about you, Carlos? Tell me about your home town.

Carlos: Yes … Yes, my home town is in the south of my country and it's a very big city. It has a population of about seven million, seven to ten million, really a lot of people. Because I like, I like the city very much because I have a lot of friends there and we can have a lot of fun. Really, you can do whatever you like. It's got facilities for sport, entertainment, whatever. But it has its bad points – the air pollution is very bad.

Examiner: That's the worst thing, is it?

Carlos: Yes, sometimes it's terrible.

Examiner: Can you tell me something about what you do in your spare time, such as your hobbies, sports and things like that? Can you tell me first, Carlos?

Carlos: Yes, in my spare time I do kick boxing. It's a martial art but really it's a sport as well – you can kick, using the feet, and also punch, using the hands. It's good for me because I'm improving my fitness, especially my legs. You can defend yourself, you can, I think you can improve and I am getting better. That's mainly what I do.

Examiner: And what about you, Maria? Do you have a hobby?

Maria: Actually, I'm not good at sports. I like to go out, so in the afternoon, for example, I go shopping.

Examiner: OK. Now, Maria, can you tell me about your plans for the future?

Maria: It's difficult to say. I haven't decided yet but I'm learning English now and maybe I can be a tourist guide.

Examiner: And what about you, Carlos? Can you tell me about your plans for the future?

Carlos: Yes, now I am a student but I have worked with my father, my father's company, we sell and buy metal, such as copper, steel, and other metals – I don't exactly know their names in English. I hope to buy and sell in the world and deal with companies in England, America, Japan, Germany. All over the world, I hope.

Examiner: Thank you. Well, let's go on to Part 2.

Unit 2

Page 20. Listening Part 2: sentence completion. Exercise 4.

Interviewer: My guest today is a young man who at the age of 27 is already a highly successful professional mountaineer. Paul Thornton, welcome.

Paul: Hi.

Interviewer: Paul, was it always your ambition to climb mountains? How did it all begin?

Paul: Well, I guess if I had to name a person, it would be Carlo Buhler. He was one of the world's greatest mountaineers and I read about him in a magazine when I was very young. It described the hardships in climbing, but also how rewarding it was to achieve a goal which you'd set yourself.

Interviewer: So you were brought up in a mountainous region?

Paul: Not at all. I come from London. But I remember being taken on a trip to Switzerland when I was about 11 years old. It was a skiing holiday with my parents and that was when I realised that I liked getting away from city life.

Interviewer: You've been climbing now for a number of years. What have been your worst moments?

Paul: I've had a few pretty bad experiences. The odd broken wrist and twisted ankle as you'd imagine. The worst time was when I fell and hurt my back quite badly. What's more, the fall pulled most of the ropes out of the rock, so I was left hanging about 500 feet off the ground. I keep that rope hanging above my desk as a reminder that it saved my life.

Interviewer: Really? But how did you get down?

Paul: I had to abseil down and then get back on foot. Unfortunately, the snow was deep and, with my injury, I could only walk very slowly. It was quite a considerable way back to the tent, so when light began to fail, I ended up spending the night on the mountain at 14,000 feet. It was a long night on a cold bed of rocks, but at least I survived.

Interviewer: Right. And what makes a good travelling companion in your opinion?

Paul: I enjoy travelling with people who have an idea of what they want to do, who've made a plan, but who are willing to change if necessary. I watch so many travellers to Nepal who don't start out with a plan and who consequently end up wasting a lot of time and seeing nothing.

Interviewer: So that's the most important thing for you?

Paul: Yeah. But I also like to have a good time and eat good food. I'm not keen on travelling on a limited budget. You have to enjoy yourself. The worst companion I ever had was a journalist who joined us on a trek to Nepal. I don't know why he was allowed to come because he just complained the whole time about the food, the fact he couldn't have a shower, things like that … The other thing is, it's best to be with people who aren't too ambitious.

Interviewer: Really?

Paul: Yes, I don't like people who put ambition before friendship, and I've seen that very often on the mountain. Sadly, many climbers are very selfish people, they let you do all the hard work for them and then they just want all the recognition.

Interviewer: And what about when you're not climbing, how do you relax?

Paul: I like music, especially Bob Marley, and I read a lot. I'm a great science fiction fan actually, although I also have to read travel books when I'm preparing for trips.

Interviewer: So where's your idea of the ideal place for a break?

Paul: I'm still searching for that, but Mendoza in western Argentina comes close. It has a great climate, terrific ice-cream and beautiful parks. The way of life there suits me, everybody is very relaxed and open. It's a great place to sit in the park and plan your next trip. I'm off there next week actually.

Interviewer: Very nice too. Thanks Paul, it was great talking to you.

Paul: Thanks.

Page 21. Speaking Part 2. Exercise 1.

Examiner: Right. Let's go on to Part 2. In this part, you each speak on your own for about a minute. I'm going to show each of you two different photographs and I'd like you to talk about them. Georgia, here are your two photographs. They show people travelling in remote areas, far away from towns and cities. Please let Iannis have a look at them. Georgia, I'd like you to compare and contrast the two photographs, saying what dangers face people when they travel in those places. You have only about a minute for this so don't worry if I interrupt you.

Page 21. Exercise 3.

Georgia: Well, I can see two very different places, a snowy, icy landscape, and a dry desert landscape. There is extreme heat and extreme cold. In the icy place, maybe it's the Arctic, they are using a – I don't know the name in English – something for transport that is pulled by dogs, but in the other photo the man is riding a horse. In the Arctic, I think it would be difficult to keep warm, you'd need lots of warm clothes. And you would need to carry lots of food. If you had an accident, it could be very serious. I mean, you could fall or even the dogs could run off and leave you alone. So you depend on them for everything. And the man in the desert depends on his horse. In that respect, they are similar situations. If the horse can't run, the man will probably die of thirst and he has to find water for the horse as well as for himself.

Page 21. Exercise 4.

Examiner: Iannis, in which place is it more difficult to survive?
Iannis: For me, in my opinion, it would be more difficult to survive in the cold place because you can't find food and you need a lot of clothes to keep you warm.

Page 21. Exercise 5.1.

Examiner: Here are your two photographs, Iannis. They show people taking part in adventurous activities. Please let Georgia have a look at them. Iannis, I'd like you to compare and contrast these photos, saying why people choose to do activities like these. You have only about a minute for this so don't worry if I interrupt you.

Page 21. Exercise 5.2.

Examiner: Georgia, can you tell me which of these activities you would prefer to do?
Georgia: Well, I think I would prefer …

Unit 3

Unit 3, page 32. Listening Part 3: multiple matching. Exercises 4 and 5.

I really love Shakespeare because the language is so different from the way we speak today. Sometimes it's a bit difficult – well, actually quite often – but you get used to it quite quickly. The love stories are my favourite, especially *Romeo and Juliet*. I think young people like me are drawn to Shakespeare by the films. I saw a version of *Romeo and Juliet* set in modern-day America – it was fantastic. And I really enjoyed that, that film called mmm … you know … *Shakespeare in Love*. When you see good films like that, it really makes you want to read the original texts in class, doesn't it?

When I was in England, it was in summer of last year, we all went on a coach trip to Stratford-upon-Avon, which is Shakespeare's birthplace, as I'm sure you know. And we saw all those wonderful old houses and also the theatre, you know, where they put on his plays. I mean, we didn't actually see a play, 'cos there wasn't really time, but I bought some real nice souvenirs. When we were back in London, we wanted to go and visit Shakespeare's Globe Theatre, it's been rebuilt, you know, and we set out one day to see it but we got completely lost and never found it.

I've only read one play by Shakespeare and that was one too many, thank you very much. It was *Julius Caesar* and I had to read it when I was at school. I've still got my school copy of it somewhere, I think. I haven't read a word of Shakespeare since then and I don't think I've missed anything, do you? And I'm not interested in seeing a Shakespeare play on stage, or even on video, either. You see, in my job, I see enough violence and dishonesty in real life without wanting to see even more of it on stage in the theatre.

My colleagues all told me I was wasting my time and it would just be too difficult for them, but I just went ahead and tried it anyway. I found that if I took them outside and got them to actually perform the scenes, instead of just reading the text, they actually got really enthusiastic. I chose *Macbeth*, which was a good choice 'cos it's full of good lines and it's got plenty of action. The response was really positive and they're begging me to do another play with them next term! Maybe we can perform it on stage for the parents at the end of term.

It's surprising how popular they still are you know. They're best-sellers, really, even after so many centuries. It's not just the plays, which exist in all sorts of different editions of course – including the cartoon comic versions – but there's literary criticism, biographies, and nowadays you've got the videos too. So we always need to keep plenty of titles in stock. 'Romeo and Juliet' is the one people are asking for now because there's a video that's just come out. And *Julius Caesar* too – it's a popular choice for teachers who want to do a play with their students.

Page 33. Speaking Part 3. Exercise 2.1.

Examiner: Let's go on. In this part of the Speaking Test, Part three, I'd like you to talk about something together for about three minutes. I'm just going to listen.
   Look at these photos, which show different learning situations. I'd like you to discuss the positive and less positive aspects of each way of learning. Then decide which <u>two</u> ways you think are the most effective.
Necip: Sorry, I don't understand what I have to do. Could you repeat it, please?
Examiner: Yes, yes, of course. Look at these photos, which show different learning situations. I'd like you to discuss the positive and less positive aspects of each way of learning. Then decide which <u>two</u> ways you think are the most effective.

Page 33. Exercises 2.2. and 2.3

Necip: Well, shall I start? Or would you like to start?

Gulay: You start.

Necip: OK. I think maybe this way, using computers is good. It is certainly increasing nowadays. What do you think?

Gulay: Yes, but this picture – a large class, classroom teaching, lots of students sitting at desks, with just one teacher – it's very common, so I'm used to it.

Necip: Mmm, and the students putting their hands up, they look very confident. They are enthusiastic, which is good. It makes a difference.

Gulay: Yes, it's OK, but actually I prefer group discussions, like in this picture, just a small group with the teacher sitting at a table.

Necip: Do you? Group discussion, yes, I agree, it's quite good. I like working in a group and expressing my own opinion. And you can hear other people's different opinions and maybe we agree with each other, or maybe not, but you can learn from this.

Gulay: And it's better if there is a teacher there to answer questions. You can ask questions and you can learn that way, you can speak together.

Necip: But when I finish lessons, I usually use the computer, I can get a lot of information that way and pursue my own interests.

Gulay: Yes, self-study. But I think that is perhaps not so good because for example, in this picture, he is using the computer alone at home and he can't communicate with other people.

Necip: I'm not sure about that. I really like computers. I mean, he can communicate with the computer!

Gulay: But it's not human, not a person!

Necip: Not a person? It doesn't matter. In my opinion, it depends on your personality. I like practical, modern things and I like working with computers very much. And actually I don't, I don't like to just sit and listen. I learn more if I do practical things.

Gulay: Like this picture – the students are doing some kind of experiment.

Necip: Yes. Or for example, I study English grammar, yes, but I prefer to speak to people because I think I can gain confidence by speaking to people. But if the teacher is good I enjoy my lessons too. What about you?

Gulay: Yes, I think you're right. It's better if you do practical things and if you can communicate with other people. So, have we decided which two are best?

Necip: Yes, I think so. I think we like working in small groups, and we like computers, yes?

Gulay: Yes.

Examiner: Thank you.

Unit 4

Page 44. Listening Part 4: multiple-choice questions. Exercises 2 to 4.

Student: Thank you very much for agreeing to let me interview you, Mr Newnham. It'll really help me with my local history project.

Peter: I'm glad to help.

Student: First of all, can you tell me what you think has been the biggest change in our town over the last 50 years or so?

Peter: Well, I suppose the biggest change is that it's physically much, much larger. And, of course, a lot more people live here now. In fact, most of the town is actually unrecognisable compared with fifty years ago.

Student: Why is that?

Peter: It's because so many buildings have been knocked down and new ones built in their place, so the whole appearance of the town has changed. A lot of this was unnecessary and very regrettable, in my view, but I'm afraid it can't be helped. We just have to put up with it.

Student: What about people's lifestyle – how has that changed?

Peter: Well, there's a lot more choice nowadays than there used to be. Just as an example, fifty years ago, soccer was about the only sport that people watched or played. But now we've got facilities for American football, baseball, basketball and even ice-hockey. And we've got our own basketball team as well as a football team.

Student: A lot of people say that the culture of the USA has had a big influence. Do you agree?

Peter: Yes, but that's nothing new. What's happening now is not so much the influence of one country, but that people want to adopt things from all over the world, from Europe and Asia as well. People travel much more nowadays and see things they like in other countries and try to copy them. And our town now has a lot of people who originally came from other countries.

All this has had a big effect on the choice of food you can buy in restaurants and shops – and a very positive one, I think. Also, if you walk around our town in the summer you see a lot of restaurants with tables outside. That's normal for you, but it used to be very unusual years ago, even in very hot weather. These changes have happened because of contact with other countries.

Student: Oh, that's interesting. I never thought of that. So are there any changes that you feel have not been so good?

Peter: Well, of course, cars are a problem. A few years ago I would have said that things were getting worse and worse, but in fact now there are more parking restrictions as well as pedestrianised areas, so I think the situation is more or less under control – though of course there's still room for improvement. You see a lot more cyclists about now, anyway. All in all, the town is a lot cleaner than it used to be, even when we take into account the pollution caused by cars.

Student: Is it really?

Peter: Oh, yes. People often complain about the litter in the streets, which is true, and it is always young people that get the blame for that. But you only have to look at old photographs to see how dirty the town used to be, mainly because of the smoke from factories and domestic fires. That's all changed. The river is much cleaner now too. You see a lot of people fishing in it, which didn't happen years ago because no fish could survive in it.

Student: The area near the river is very popular now, isn't it?

Peter: It definitely is. In fact, you could say that the centre of town has moved. It used to be the square in front of the town hall, that's the actual physical centre. It's the place people used to meet. But now, if you ask where the town centre is, people will direct you to the river. That's where a lot of people congregate in the evening, young and old, to walk along the riverbank, meet their friends and enjoy their leisure time.

Student: How did people spend their leisure time fifty years ago?

Peter: Well, …

Page 45. Speaking Part 4. Exercise 1.

Examiner: In this part of the Speaking Test, Part 3, I'd like you to talk to about something together for about three minutes. I'm just going to listen.

Look at these pictures. I'd like you to imagine that in the town where you live, there are plans to build two of the five amenities that you see in the pictures. Discuss how useful each amenity would be. Then decide which two you would choose and why you would choose them.

Ewa: I'm sorry, I didn't quite catch that. Could you say it again, please?

Examiner: Yes, yes, of course. Look at these pictures. Imagine that in the town where you live, there are plans to build two of the five amenities in the pictures. I'd like you to discuss how useful each amenity would be. Then decide which two you would choose and why you would choose them.

Page 45. Exercises 4.1 and 4.2

Ewa: Well, I chose the park and the swimming pool. A park is good, because you can go there and relax. And a swimming pool would be very good for exercise and keeping fit. But I'm not sure … was it the theatre or the skateboarding area you liked, Rajmund?

Rajmund: Yes, I like the skateboarding area. Young people can go there and have a lot of fun.

Ewa: And what else?

Rajmund: I agree with you about the swimming pool.

Ewa: So that was the conclusion we reached, definitely the swimming pool and then either the skateboarding area or the park.

Examiner: Thank you. What objections might people have to some of these amenities?

Ewa: Well, I think that generally they will be popular, especially the sporting facilities, but if a place gets very crowded, sometimes people object, especially if there's lots of traffic. If you live near these things, you may not be so keen on them.

Rajmund: And noise – it can be a problem sometimes.

Ewa: Which places do you think are worse for noise, Rajmund?

Rajmund: Well, for example, if something is going on all night, like theatre or other entertainment, maybe people who live in the area can't sleep.

Ewa: Yes, that's a good point. You might hear a lot of shouting and laughing. So I think places like this should be separate from residential areas. And also, there is a problem of litter. People can drop litter in the park like cans and things. That can be quite terrible sometimes.

Examiner: Can you think of any other reasons why some people may not want these amenities?

Ewa: Well, let me see. There is the question of danger, for example with skateboarding, there might be accidents because skateboarders go very fast. I know old people sometimes complain about that. Do you think there is a solution to that problem, Rajmund?

Rajmund: You can build the area so that it is only for skateboarders and nobody walks there. Then it will be safe and not cause any problems.

Ewa: Yes, I agree with that. It will be better for the skateboarders too.

Examiner: What amenities are absolutely essential in every town, in your opinion?

Ewa: Well, I think that theatres and concert halls are essential because things like drama and music are important to a lot of people. My town really needs a new concert hall with high-quality sound. And sometimes it can be good to have a festival so that everyone in the town gets involved. Do you agree, Rajmund?

Rajmund: Yes, that's right. And also you need sports facilities, both for playing sport yourself and also watching professional sport.

Ewa: Yes, it makes a big difference if you have top-quality sport taking place in your town. And I also think that an art gallery and a museum are important because every town needs a place where you see what happened in the past. And you can see works of art from the past and the present, because I think that modern artists need a place to show their work. Those things give you a sense of history and make you proud of where you live, don't you think, Rajmund?

Rajmund: Yes, I agree, I think these things are very important.

Examiner: Thank you very much. That's the end of the Speaking Test.

Unit 5

Page 58. Listening Part 4: true or false? Exercises 1 and 2.

Dan: Hi, Mel, I haven't seen you for a while. How are things with you?

Mel: Oh, I'm OK. Broke, as usual, but apart from that, everything's fine. You?

Dan: Yeah, not too bad. That's a really cool T-shirt you're wearing. Where did you get it?

Mel: I got it mail order, actually. It's a catalogue that has lots of designer stuff much cheaper than in the shops. It's the real thing, though, not a rip off or anything.

Dan: Mmm. It really suits you anyway. So how much do you actually spend on clothes, Mel?

Mel: That's a funny question. What makes you ask me that, Dan? Do I look as if I buy cheap clothes or something?

Dan: Sorry, I didn't mean that. No, it's just that my mum reckons I spend more on clothes than the average teenager, but personally, I just don't see it.

Mel: Well, she may have a point actually. I always think there are two ways of looking at it. On the one hand, there are people who like clothes but maybe don't buy a lot of them because they choose very carefully, you know, they buy the top designer labels and all that. Good quality stuff.

Dan: Expensive stuff, you mean.

Mel: Yeah, if you like. I mean, my sister's like that. She doesn't go shopping very often, but she thinks about what she's buying and so she doesn't make many mistakes. She gets good value for money.

Dan: It all gets worn, you mean?

Mel: Exactly.

Dan: Perhaps I should tell my mum that that's what I do, then she'd understand why I need to buy good stuff.

Mel: But how often do you go shopping?

Dan: Oh only at weekends, but I do tend to buy something each week, and I suppose some weeks I buy quite a lot of stuff.

Mel: Right. Well, you actually sound more like me than like my sister. To go back to what I was saying. I'm the second type. I mean, what I really like is shopping. I go every week and I always end up buying something. But half the time I get home and realise that what I've bought is a mistake, and it doesn't suit me or whatever, so I never wear it.

Dan: But don't you try things on? I always get my friends to say what they think.

Mel: Well, yeah, so do I, but that's half the problem. They're always saying, 'Yeah go on, it's great Mel, buy it,' but then they're not the ones who have to pay for it, are they?

Dan: Right. I think my mates are usually quite straight with me actually. My problem is really my brother. You see, he's really the opposite to me. I mean, he never goes shopping, he just wears the same stuff day in day out and couldn't care less about designer labels.

Mel: That must make your mum happy?

Dan: Exactly. She can get him a cheap shirt from the market with a fake label on and it costs her next to nothing.

Mel: But what do his friends think? People must notice.

Dan: Well, basically, my brother's mates are into computers. They spend ages chatting to people on the net and designing new games and all that. None of them are bothered about clothes.

Mel: Sounds like you and me have got the same problem. We spend half our time shopping and the other half worrying about what people think of what we've bought.

Dan: But it's important what people think of you, Mel. I wouldn't want to be like my brother.

Mel: Nor would I actually. I wouldn't want to be like my sister either. Come on, let's go down the shops and see what's new.

Dan: Good idea!

Unit 6

Page 71. Listening Part 3: multiple matching. Exercises 2 and 3.

It was great. Everyone from the class had brought either some food or something to drink and so Marie hadn't had to do much of the work herself. She's really lucky because her family have given her some lovely things as presents, which always makes a good start in a new place. One room was still completely empty though and we used that for dancing way into the night. Fortunately the next day was a public holiday, so we didn't have to get up and go into college.

I've never been to a party like it before – at least not in somebody else's home. But apparently Peter's mother had insisted on making all the arrangements herself. Most of Peter's friends from college were there, which was nice because we hadn't met them before. Peter's already got a job sorted out, so it'll be strange him working while Louise is still coming to class. They won't actually be getting married for a while because, although they're the same age more or less, Louise's birthday is much later in the year and so she's still got another term to do at school.

In the end, we all went out to a restaurant because although everyone wanted to do something to celebrate, no one had really thought to organise anything in advance. It was the same place I went for my last birthday party so I knew it was good and fortunately they'd had a retirement party cancel at the last minute so they managed to fit us in. After all that hard work, it was nice to relax together. You know, some people had even gone into the library to study on the public holiday, would you believe it! We were all just so relieved that it was all over and now we can relax until after the long holiday.

It came as such a shock. We'd been intending to go out for Marilyn's birthday, of course, but then she broke the news to us and so we brought the evening forward to celebrate this instead. All her family were getting together the next day and apparently they were just as shocked as us because the wedding took place over there and in secret! It's incredibly romantic, isn't it? And just think, she'll have a new life in a new country by the time we're all back at college next term. I shall miss her though.

Of course, it only happens once in your life and so I wanted it to be a big party and I knew that all the exams would be over by then, even though it wouldn't be the end of term for a couple of weeks yet. My boyfriend lives in a flat with two other students and he said we could have the party there, which was great, and it was nice to actually have it on the day itself. I'll be having another celebration with my family, of course, but we'll do that when everyone comes home for the public holiday at the end of the month. So, I've still got some more presents to look forward to then, I hope!

Unit 7

Page 83. Listening Part 4: multiple-choice questions. Exercises 3.1 and 4.

Interviewer: I'd like to welcome Rachel Anderson, Britain's first licensed female football agent. How did you become a football agent, Rachel?

Rachel: It was by accident really. Eight years ago I was on an aerobics teaching course and after class one day, I was talking about West Ham Football Club. One of their players, Julian Dicks, was being criticised by the tabloid newspapers and I was angry because he was the best footballer I'd seen and the papers were giving him a hard time. I discovered later that his wife was one of the people listening to me. I was embarrassed, as you can imagine, but she said I was right. She said Julian didn't deal with the press very well and she asked me for advice on dealing with the media. Then a bit later Julian challenged me to be his agent for a year.

Interviewer: Mmm, I see. So can you explain what a football agent does?

Rachel: Well, from seven in the morning until, sometimes, eleven at night, I talk to club chairmen, players, lawyers and the press. I have thirty-one players from fifteen different clubs. If a player is happy at a club, I have to make sure they become well-known, so for example I work to get them sponsorship deals.

Interviewer: I see.

Rachel: I also find new clubs for unhappy players, that means working on transfer deals, and I take care of press engagements. I always encourage players to have a back-up career in case they're injured. And I try to point them in the right direction financially. I want them to understand they need to save money instead of buying another expensive car.

Interviewer: Now, do you mind if I ask how much does one earn as an agent?

Rachel: Er, upwards of £100,000. One good year I made £500,000. But I do have a lot of expenses. I travel a lot – I take around three flights a week – and I have five people working for me. And the players don't pay any of my expenses. As their agent, they give me three per cent of everything they earn. But I might work for a player for two years before asking them to pay me anything. That way I can get good players very early on.

Interviewer: Ah. So have you always loved football?

Rachel: As a young girl, I wasn't supposed to be interested in football. My family were rugby fans and football was considered unacceptable! But I used to sneak off to football matches with the boys from school. Then in my late teens I worked for three years for the president of the International Football Federation. He took me to some matches and that re-awakened my love of the game.

Interviewer: Have you ever played football yourself?

Rachel: Certainly not. At my school, girls only played 'hard' games like hockey or netball. The sort of games where you get serious injuries. None of the 'soft stuff' that goes on on the football field!

Interviewer: Is it difficult being a female agent in a man's game?

Rachel: The only problem I've encountered was when I was banned from the annual dinner of the Professional Footballers Association. I'd been invited by one of my clients, but I was told that the dinner was a male-only event. Even though I live, breathe and work in football, I wasn't allowed in.

Interviewer: So what did you do about it?

Rachel: I took legal action. When the case was heard, the PFA argued that as it was a private dinner, not a public occasion, they could ban women and whoever else they wanted to. The court hasn't made a decision yet.

Interviewer: Did you have to change to fit into the footballing world?

Rachel: I made a conscious effort not to behave like a man. I'm not that kind of person and I don't need to be a man to get respect.

Interviewer: Would you like to see more women working in football?

Rachel: Only if they're good enough at what they do. They should only succeed on their merits, but as in most walks of life, women in football have to do that much more than their male colleagues to be successful.

Interviewer: And how often do you watch a match?

Rachel: I watch three or four games a week. If I'm deciding whether to represent a player, I have to see him play. The first thing a manager will ask if I'm trying to fix a deal is 'Have you seen him play?'

Interviewer: Now, what does your family think of your career?

Rachel: I think they're proud of me. I'm away a lot but my husband is very tolerant. My children are university students and well I think their friends respect them because they have a mother who knows the best footballers.

Interviewer: Rachel Anderson, thank you very much for talking to me.

Rachel: Thanks.

Unit 8

Page 94. Listening Part 2: note-taking. Exercise 2.

Presenter: Good evening. My subject tonight is travel in the 21st century, or to be more precise, holidays in the 21st century. According to the World Tourism Organisation, the holiday trade is going to be a boom industry in the coming decades. For a start, the organisation predicts a big increase in the amount of holiday travelling we do. It estimates that there will be an increase in the number of holiday trips taken around the world, and that the number of trips will go up by 4.1 percent each year. If you consider that there are already hundreds of millions of holiday trips each year, then this is a big increase.

As a result of this increase, the organisation reckons that travel and tourism will soon become the world's largest industry, overtaking even information technology in terms of the amount of money it makes. Tourism is already larger than manufacturing in most parts of the world, including Britain, employing far more people.

So more people will be making more holiday trips to more places in the years to come. But that is not the only change that the organisation predicts. The type of holidays that people take is also likely to change. In the 20th century, although many types of holiday were on offer, and sightseeing and activity holidays have always been popular with certain groups, it was the classic beach holiday that really attracted the largest groups of holidaymakers. That was where the biggest growth occurred, and with it the familiar development of tourist facilities in coastal resorts.

In the 21st century, however, tourists may well be looking for a different type of holiday experience. There is a tendency for people to be less attracted to hotels, for example, as self-catering accommodation becomes more popular. People don't necessarily want to be tied to fixed mealtimes, fixed menus, and the restrictions of small hotel bedrooms. They are willing to be more adventurous and independent, choosing to cook for themselves or eat out in restaurants. Indeed, 21st-century tourists will increasingly be looking to sample the local culture when visiting other countries, particularly things like food and music.

In the same way, tourists are increasingly looking to travel around more in the countries they visit. But they are less keen to do this as part of organised groups, climbing on and off tour buses at the major sights. The 21st-century tourist is more interested in having a hire car, so that the country can be explored in depth and at the pace of each individual or family group.

And tourists are becoming more interested in variety. Some holiday packages already include the chance to stay in more than one resort. A week by the sea, followed by a week in the mountains, for example, has long been a popular option. But now people are becoming more interested in visiting two different countries during one holiday. A week on safari in Africa followed by a week on an Indian Ocean island is predicted to become the 21st-century version of the two-centre holiday. People of all ages are also keen to include an activity in their holiday package. Scuba diving is an example of one that is becoming increasingly popular.

So why are these changes occurring? Clearly travel is getting easier and cheaper, but people's working lives are also changing. Stressed office workers need to relax on holiday, but they don't necessarily need to sit around doing nothing, they need exercise. Also, people are becoming much more aware of what is available to them in terms of holiday choices. With access to the Internet, they are no longer dependent on travel agents and the information in brochures, but can find out for themselves all about both the places they will visit and the packages on offer. They therefore have more choice.

So, these are the changes that are predicted …

Unit 9

Page 108. Listening Part 2: sentence completion. Exercise 4.

Presenter: Good evening. The topic of my talk today is that most famous of mysteries, the Bermuda Triangle. Most people have heard of it, but few people, if anyone, can really tell you what it is. Well, I suppose that's the nature of mysteries, isn't it?

Let's start with a few facts. The Bermuda Triangle is an area in the Atlantic Ocean that lies roughly between Florida in the USA and the islands of Bermuda and Puerto Rico. In the past 500 years, there have been an amazing number of strange events in this area, as many as one thousand according to some people. And we're talking about quite a large area, of course, over 500,000 square miles in fact.

The name 'Bermuda Triangle' was first given to this area in 1964 when a magazine article was published on the subject. But the idea that such an area as the Bermuda Triangle actually existed only really took off in the public imagination following a book with that title published in 1974. This book told of more than 50 ships and 20 planes lost in the area in the 20th century alone and it put forward various theories to explain this, including freak weather conditions, undersea earthquakes and even the actions of aliens from outer space.

One of the most publicised of these mysteries was the disappearance of five US Navy aeroplanes that were lost on a training flight in 1945. Flight 19, as the operation was called, left Fort Lauderdale in Florida at around two o'clock in the afternoon to perform a practice low-level flight over the sea and then return home. The weather that day was described as moderate and there was nothing unusual about the flight. In command was Lieutenant Charles Taylor, a senior instructor. Although trainees, the four other pilots had a fair amount of experience with around 400 hours of flying experience each.

At around 4 pm, came the first sign that Flight 19 was in trouble. Charles Taylor radioed to say that he was unsure of his position and that his compass had ceased to function. It appears that, confused by his lack of instruments, and in increasingly bad weather, Taylor took the wrong decision and instead of heading back towards Florida, led the other planes further out to sea.

By 4.45, it was obvious to the officers back in the control tower at Fort Lauderdale that Flight 19 was hopelessly lost. They could hear Charles Taylor and his trainees communicating with each other by radio, but in the days before more sophisticated communications, they were unable to help them. In desperation, at 6.20 they responded by sending out a flying boat to search for the missing planes and guide them back to Florida. A growing storm made this job very difficult and they were never found. The last message from Flight 19 came at 7.04. Shortly after this, it was calculated, the planes must have run out of fuel. The officers then sent two further planes out in a last attempt to find survivors. To add to the mystery, one of these planes never returned and is thought to have crashed into the sea.

The disappearance of Flight 19 is probably the most famous mystery connected with the Bermuda Triangle. But actually, there's no evidence for a mystery at all. All the tragic events can be explained. The US Navy's original report put the disappearance down to human error. Taylor's mother, however, always refused to accept this and eventually convinced the Navy to change its explanation to 'causes or reasons unknown'. Despite the many fanciful theories about the Bermuda Triangle, and the attempts to link this story with other mysterious disappearances in the area, my view is that it was probably the result of a combination of bad luck and unexpected bad weather, in a time before pilots had reliable technological aids to guide them.

Page 108. Exercise 5.

Question 5

At around 4 pm, came the first sign that Flight 19 was in trouble. Charles Taylor radioed to say that he was unsure of his position and that his compass had ceased to function.

Question 8

The last message from Flight 19 came at 7.04. Shortly after this, it was calculated, the planes must have run out of fuel.

Question 9

All the tragic events can be explained. The US Navy's original report put the disappearance down to human error.

Question 10

Despite the many fanciful theories about the Bermuda Triangle, and the attempts to link this story with other mysterious disappearances in the area, my view is that it was probably the result of a combination of bad luck and unexpected bad weather, in a time before pilots had reliable technological aids to guide them.

Unit 10

Page 120. Listening Part 3: multiple matching. Exercise 2.

Basically, I couldn't do without it, given the work I do. I mean, the last thing I want is interruptions all the time, and believe me these days, even if you do work from home, people really expect you to be available all the time. At the end of each day, I send a quick report to my bosses and that's when I check my message box and get back to anyone who's contacted me. I get piles of demo discs sent in by bands every week. They're all after getting a recording contract with us and my job is to listen and work out whether they're in the running or not.

I'm on the road a lot and that's when I find it really useful. I wouldn't like to calculate how many hours I spend in that van going from gig to gig. My actual work involves catching up with bands when they're performing, and then getting back to the company if I think any might be worth getting a demo disc from. Of course, once they get to know who you are, they're always pressing them into your hands in any case. So that's what I listen to a lot of the time. It's good to double check anyway, because they're often much better on them than at the live gigs.

I'm actually on the promotional side. I'm off around the radio stations and retail outlets, trying to get airtime and making sure our bands are getting the right exposure. Obviously, I need to make a lot of appointments, and arrangements are always getting changed at the last minute, so it really allows me to make good use of my travelling time. I know that they're annoying if they go off at the wrong moment, but on the whole I wouldn't be without it. I've even thought of getting a portable computer to take round as well, but to be honest I've got enough to carry and as long as I can keep in touch with people, I'm OK.

Although I work from Head Office, I often have to go out to the bands because they have really tight schedules. My job is actually to draw up contracts and calculate percentages of royalties on projected sales, all that sort of thing. As this is a very tricky area, I need all the details at my fingertips and that would mean carting round a lot of paperwork. As I travel by train a lot, this is much better. I can even print stuff out, and on the way home I can get the details of the meeting down before I forget, because good record-keeping is essential.

A lot of the bands we use are quite young and so they employ me to liaise with schools and parents and so on. Kids and parents tend to do their talking at weekends, so I always make sure they've got my home number in case there's a crisis. I never know what's going to land in my lap next! Planning things like promotional tours involves working out just the right moment so as not to interfere with schools, family holidays, etc. and this can be quite tricky. At least with this I can always be reached but it lets me decide who to get back to immediately and what can wait until I get back to the office on Monday morning.

Unit 11

Page 132. Listening Part 2: sentence completion. Exercise 2.

Anna: Good evening. My name's Anna Fordham and I'd like to thank you all for coming along to hear me this evening. Now, I know that many of you here are very concerned about the environment in which we live and that's why I've come to talk about a very exciting new project that really deserves your full support. It's called the National Cycle Network and I think it's something that's going to make a great difference to our lives.

For a number of years, we have been growing more aware of the problems that arise from our increasing use of, and dependence upon, the motor car. Now, many people tell you that they would like to use public transport, but this is neither efficient nor reliable enough for their needs, particularly for those who live outside the big cities and travel in each day to work. Other people will tell you that they would very much like to use bicycles instead of cars, but they are reluctant to do so because of the safety considerations. There is always the physical danger of being involved in an accident and, considering the level of traffic, who can blame cyclists if they feel very vulnerable. What's more, people living in cities feel particularly put off by the dangers of riding through all the pollution given out by the motorised traffic, and this is something, of course, which affects people on foot too.

Well, finally, we have the answer. What this group is planning for Britain is something that will allow cyclists to take possession of their own dedicated routes where it will be safe to cycle away from the danger and dirt produced by cars. Literally hundreds of miles of attractive cycle routes will be

built across the country. And these routes will not just be for leisure cycling, they will also be aimed to help commuters to get to work. The network will be the most extensive nationwide construction project of the next decade. When completed, the network of cycle routes will mean that 20 million people in this country will be within ten minutes' cycle ride of their nearest route.

And don't imagine that whole areas of countryside are going to be spoilt to make way for these new routes, as is often the case when new roads are constructed. As well as being smaller and cleaner than roads, these routes will make full use of existing features such as paths along rivers and canals and old railways that are no longer in use. Half the network will take advantage of such existing routeways.

The project will also bring other advantages. Don't forget the Medical Association strongly recommends cycling and walking on health grounds and hopefully people will be encouraged to both walk and cycle by the existence of these routes. This may even mean that people use their cars less and so we all breathe cleaner air as a result, who knows?

The routes are also designed so that young people can use them safely. The whole network will be designed with a view to unsupervised youngsters from 12 years old upwards being able to use them. Even younger children will also benefit, of course, and there will be special facilities for mothers with pushchairs as well as for disabled people in wheelchairs.

The network will also bring other benefits. It will be a national asset, increasing prosperity through things like tourism, which will be encouraged in a sustainable way. And, of course, thousands of jobs are being created as a result of schemes like this.

So, that is the basic idea. Before I go on to tell you some of the proposals for routes in this area, are there any questions?

Unit 12

Page 144. Listening Part 4: yes/no answers. Exercises 3 and 4.

Presenter: These days, when there's so much pressure on young people to get qualifications and pursue a career, the thought of taking a year off between school and further education, what's called a gap year, may seem like a luxury they can't afford. With me I have James Green and Kelly Thomas, who've done just that. James, was it a good use of your time?

James: Well, of course, it's not exactly time off. It's excellent experience, you know, you come back more mature, more able to cope with life and everything. And universities and colleges, even lots of employers, are actually in favour of the idea, as long as you can convince them you've spent your time wisely, you know, they're not impressed if you've just messed about for a year or something.

Presenter: Right. So, what did you do?

James: I wanted to travel, but it took me a while to sort out the details. My parents aren't that well off, so, although they didn't mind me going, they weren't going to pay for me to have an extended holiday or anything.

Presenter: I can imagine. So how did you decide where to go?

James: I saw an advertisement in a magazine. They wanted people to teach English to little kids in a mountain village in the Himalayas. I had to pay for my ticket out there, but I had a job to go to. After that, I never looked back. Once there, I found I had real responsibility for things, you know, there was no one to fall back on but myself. It was great in terms of building my self-confidence and I discovered I did actually have quite good judgement, even if I made the odd mistake along the way.

Presenter: Did you do that all year?

James: No, I met some people doing an environmental survey and joined them. One thing just sort of led to another and before long I was leading a whole group of people. It was brilliant experience, although it was sad leaving the school of course. But I didn't feel too guilty because they found someone else who'd got teaching experience, so it's not as if the kids lost out.

Presenter: Kelly, did you find it easy to plan the year?

Kelly: Well, I knew what I wanted to do. I really wanted to live in another country and learn a language really well. What terrified me was the thought of going on my own. Most of my friends had other ideas. They wanted to travel more widely, or do particular jobs or sports, whereas I just wanted to live somewhere else. I realised it would be a mistake to go and do something I didn't want to do, just to be with them.

Presenter: So what was the solution?

Kelly: Well, I realised the best thing for me was getting one of those jobs where you live with a family, you know, looking after children and helping with the housework and, in the end I signed up with an agency.

Presenter: And was that a good idea?

Kelly: I found the information they gave me very helpful. It really got me started. They paired me up with another girl and we went out together. As we both had jobs in the same town, the idea was that we'd see each other in our free time. I don't think I'd have gone otherwise.

Presenter: So you had some support when you got there?

Kelly: Well, as it happened the girl hated her family and only lasted a week before she flew home, but it didn't matter. As soon as I walked through the door, I realised my family was going to be great. They introduced me to all their friends and took me everywhere with them, even on holiday. It wasn't really like a job at all. And the best thing was I hardly spoke a word of English all the time I was there, so I'm really fluent in the language now.

Presenter: But it would have been so easy to be put off, wouldn't it?

Kelly: Oh yes. I mean it could've been very different. I'd do it again, but I don't suppose I'd be quite as lucky another time.

Presenter: OK. Well, thank you James and Kelly. In the next part of the programme ...

Practice exam

Page 169. Listening Part 1: extracts.

One.

Mother: Ben was just born untidy. As a child, he was the least likely to help with the tidying up. It's even worse now. OK, so I'm not falling over his toys any more, but the stuff he leaves around has got bigger. Now it's huge trainers and bags full of dirty sports equipment. He never wants to throw anything away and if I didn't force him to, he'd be wading knee deep in debris. But I've learnt to live with it over the years. I used to hope that having friends over would encourage him to clean up his room. Now I realise that among teenage boys, the messier the bedroom, the greater the street cred.

Two.

Presenter: 15-year-old Adam Mackintosh has built his own house 12 metres up in the branches of a tree in his parents' garden. As Adam explained, this really is a 'green' house.

Adam: Everything is solar-powered. I've got central heating, lights, a hi-fi, as well as running water. The house is secured by ropes and so no nails have been banged into the tree. My pals think it's really weird that I'd rather spend time up here than playing the latest console games or going clubbing, but I really got a lot out of building it. The only worry is when the wind is strong, then the whole thing moves about a bit.

Three.

Summer, yes I remember summer – unfortunately a lot of the time I work on company contracts which always seem to start in winter so that we're digging foundations with freezing hands and up to our knees in mud. Come summer, the main structure's up and I'm inside sorting out the finishing touches. When I do get out of doors, of course, I remember why I wanted to do this – even at school I knew that I couldn't sit behind a desk all day. Then I'll drive past something I've worked on and that sense of pride kicks in. I love the idea of leaving something lasting behind me.

Four.

I'm sorry but my schedule's been changed. I won't get back at all tonight. There's nothing I can do about it ... but, you know I'm not in a position to argue, I have to do what I'm told ... yes, I know I said I'd look after Olivia and I know how important the final of the competition is to you ... but surely you can find someone else. ... OK, but if I lose my job over this ... yes it is that important. ... OK thanks, I really appreciate that ... and, look, I promise this won't happen again ... really.

Five.

Man: Andrea! I'm over here.

Woman: Hi, sorry I'm late, I was held up on the motorway, and then I couldn't get parked anywhere.

Man: That's OK, but I thought I'd come in and find our table in case they gave it to somebody else.

Woman: Good idea. It's not like the theatre where you book actual seats. I've known them let the place fill up, even when people have phoned to book.

Man: Yes, or you get stuck in a corner because that's all they have left. Anyway, we don't want to be late for the concert, so shall we see if we can order?

Woman: Yes, the curtain goes up at eight, so we haven't got long.

Six.

From my point of view, I enjoy going to the ice-hockey rink each week to train and play. I learn skills and other stuff and have a good time with the other players on the team as well. In the game itself, there are a lot of rules against rough play. If anyone starts picking on another player, then they may have to sit in the penalty box while the rest of the team plays short-handed. Coaches get really annoyed when that happens, and you come to respect that, which is a good thing. But actually as we're all wearing protective clothing, it's pretty hard to get hurt.

Seven.

Presenter: And now over to Ray Yelland at the weather centre.

Ray: Well, today's going to start off a bit cloudy with just the outside possibility of rain immediately after lunch. Temperatures are about normal for the time of year and despite the light winds from the southwest, it's going to feel fairly warm.

Then, as the day wears on, we can expect the cloud to break up a little and we may even get a hint of sunshine. But it would be a mistake to venture out without an umbrella because, although there may be moments of brightness, the possibility of getting caught in the odd shower is going to increase as the day goes on.

Eight.

I love music, but I feel very strongly about the stuff they play in the supermarket where I work. It's on all day and it drives me mad. We are allowed to turn it off, but then we have to have the radio instead and that's even worse. It's easier to shut the music out because it's so boring. I guess it has a purpose, perhaps it makes people feel more at ease. It makes me feel ill. A lot of it contains well-known songs, but badly-done, with panpipes. It's bad taste of the highest order, mostly made by computer; I'm a firm believer that music's much better when composed by a human being.

Page 170. Listening Part 2: sentence completion.

Interviewer: And my first guest today is the crime writer, Lynda Norton. Lynda, welcome.

Lynda: Hello.

Interviewer: Now you're in London for the publication of your latest novel, aren't you?

Lynda: That's right.

Interviewer: After the success of your Inspector Benson series, which included bestsellers such as 'Murder at the Hotel' and 'Mystery on the Beach', your new novel, which is called 'A Strange Case', has a new detective. Why is that?

Lynda: Well, first of all, Anna, who's the main character, is after all only twelve years old. We see the events surrounding the mystery through her eyes, but she doesn't actually solve the crime and she is not a detective. I thought it would be interesting to understand a mystery from a child's point of view, but it's not a children's adventure story or anything like that. It's just another way of telling the story.

Interviewer: And just reading the first few pages, I notice that the novel is actually set in Cambridge.

Lynda: Well, it starts in Cambridge, but most of the action actually takes place in Italy, and there are scenes in London and Ireland too.

Interviewer: Yes, of course, and I think you had first-hand experience of living abroad as a child, didn't you?

Lynda: Well, when I was five, I lived in Rome with my family for a few months.

Interviewer: So is the novel autobiographical in any way?

Lynda: Well, no. There was no actual crime, but obviously some of the scenes that Anna describes, some of the things that happen to her are based on fact, although not necessarily on my own memories. More of an influence were the stories about that period that my mother used to tell my brother and me, when we were back in England. The plot of the novel itself is quite imaginary, however.

Interviewer: What made you start writing crime novels in the first place?

Lynda: Well, originally, I started off writing romantic fiction, and although most of those novels were published, they weren't very successful. So I started doing some travel writing to make money, and stories for magazines, that sort of thing. The crime writing began when I wrote a short story, oh about ten years ago, which I entered for a competition.

Interviewer: Really?

Lynda: Yes. It didn't win, but one of the judges, a well-known author, said to me: 'You've got the first chapter of a crime novel there, you know.' And so I went home and worked on it and that was the first Inspector Benson novel.

Interviewer: Which has now been filmed for television?

Lynda: That's right.

Interviewer: Do you like the television version?

Lynda: Well, I helped with the writing of the screenplay, which was great fun actually, but I didn't have any influence over the other things, like choosing the actors.

Interviewer: So what did you think of the actor who plays Inspector Benson?

Lynda: Oh he's a very good actor.

Interviewer: But?

Lynda: Well, although he's very good-looking, and has been a great success, I suppose in my mind he was an older man, you know. But I have no complaints really. He's fine.

Interviewer: And what's coming next? Is Anna going to feature in any more novels, or is it back to Inspector Benson?

Lynda: Neither actually. I so enjoyed writing about Anna that I'm going to try something else new in my next book. Having done both thrillers and love stories, I thought it was time to try my hand at science fiction. I've just finished it, although we haven't decided on the title yet.

Interviewer: And can we expect to see that in the shops soon?

Lynda: Well, I finished it in July, so if all goes to plan it should be in the shops by next March.

Interviewer: By which time you'll have started another one?

Lynda: Who knows, but I've promised my publisher a new Inspector Benson novel by next October, so I'll have to get down to that soon.

Interviewer: Lynda, thank you very much. And if you'd like to buy a copy of …

Page 171. Listening Part 3: multiple matching.

Basically, we have road managers who look after our instruments, the equipment and things, but we have to take suitcases for our personal stuff, you know. I take one or two cases depending on the length of the trip. The first's a black canvas holdall which I try to take on the plane as hand luggage. It's great because it's got so many zips and compartments and that helps me to know where everything is and keep it tidy. I've also got a massive black suitcase with wheels and handles on each side – for my clothes. That's a really good one because it doesn't get crushed and so my clothes arrive looking relatively decent.

I always take CDs because I like to arrive at a hotel and play some familiar music. But I often don't start packing until about midnight the night before we're leaving. Then, of course, I realise that certain things I want to take need washing and so I always regret not getting organised sooner. I try to fold my clothes as neatly as I can, but they always end up looking like a bag of dirty washing by the time I unpack, no matter how careful I am, and I always arrive at the hotel and find that I've forgotten something crucial, like socks or my soapbag.

I once took a cowboy hat on tour that I don't even wear at home. I never even put it on, but had to carry it round for three weeks because I didn't want to crush it. Then I went and left it in a taxi on the way to the airport on the return journey. I never saw it again. I'm afraid I'm well-known for packing far too much stuff, especially clothes, even on short trips. I never know what I might feel like wearing. I also like to take lots of things like batteries and sticking plasters, there's always someone who needs them and it's nice to able to help.

It's incredible the stuff you end up carrying round with you. You really only realise it when your case goes missing. It happened to me once. I got off the plane at Manchester and my luggage didn't arrive. I had to fill in a form saying what it looked like. And, you know, I couldn't remember if it was blue or black – I'd never taken that much notice. Then I had to make a list of all the things that were inside. That was really difficult! Fortunately, it turned up a few hours later. It had somehow managed to miss the flight. We'd been fairly late that day ourselves, and I guess that was how it happened.

These days, I just throw a few things in a suitcase at the last minute, because the more time you allow for getting ready for a trip, the longer it'll take. I'm quite disciplined though, and I try not to take any more than I need. And to be honest, I rarely leave out anything important. What's more, I used to come back with more than I'd taken, you know, worthless souvenirs, not to mention all the little bottles of shampoo and pens and things you get free in hotel rooms. I found I never used them when I got home, so I've had to stop myself slipping them into my soapbag as I leave.

Page 172. Listening Part 4: multiple-choice questions.

Interviewer: In the studio today, I have the young British film actress, Kate Brompton, whose latest film, *Dancefloor*, was the first that she's made in the USA. Kate, in that film, you play a girl who shares a flat with some other students and has a wonderful time. Were you able to draw on your own experience of flat-sharing?

Kate: You're joking! I'm just not good at things like that. Maybe it's because I've got four brothers. You get quite protective of your own space. I was the oldest and they just seemed to keep arriving right up until I was nine or ten. I never actually had to share a room or anything, but there was always that fear that I might be made to, especially if the next one to come along had been a little sister. No, Jenny, the character in the film, was an only child, so it was a big adventure for her. I've never even tried to share a flat.

Interviewer: You're not one of those actresses who's always out and about either, are you?

Kate: Almost wish I was. I admire people who do all the work and then all the partying as well. But if I've been filming all day, the last thing I want to do is dress up and go out. I want to put on my pyjamas, sit at home and relax, because the work takes a lot out of me. I need to recharge my batteries, maybe other people don't. In any case, although I have friends that I like seeing, I've gone off all the partying. I know it's good to get your photo in all the magazines, but really those big celebrity parties can be a bit of a bore. Everyone's very nice to you, but you don't really know anyone well enough to have a proper laugh. So, you know, it's just more fun going out with a few close friends sometimes.

Interviewer: Your boyfriend, Phil, is also an actor – does it help, him being in the same business?

Kate: I think so, on the whole. It means we understand each other's lifestyle. The sad thing is that you can't count on either of you being free at any given moment. If I finish a job and feel like going on holiday, the chances are he's just started something and so we can't. We hardly get any time together actually. Now I realise why my parents said: 'Why don't you get a nice nine-to-five job where you can plan things and know how much money you're earning?' They're both in showbusiness and that was their main reservation when they saw how keen I was to act. But I thought, 'Why would anybody care about that?' Now I realise what they were talking about.

Interviewer: What was it like filming *Dancefloor* in New York? Was it hard being the only British actor?

Kate: Only a bit. I mean, you get tired of colleagues saying, 'Oh, your accent is so nice,' and I did feel quite a long way from home, but it was nice too. New York has aspects that are quite like London; lots of different kinds of people – no one from New York is really from New York, you know, so I never feel like an outsider there. I've found another place I feel at home in.

Interviewer: Is that important to you?

Kate: Oh yeah, it is. I've got loads of friends there, really brilliant people who I would just love to phone up and go and have a cup of tea with or something, but, you know, I wish it was nearer, so I could go for weekends.

Interviewer: Loads of British actresses go to Hollywood to try and make a fortune. I can't imagine you doing that.

Kate: I can't imagine it either! I just feel that if you can do work that you're interested in and can be proud of, then that's enough. You know, as long as you can pay the bills, I don't need to make $10 million and I don't need to be the most famous person in the world. In fact, I'd rather not be.

Interviewer: Well, that's all we have time for. Kate Brompton, thank you.

Kate: Thank you.

Unit 1 Test

1 Lexical cloze

Choose which answer A, B, C or D best fits each space.

1 All members of the team played a vital .... in the success of the campaign.

   A job B help C role D game

2 He took the part in the film .... it did not pay very well.

   A however B although C as though D apart

3 The film researchers needed .... to many historical documents.

   A access B get C reach D permission

4 I recently .... someone saying that there is to be yet another space adventure film.

   A overheard B listened C noticed D remarked

5 The filming in the café attracted a crowd of ....

   A viewers B watchers C onlookers D audiences

2 Gapped sentences

Think of the word which best fits each space.

1 As they are children they don't .... to pay tax.

2 I'm .... to go to the circus when it next comes to town.

3 The style of that painting is reminiscent .... the early twentieth century.

4 We bought front row tickets in .... of the fact that they were very expensive.

5 There are plenty of seats so there's no need to buy tickets .... advance.

3 Key word transformation

Complete the second sentence so that it has a similar meaning to the first sentence, using the word given. Do not change the word given. You must use between two and five words, including the word given.

1 In my opinion the film will not succeed.

   think

   I .... will succeed.

2 The musical opened ten years ago.

   showing

   The musical .... for ten years.

3 I like musicals better than plays.

   prefer

   I .... plays.

4 'Where are you from?'

   come

   'Where .... from?'

5 What is the starting time of the Saturday afternoon performance?

   on

   What time .... Saturday afternoon?

4 Error correction

Some of these sentences are correct and some have a word which should not be there. Cross out the extra words.

1 Can you tell me what he looks like?

2 I will to come and help with the scenery.

3 I am agree that the exhibition was dull.

4 I have been seen that film five times.

5 The play was a failure despite of good reviews.

5 Word formation

Use the word given in capitals at the end of each sentence to form a word that fits in the space.

1 You can't make a film without ....   **FUND**

2 Researchers are looking into how .... television is.   **INFLUENCE**

3 That review was very .... written.   **THOUGHT**

4 His .... in films as a child has given him great self confidence.   **INVOLVE**

5 Although the director was .... , the film was a great success.   **EXPERIENCE**

Unit 2 Test

1 Lexical cloze

Choose which answer A, B, C or D best fits each space.

1 It was very .... of you to make the whole group do what you wanted to do.

   A brave   B selfish   C ambitious   D sensible

2 The leader waited .... the whole team had caught up.

   A before   B while   C until   D after

3 I would like to be .... exactly what the risks are.

   A know   B said   C told   D found out

4 You shouldn't walk in the mountains without .... clothing.

   A right   B normal   C correct   D suitable

5 The ship's captain needed to find a .... of strong, healthy and brave men.

   A crew   B staff   C troop   D band

2 Gapped sentences

Think of the word which best fits each space.

1 Are you interested .... learning to ski?

2 Tom had always wanted to take .... caving.

3 I was at the foot of the mountain .... I heard the avalanche.

4 They didn't start the climb .... they had checked all the equipment.

5 .... the time we arrived, everybody had gone.

3 Key word transformation

Complete the second sentence so that it has a similar meaning to the first sentence, using the word given. Do not change the word given. You must use between two and five words, including the word given.

1 During my stay in Australia, I saw an advertisement for a round-the-world drive.

   while

   I saw an advertisement for a round-the-world drive .... in Australia.

2 We set off and ten minutes later we got lost.

   had

   We got lost ten minutes .... off.

3 Did Shackleton write a diary of his expedition?

   wrote

   I wonder .... a diary of his expedition.

4 I'd like to know how long we will be away.

   grateful

   I'd .... you could tell me how long we will be away.

5 I find the subject of exploration very interesting.

   keen

   I .... the subject of exploration.

4 Error correction

Some of these sentences are correct and some have a word which should not be there. Cross out the extra words.

1 I wonder if you could tell me how much do I have to pay.

2 After I had watched the instructor's demonstration, I tried to put on my own equipment.

3 Could you tell me what the cost of the expedition?

4 I was wonder how long the drive to the mountains will take.

5 The explorers ran out of supplies and then they had decided to turn back.

5 Word formation

Use the word given in capitals at the end of each sentence to form a word that fits in the space.

1 My sister has always been .... of dogs.   TERRIFY

2 As it's so late, I think it would be .... to take a taxi home.   SENSE

3 It was .... to take the children swimming without a lifeguard.   RESPONSIBLE

4 There were so many .... that I didn't know which to choose.   ACTIVE

5 Our .... taught us some basic safety rules before we went into the caves.   INSTRUCT

Unit 3 Test

1 Lexical cloze

Choose which answer A, B, C or D best fits each space.

1   It's not .... spending a lot of money on books because you can use the library.

    A use **B** value **C** point **D** worth

2   Tom enjoys history but he doesn't want to .... an exam in it.

    A pass **B** write **C** take **D** make

3   After being ill, it took Susan a long time to .... up on her school work.

    A make **B** catch **C** turn **D** finish

4   The students thought they were being asked to study too many ....

    A subjects **B** matters **C** lessons **D** departments

5   Students tend to .... a lot of time chatting.

    A pass **B** spend **C** make **D** use

2 Gapped sentences

Think of the word which best fits each space.

1   Mike insisted .... going to university in another city.

2   Some people are very good .... doing homework and watching television at the same time.

3   Could somebody .... a decision quickly as we have to leave soon?

4   If I were you, I .... stay on at school a bit longer.

5   You won't pass your exam .... you work a bit harder.

3 Key word transformation

Complete the second sentence so that it has a similar meaning to the first sentence, using the word given. Do not change the word given. You must use between two and five words, including the word given.

1   Stella did not take up the offer of a sports scholarship.

    turned

    Stella .... of a sports scholarship.

2   I'm sure we studied this unit last year.

    remember

    I .... this unit last year.

3   If you don't study computing, you might find it difficult to get a job.

    unless

    You might find it difficult to get a job .... computing.

4   You can study another language if you get good results in your English exam.

    provided

    You can study another language .... well in your English exam.

5   I can't go out tonight because of all my homework.

    have

    I can't go out tonight because I .... my homework.

4 Error correction

Some of these sentences are correct and some have a word which should not be there. Cross out the extra words.

1   The teacher made the children to stay in after school to clean up.

2   I'd rather not play in the school team on Saturday.

3   Are you looking forward to enjoy the school holidays?

4   If you will go to that school, you'll have to wear a uniform.

5   The students really liked to having more independence.

5 Word formation

Use the word given in capitals at the end of each sentence to form a word that fits in the space.

1   Shakespeare is one of the world's most famous .... **PLAY**

2   It seems to be .... for members of that family to study law. **TRADITION**

3   Sam always thought he was .... at Maths until he won that prize. **HOPE**

4   If you want to be a doctor, you will have to study .... as well as the other sciences. **CHEMIST**

5   Frank always found music and art lessons the most .... at school. **ENJOY**

Unit 4 Test

1 Lexical cloze

Choose which answer A, B, C or D best fits each space.

1 Each time they .... down a building something taller goes up in its place.

A put B push C pull D turn

2 There's a wonderful flat for sale at the top of the tallest apartment .... in the city.

A house B block C home D tower

3 The local skating .... is very popular with teenagers in the evenings.

A place B pitch C court D rink

4 Living in the mountains was wonderful at first but when the winter came our enthusiasm soon .... off.

A ended B wore C finished D turned

5 It's a great .... more convenient to live in the city centre than in the suburbs.

A deal B much C amount D far

2 Gapped sentences

Think of the word which best fits each space.

1 Tom recently built his own house, ... was extremely hard work.

2 .... a student you will find it difficult to find a place to live that you can afford.

3 The more ethnic communities there are in a city, ... more interesting it is to live in.

4 Living in the city centre, it is difficult to get away .... the hectic lifestyle.

5 Which is the .... expensive city in the world?

3 Key word transformation

Complete the second sentence so that it has a similar meaning to the first sentence, using the word given. Do not change the word given. You must use between two and five words, including the word given.

1 Our new house is not as big as the old one was.

than

Our old house .... the new one.

2 Mary's house was flooded recently and she now lives further up the hill.

whose

Mary, ... , now lives further up the hill.

3 No city in the world has such an efficient transport system as this one.

most

This city .... transport system in the world.

4 We have looked at many houses and we found some of them very interesting.

which

We have looked at many houses, ...
.... very interesting.

5 I have never been to such a polluted place.

ever

It is the most polluted .... been to.

4 Error correction

Some of these sentences are correct and some have a word which should not be there. Cross out the extra words.

1 The twins didn't like living in the country because it was too much quiet.

2 It's much more cheaper to live in an apartment than a house.

3 Let's go away on holiday while the house is being done up.

4 My grandparents preferred to stay in their own house, which it was by the sea.

5 Many young people are leaving the villages for the livelier cities.

5 Word formation

Use the word given in capitals at the end of each sentence to form a word that fits in the space.

1 The traffic will improve when they
.... the road.   WIDE

2 The traffic pollution is ....
wildlife in the city.   DANGER

3 The road repairs are causing serious
....   CONGEST

4 Our village is the .... in
the area.   FRIEND

5 The local restaurants have a very
.... atmosphere.   WELCOME

Progress test 1

1 Lexical cloze

For Questions 1–15, read the text below and decide which answer A, B, C, D best fits each space. There is an example at the beginning (0).

Example:

0   A includes   B involves   C contains   D makes

MAKING A CARTOON

Making a full-length cartoon film (0) ......*B*........ the highly skilled work of a large team of artists. (1) .... , an artist produces some quick drawings to catch the (2) .... before detailed work on the story can begin. These artists are talented illustrators who can visualise the look of the film, (3) .... their work is not used in the (4) .... film. Then the story is sketched out as a (5) .... of drawings. If the ideas are approved, the (6) .... stage is a more detailed sketch with the dialogue included. The (7) .... is a full storyboard, ready for the director to work from.

The director's work is to (8) .... ideas already mapped out and look (9) .... the animators and the voice casting. The soundtrack is done first and the storyboard is adapted to (10) .... it. Only then is the visual part of the film put into (11) .... production. Each character has its own animator who knows (12) .... detail of the character. They draw the (13) .... positions of their characters and other artists draw the rest of the positions to match. Then there are painters who draw the background. However, nowadays computer generated artwork is (14) .... a large part in this process. Drawings are scanned into the computer, which then gives them (15) .... This saves many hours of hand painting for every position.

1	A At first	B First thing	C First of all	D In the beginning
2	A sense	B feeling	C scene	D scenery
3	A or	B although	C since	D because
4	A whole	B done	C made	D finished
5	A series	B bunch	C team	D crowd
6	A then	B further	C next	D after
7	A end	B result	C final	D following
8	A carry out	B carry on	C set up	D set out
9	A up	B out	C after	D to
10	A match	B go	C finish	D equal
11	A complete	B whole	C full	D total
12	A every	B all	C main	D a
13	A most	B each	C main	D all
14	A doing	B playing	C making	D putting
15	A movement	B change	C development	D difference

2 Structural cloze

For Questions 16–30, read the text below and think of the word which best fits each space. Use only one word in each space. There is an example at the beginning (0).

Many of our winter customs go back to Roman times and before. One of (0) ....._these_..... is the custom of collecting evergreens (16) .... the house. The people of ancient Rome worshipped the sun and they believed Saturn to (17) .... the god of all growing things. His special festival was held (18) .... the middle of winter. (19) .... Romans decorated their houses (20) .... the branches of evergreen trees and bushes to remind Saturn (21) .... send crops and plants as food the following spring. This festival was (22) .... Saturnalia and it was the custom to give evergreen plants (23) .... presents.

In northern countries in winter there (24) .... little sun and the days are short. People used to light fires (25) .... hold ceremonies (26) .... this time of year, hoping to give the sun back (27) .... strength. As time went by, people gradually stopped worshipping Saturn and the sun (28) .... they continued with many (29) .... the ancient winter customs. In many countries the Christmas tree is now traditional and people often light candles to brighten (30) .... their homes.

3 Key word transformations

For Questions 31–40, complete the second sentence so that it has a similar meaning to the first sentence, using the word given. **Do not change the word given. You must use between two and five words, including the word given.** Here is an example (0).

Example:

0   You must do exactly what your teacher tells you.

   carry

   You must ......_carry out your teacher's_...... instructions exactly.

31   My advice is to stay on at school another year.

   would

   If I .... stay on at school another year.

32   How much is the flight without the accommodation?

   cost

   Could you tell me ....
   without the accommodation?

33   There are not as many theatres in Liverpool as in London.

   than

   There are .... in London.

34   Why don't you go to Italy by train?

   suggest

   I .... to Italy by train.

35   I would like to go on a trip to the Antarctic.

   interested

   I .... on a trip to the Antarctic.

36   Work started on the new theatre 5 years ago.

   working

   They .... on the new theatre for five years.

37   Can you find out the time of the film on Sunday?

   when

   Can you find out .... on Sunday?

38   You need to decide what course you are going to do next year.

   decision

   You need to .... what course you are going to do next year.

39   What do you intend to do with all your old climbing equipment?

   are

   What .... with all your old climbing equipment?

40   I have never seen such a bad film.

   ever

   It was the .... seen.

4 Error correction

For Questions 41–55, read the text below and look carefully at each line. Some of the lines are correct and some have a word which should not be there.

If a line is correct, put a tick (✔) in the space by the number. If a line has a word which should not be there, write the word in the space by the number. There are two examples at the beginning (0 and 00).

STUDYING IN AUSTRALIA

0	*up*	With rising up fees at European universities, Australia is
00	✔	now becoming a definite option for people who want to
41	....	save money and have the new experiences while studying.
42	....	Universities are based on the British model in terms of
43	....	structure and teaching and links with Britain are still being
44	....	strong. However they are not just as imitations of the older
45	....	universities; they now have been a noticeable academic and
46	....	organisational flavour of their own. Educational standards
47	....	are high and in many ways Australia is up ahead of Britain
48	....	in the development of world class higher education.
49	....	What about to living in Australia? People from all over the
50	....	world are warmly welcomed and accepted as if equals.
51	....	People they work hard but also know how to relax and have a
52	....	good time. As for the cost of living, Australia is more cheaper
53	....	than Britain for food, rent and basic clothing but other things are
54	....	not such a good value, for example imported clothing and cars.
55	....	Australia is definitely worth it considering for a good time and a
		world class degree.

5 Word formation

For Questions 56–65, read the text below. Use the word given in capitals at the end of each line to form a word that fits in the space in the same line. There is an example at the beginning (0).

The world's great long (0) ....*distance*.... rail journeys can be an   **DISTANT**
adventure in themselves. On these journeys, (56) .... marks   **ARRIVE**
the end rather than the (57) .... of the adventure. One example   **BEGIN**
is the Trans-Siberian (58) .... It stretches from Moscow in the   **RAIL**
west, all the way to the (59) .... coast of China and can take up   **EAST**
to ten days. During these ten days the (60) .... feels he has   **TRAVEL**
gained first-hand (61) .... of a vast continent. There is also the   **KNOW**
(62) .... of spending the night in a hotel somewhere along the route   **POSSIBLE**
and catching the next train as it passes through. Part of the (63) ....   **FASCINATE**
is not only the (64) .... but also the local people, who greet the   **SCENE**
train as their only (65) .... with the rest of the world as it brings in   **CONNECT**
supplies and mail.

Unit 5 Test

1 Lexical cloze

Choose which answer A, B, C or D best fits each space.

1 They are building a new shopping .... next to the motorway.

   A block B site C town D mall

2 Young children are becoming more and more fashion ....

   A aware B conscious C following D trendy

3 If you don't like it, take it back to the shop and get a ....

   A refund B recharge C return D replace

4 What .... of car are you thinking of buying?

   A brand B make C label D mark

5 Parents .... to pay more attention to what their children are doing.

   A must B should C ought D could

2 Gapped sentences

Think of the word which best fits each space.

1 Don't buy those shoes – they're made .... plastic.

2 I recommend that you buy the best that you .... afford.

3 I bought three pairs of jeans because they were .... special offer.

4 Your room will look better if you just have a .... colours.

5 Paul returned his broken television to the shop and asked for his money ....

3 Key word transformation

Complete the second sentence so that it has a similar meaning to the first sentence, using the word given. Do not change the word given. You must use between two and five words, including the word given.

1 It was not necessary to buy all that food for six people.

   need

   You .... all that food for six people.

2 I think it would be a good idea to get rid of some of that old furniture.

   suggest

   I .... rid of some of that old furniture.

3 'This fridge will last a lifetime', said the sales assistant.

   claimed

   The sales assistant .... last a lifetime.

4 It is not necessary to pay until the goods are delivered.

   have

   You .... until the goods are delivered.

5 The new bookshops offer several services in the same building.

   one

   The new bookshops offer several services .... roof.

4 Error correction

Some of these sentences are correct and some have a word which should not be there. Cross out the extra words.

1 You really must to go to the supermarket today.

2 Julia asked the sales assistant for an advice about the cameras.

3 Mike has never been able to resist buying the latest discs of his favourite bands.

4 I wanted some of trainers like yours but they didn't have any in stock.

5 I think it would be a good idea for you to talk to him face to face.

5 Word formation

Use the word given in capitals at the end of each sentence to form a word that fits in the space.

1 The new arrangement of furniture makes the room look much more .... SPACE

2 When they were first married they only just had enough money to buy the basic .... NECESSARY

3 If you are .... with our product, you may return it within 10 days. SATISFY

4 The company received a lot of .... about the poor quality of their goods. COMPLAIN

5 Tom has very few possessions because he prefers his room to be .... CLUTTER

Unit 6 Test

1 Lexical cloze

Choose which answer A, B, C or D best fits each space.

1 My aunt .... me that I should try and talk to my father.

A suggested B told C allowed D forbade

2 Going to parties is a good way to .... new people.

A meet B know C look D search

3 We will have a chat about the problem .... dinner.

A while B meanwhile C when D during

4 My brother .... to come and help us prepare the room for the party.

A said B told C promised D stated

5 My father .... in a small village in the Scottish Highlands.

A brought up B raised C grew up D born

2 Gapped sentences

Think of the word which best fits each space.

1 My parents told me off .... arriving home at 2 o'clock in the morning.

2 Please explain .... me why you didn't let us know you weren't coming.

3 Please try to be here .... the beginning of the party.

4 Tom and Sue couldn't .... to an agreement over who should babysit their younger brother.

5 When we were children we .... always listen for our father's key in the door.

3 Key word transformation

Complete the second sentence so that it has a similar meaning to the first sentence, using the word given. Do not change the word given. You must use between two and five words, including the word given.

1 Alan said he didn't tell my secret to Mark.

telling

Alan .... my secret to Mark

2 'Please tidy your room or I'll punish you,' said my father.

if

My father threatened .... didn't tidy my room.

3 My grandmother thought it would be better for me to stay at home while my mother was ill.

advised

My grandmother .... at home while my mother was ill.

4 When my older sisters got married, I had to adjust to being an only child.

used

When my older sisters got married, I had .... an only child.

5 In spite of their very busy lives, my parents always made time to listen to my problems.

although

My parents always made time to listen to my problems .... very busy lives.

4 Error correction

Some of these sentences are correct and some have a word which should not be there. Cross out the extra words.

1 Tom admitted me that he had lied.

2 At firstly, I apologise for criticising you.

3 The twins went to the pop concert despite of their parents' protests.

4 Our group of friends all promised to keep in contact when we left school.

5 When I was small I was used to live with my grandparents.

5 Word formation

Use the word given in capitals at the end of each sentence to form a word that fits in the space.

1 His behaviour is making his parents very ....   ANXIETY

2 The wedding .... was great fun, with a lot of music and dancing.   RECEIVE

3 I am surprised that they are friends because their .... are so different.   PERSONAL

4 Young people sometimes have to decide between .... to their friends and to their family.   LOYAL

5 In a large family it can be very difficult to find ....   PRIVATE

Unit 7 Test

1 Lexical cloze

Choose which answer A, B, C or D best fits each space.

1 They are making an old car park into an extra football .... for the school.

A court   B pitch   C place   D track

2 The most important thing is to ensure that you have a(n) .... diet.

A balanced   B even   C equal   D organised

3 Stress is often .... by pressure from friends.

A made   B caused   C led   D brought

4 If you have a cough, why don't you .... some medicine?

A take   B eat   C drink   D use

5 Many forms of cancer can now be ....

A healed   B recovered   C cured   D dealt

2 Gapped sentences

Think of the word which best fits each space.

1 Sometimes it is difficult to face .... to problems at school or work.

2 Her doctor advised her to go .... a diet.

3 I have started to go for a run every morning in order .... get fit.

4 It can take several weeks to recover .... a bad case of flu.

5 The new sports centre is .... built at the moment.

3 Key word transformation

Complete the second sentence so that it has a similar meaning to the first sentence, using the word given. Do not change the word given. You must use between two and five words, including the word given.

1 The demands of the education system make teenagers work very hard.

made

Teenagers .... very hard by the demands of the education system.

2 My father started to work less because he didn't want to make himself ill.

so

My father started to work less .... to make himself ill.

3 'Please don't interrupt me, I'm busy,' he said.

be

He didn't .... because he was busy.

4 I don't know what to do about the problem of student stress.

cope

I don't know .... the problem of student stress.

5 Somebody gave Ben a cycling machine for his birthday.

was

Ben .... a cycling machine for his birthday.

4 Error correction

Some of these sentences are correct and some have a word which should not be there. Cross out the extra words.

1 I get up early for to go to the gym before work.

2 £1,000 has been donated to the school for them building a new sports hall.

3 Sam broke up his leg while playing football.

4 My uncle is looking forward to be being given a new treatment for his arthritis.

5 The whole class turned up in the hope of being chosen for the team.

5 Word formation

Use the word given in capitals at the end of each sentence to form a word that fits in the space.

1 If you got some more exercise, you would be much ....   HEALTH

2 Sarah showed a lot of .... in overcoming her illness.   DETERMINE

3 Not enough is being done to improve the .... of young people.   FIT

4 Test your muscles by lifting those ....   WEIGH

5 Before the race, you need to do exercises to .... your leg muscles.   STRONG

Unit 8 Test

1 Lexical cloze

Choose which answer A, B, C or D best fits each space.

1 From the safety of the .... platform, we watched the crocodiles being fed.

   A sighting B viewing C looking D seeing

2 London is .... to Paris by a high speed railway line.

   A joined B arrived C linked D reached

3 I'd love to go to Australia, but it's a very long .... from Europe.

   A travel B tour C trip D journey

4 Leave plenty of time to get to the airport in case you get .... up in traffic.

   A held B restricted C stopped D slowed

5 On a sunny weekend many city people .... for the coast.

   A go B set C make D drive

2 Gapped sentences

Think of the word which best fits each space.

1 Neither the tourists .... the locals go to that area after dark.

2 There is a .... deal of snow expected this year.

3 There are hardly .... tourists around at this time of year.

4 You ought not .... have stayed in the sun so long.

5 It's a beautiful avenue, lined .... poplar trees.

3 Key word transformation

Complete the second sentence so that it has a similar meaning to the first sentence, using the word given. Do not change the word given. You must use between two and five words, including the word given.

1 There are mountains all around the village.

   by

   The village .... mountains.

2 There are not many animals left in the forest.

   only

   There are .... animals left in the forest.

3 We have a choice between going on a safari or a skiing holiday.

   either

   This year we .... a safari or a skiing holiday.

4 Have you ever visited another country for a holiday?

   abroad

   Have you ever .... for a holiday?

5 It would have been better to book a hotel in advance.

   should

   We .... a hotel in advance.

4 Error correction

Some of these sentences are correct and some have a word which should not be there. Cross out the extra words.

1 I want to visit each of country in Europe.

2 You needn't to have brought all those warm clothes.

3 It took a long time to clean up the rubbish after the festival.

4 I dropped off my camera while I was running along the beach.

5 Several Greek islands are very small indeed.

5 Word formation

Use the word given in capitals at the end of each sentence to form a word that fits in the space.

1 Tourism is driving away the .... in many areas. WILD

2 There should be more .... research into the effects of tourism on the environment. SCIENCE

3 I have a .... for a single room for three nights. RESERVE

4 There are .... few visitors to this beautiful island. SURPRISE

5 The view from the top of the mountain is .... SENSE

Progress test 2

1 Lexical cloze

For Questions 1–15, read the text below and decide which answer A, B, C or D best fits each space. There is an example at the beginning (0).

Example:

0   **A** in   **B** on   **C** of   **D** at

THE GRAND CANYON

The Grand Canyon is one of the natural wonders (0) ....*of*.... the world. It was
(1) .... by the Colorado River, which carved its way through the
(2) .... coloured layers of rock making a gap over 1.5 kilometres
(3) .... Its sides are steep cliffs and some of the peaks look (4) ....
towers, castles and temples.

A fantastic adventure for anyone with (5) .... time in which to experience
the Grand Canyon would be to take a sightseeing flight (6) .... the area. The
small twin engine planes have huge panoramic windows perfect for (7) ....
photographs. It is (8) .... to book an overnight tour if you want to stay
(9) .... at the Canyon but do not want to drive. This way you can
(10) .... the spectacular sunset and sunrise and fit in a(n) (11) .... day
exploring the Canyon trails (12) ....

You can also witness the dazzling lights of (13) .... Las Vegas by night with a
breathtaking helicopter flight. The tour (14) .... approximately an hour and
(15) .... transport from your hotel to the airport and 20 minutes in the air.

1	A done	B set	C created	D built
2	A different	B several	C much	D varied
3	A down	B deep	C far	D below
4	A as	B if	C up	D like
5	A restricted	B limited	C reduced	D small
6	A above	B in	C over	D on
7	A making	B putting	C taking	D doing
8	A possible	B probable	C likely	D suitable
9	A more	B further	C extra	D longer
10	A look	B watch	C notice	D glance
11	A whole	B all	C total	D utter
12	A by foot	B on foot	C with feet	D by feet
13	A nearby	B near	C close	D next
14	A spends	B lasts	C covers	D makes
15	A contains	B has	C includes	D covers

2 Structural cloze

For Questions 16–30, read the text below and think of the word which best fits each space. Use only one word in each space. There is an example at the beginning (0).

New York is known (0) ....*as*........ the city that never sleeps but Madrid is (16) .... same. The main difference is the Latin charm (17) .... is added. Enjoy long evenings with food and dancing but save your energy (18) .... shopping. Shopping is one of the (19) .... popular attractions of Madrid. For leather goods you can pay around 20 per cent less (20) .... in many other European countries. Many visitors make a point of (21) .... several pairs of shoes at bargain prices. Madrid has everything (22) .... megastores to trendy second-hand clothes stalls and if you visit at Christmas, you (23) .... see decorations wherever you look. Many of these are beautifully made (24) .... hand and would make wonderful souvenirs (25) .... take home for a special festive atmosphere.

Shopping here is accompanied (26) .... great entertainment. There (27) .... artists and musicians among the market stalls and people play dominoes behind the Palacio de Cristal. However, when the busy streetlife gets (28) .... tiring for you, you can relax in some of the world's finest art galleries, enjoying the air conditioning as (29) .... as the works of Spain's great artists (30) .... as Picasso and Goya.

3 Key word transformation

For Questions 31–40, complete the second sentence so that it has a similar meaning to the first sentence, using the word given. **Do not change the word given.** You must use between two and five words, including the word given. Here is an example (0).

Example:

0   You must do exactly what your teacher tells you.

   carry

   You must ......*carry out your teacher's*...... instructions exactly.

31   It was not necessary to shout at him like that.

   need

   You .... at him like that.

32   A healthy lifestyle can prevent most diseases.

   be

   Most diseases .... a healthy lifestyle.

33   'We will deliver the sofa this afternoon,' promised the shop assistant.

   delivered

   The shop assistant promised the .... afternoon.

34   I still find it strange to drive on the left.

   used

   I still have .... on the left.

35   They drove to town because they wanted to buy new clothes for the college disco.

   order

   They drove to town .... new clothes for the college disco.

36   'I did not borrow your dress,' said Mary to her sister.

   denied

   Mary .... dress.

37   Those shoes are too narrow for my feet.

   wide

   Those shoes are .... for my feet.

38   I haven't got time to travel around the world.

   would

   If I .... travel around the world.

39   I like the countryside better than the town.

   prefer

   I .... the town.

40   I do not have the same opinion as you.

   agree

   I .... you.

4 Error correction

For Questions 41–55, read the text below and look carefully at each line. Some of the lines are correct and some have a word which should not be there.

If a line is correct, put a tick (✔) in the space by the number. If a line has a word which should not be there, write the word in the space by the number. There are two examples at the beginning (0 and 00).

0	*to*	The fact that over to12 million people a year visit theme
00	✔	parks in Britain proves that being scared out of our senses
41	....	it is something we are prepared to pay a lot of money for.
42	....	Racing towards the ground at 140 kilometres per hour with
43	....	just a metal bar across your knees is not that what everyone wants,
44	....	so theme parks try to provide something for everybody.
45	....	Alton Towers which is set in a large wooded park and has more
46	....	rides to make you scream than the any other theme park in Europe,
47	....	but there are and also shows to watch, a lake to row on, grass to
48	....	picnic on and slower than rides for the very young. It is teenagers
49	....	and young adults who compete with each other to go on the
50	....	scariest rides, while grandma enjoys herself the parkland. People are
51	....	prepared to travel long distances far from all corners of the country
52	....	to spend there a day at the park. It's a popular way of celebrating
53	....	children's birthdays and at the end of the school year. The addition
54	....	of new rides in year after year means that people will always
55	....	want to return back to test their nerves even further.

5 Word formation

For Questions 56–65, read the text below. Use the word given in capitals at the end of each line to form a word that fits in the space in the same line. There is an example at the beginning (0).

The modern (0) ....*living*.......... room is expected to fulfil many functions.	LIVE
(56) .... is the main one, and this could mean talking to friends,	RELAX
enjoying music or reading a book. In (57) .... , someone might	ADD
want to eat there or stay (58) .... Children will want to play there,	NIGHT
and do their (59) .... on the floor, while keeping their toys within	HOME
easy reach. (60) .... , when the children become teenagers, they will	LATE
want to chat and eat snacks. Therefore, every item needs to be (61) .... ,	ATTRACT
comfortable and hardwearing. There needs to be (62) .... for a	STORE
television, an audio (63) .... system, perhaps also a computer,	ENTERTAIN
while the room remains (64) .... enough for people to move around.	SPACE
With some thought and (65) .... design, a room can serve a changing	CARE
family for many years.	

Unit 9 Test

1 Lexical cloze

Choose which answer A, B, C or D best fits each space.

1 The .... of oil has changed the economy of many countries around the world.

   A invention B find C discovery D search

2 I have .... to the conclusion that there may be life on other planets.

   A brought B fallen C come D found

3 Could an alien civilisation be a .... to life on earth?

   A warning B threat C change D damage

4 Scientists .... that they knew the cause of the explosion.

   A denied B refused C rejected D declined

5 What do you think is the most .... explanation for those strange lights in the sky?

   A possible B likely C expected D liable

2 Gapped sentences

Think of the word which best fits each space.

1 We might .... been visited by aliens in the past.

2 Please pay this bill immediately, unless you have already done ....

3 Despite .... very frightened, we went into the forest to investigate the strange lights.

4 They stared .... horror at the creature that came out of the cave.

5 What do you make .... the shadow in the corner of the picture?

3 Key word transformation

Complete the second sentence so that it has a similar meaning to the first sentence, using the word given. Do not change the word given. You must use between two and five words, including the word given.

1 It's possible that she was not telling the truth.

   may

   She .... telling the truth.

2 He went further because he didn't realise the weather was getting worse.

   realising

   He went further, ... the weather was getting worse.

3 When he saw the shapes in the sky, he called for help.

   on

   He called for help .... the shapes in the sky.

4 It's impossible that the sounds came from the house.

   have

   The sounds .... from the house.

5 I thought I heard someone knocking on the door but then I discovered it was the wind.

   turned

   I thought I heard someone knocking on the door but it .... the wind.

4 Error correction

Some of these sentences are correct and some have a word which should not be there. Cross out the extra words.

1 You can't have been seen a ghost.

2 The recent sightings have brought up to light many others.

3 Not having seen my friends leave, I thought they were hiding somewhere.

4 Nobody can come up with an adequate explanation for the crop circles.

5 Having been discovered the gold, they decided to keep it a secret.

5 Word formation

Use the word given in capitals at the end of each sentence to form a word that fits in the space.

1 On the night of the storm, the .... of the animals was very strange.   BEHAVE

2 Most .... things seem to happen at night.   MYSTERY

3 The children were very .... that they had discovered such important prehistoric caves.   PRIDE

4 The sound of .... was coming from the spaceship.   LAUGH

5 The research project failed because of your ....   LAZY

Unit 10 Test

1 Lexical cloze

Choose which answer A, B, C or D best fits each space.

1 If a computer breaks down, you may lose all the information that is .... on it.

   A held   B maintained   C stored   D stocked

2 Microwaves are very .... because you can heat up a meal in a couple of minutes.

   A convenient   B suitable   C comfortable
   D adequate

3 They use a camera to .... the stadium during a football match.

   A record   B look   C scan   D move

4 Someone has .... all the money from the safe.

   A robbed   B burgled   C stolen   D thieved

5 The prisoner was .... free after his appeal was successful.

   A made   B allowed   C let   D set

2 Gapped sentences

Think of the word which best fits each space.

1 I have no idea what I will .... doing in twenty years' time.

2 The thief gave himself .... to the police.

3 I am sorry to hear that you have .... your car stolen.

4 Burglars often take advantage .... the holiday season to find empty houses.

5 Don't be impatient. I promise the work .... be done by six o'clock.

3 Key word transformation

Complete the second sentence so that it has a similar meaning to the first sentence, using the word given. Do not change the word given. You must use between two and five words, including the word given.

1 They promised the new equipment would arrive by Monday.

   due

   The new equipment .... on Monday.

2 I would recommend the immediate installation of an alarm.

   have

   You should .... immediately.

3 The thieves revealed themselves by the mud on their clothes.

   gave

   The thieves .... by the mud on their clothes.

4 The police had the most up-to-date technology available to them.

   make

   The police were able .... the most up-to-date technology.

5 We will be tired after the 10 hour drive.

   been

   We will be tired because we .... 10 hours.

4 Error correction

Some of these sentences are correct and some have a word which should not be there. Cross out the extra words.

1 Pickpockets usually get off away without being punished.

2 When you retire, how long will you have been being here?

3 It's a nuisance that they haven't had the photocopier repaired yet.

4 I'm sure that such a device may has been invented already.

5 Can you suggest reasons for why the money isn't there?

5 Word formation

Use the word given in capitals at the end of each sentence to form a word that fits in the space.

1 If you have had a .... , you can claim on your insurance.   BURGLE

2 There are 15 computers on our ....   NET

3 The store detectives are there to catch ....   SHOP

4 The tiny .... in this electronic gadget can detect anxiety levels.   SENSE

5 Some people keep dogs for ....   SECURE

Unit 11 Test

1 Lexical cloze

Choose which answer A, B, C or D best fits each space.

1 There are now tourist resorts all along the north .... of the country.

   A beach   B shore   C coast   D seaside

2 The changes in the weather are .... to have been caused by global warming.

   A accepted   B allowed   C expected   D believed

3 There are many other endangered species .... the panda.

   A also   B in addition   C too   D besides

4 All over the world we are .... down too many trees.

   A cutting   B knocking   C pushing   D breaking

5 I'm sure the earth will have very few resources left ....

   A lastly   B at last   C in the end   D at the end

2 Gapped sentences

Think of the word which best fits each space.

1 Many people laugh .... the idea of dolphins helping humans.

2 We need to cut down .... the amount of fuel we use.

3 The hurricane is reported to .... moving towards the coast.

4 If I had known, I would .... done something earlier.

5 We should do more to protect .... environment.

3 Key word transformation

Complete the second sentence so that it has a similar meaning to the first sentence, using the word given. Do not change the word given. You must use between two and five words, including the word given.

1 People say that the earth's temperature is rising.

   said

   The earth's temperature .... rising.

2 Soon we won't be able to swim in the sea any more.

   longer

   Soon we .... to swim in the sea.

3 People must accept that we cannot continue to use private cars.

   face

   People must .... that we cannot continue to use private cars.

4 The police caught the thief by using dogs.

   not

   If the police.. , they wouldn't have caught the thief.

5 We are now short of raw materials because people didn't take care of them in the past.

   be

   We .... raw materials, if people had taken care of them in the past.

4 Error correction

Some of these sentences are correct and some have a word which should not be there. Cross out the extra words.

1 We will soon have used up all the coal in the local mines.

2 It is been reported that animals can help disabled people.

3 You won't see the animals unless if you keep very quiet.

4 If the cities will continue to grow, we will have to change the way we live.

5 If we had had the opportunity, we would have tried to save the animals from the flood.

5 Word formation

Use the word given in capitals at the end of each sentence to form a word that fits in the space.

1 Animal rights campaigners have sent a .... letter to the government.   **THREAT**

2 It will be .... if we run out of oil.   **DISASTER**

3 During the storm, some houses were struck by ....   **LIGHT**

4 The main reason for keeping pets is ....   **COMPANION**

5 Limiting the traffic in the town centre would be .... to the local residents.   **BENEFIT**

Unit 12 Test

1 Lexical cloze

Choose which answer A, B, C or D best fits each space.

1 Why don't you save the money you .... from your Saturday job?

A pay B earn C win D gain

2 It's important to keep your computer skills ....

A up-to-date B in fashion C trendy D latest

3 Sam loves his job .... it doesn't pay very well.

A despite B however C nevertheless
D although

4 I think Mike is very .... at his job.

A suitable B good C ambitious D responsible

5 If you had the .... , would you apply for promotion?

A opportunity B occasion C prospect
D ability

2 Gapped sentences

Think of the word which best fits each space.

1 It's time you .... for a new job.

2 Sue resigned from the job because .... was boring.

3 I'd rather you .... not leave early today.

4 There is a serious lack .... employment in the northern cities.

5 I wish you .... let me make my own decisions.

3 Key word transformation

Complete the second sentence so that it has a similar meaning to the first sentence, using the word given. Do not change the word given. You must use between two and five words, including the word given.

1 He lacks experience and qualifications.

neither

He .... qualifications.

2 I would like my boss to show more gratitude.

wish

I .... show more gratitude.

3 Joanne is sorry that she didn't finish her university course.

wishes

Joanne .... her university course.

4 There is a miners' strike because of low pay.

gone

The miners .... because of low pay.

5 I realise I shouldn't have resigned so quickly.

regret

I .... so quickly.

4 Error correction

Some of these sentences are correct and some have a word which should not be there. Cross out the extra words.

1 I'd rather to get a job than study any more.

2 Don't give her the job if you don't trust with her.

3 In the conclusion, it's better to do a job that you like than to get a lot of money.

4 If only I had more holiday, I would go around the world.

5 If you want to get better, just keep in practising.

5 Word formation

Use the word given in capitals at the end of each sentence to form a word that fits in the space.

1 There is a lot of .... on people to work long hours. **PRESS**

2 Many people can now look forward to a long .... **RETIRE**

3 Annie loves her work because she meets people from a wide .... of backgrounds. **VARY**

4 The course was .... because the people were so interesting. **MEMORY**

5 He is difficult to work with because he is so .... **COMPETE**

Progress test 3

1 Lexical cloze

For Questions 1–15, read the text below and decide which answer A, B, C or D best fits each space. There is an example at the beginning (0).

Example:

0   A dozens   B some   C many   D several

STONEHENGE

Stonehenge is still a mystery. 4,000 years ago (0) ....*A*........ of enormous stones were (1) .... like a series of doorways in a perfect circle. They were also placed in line with the rising and (2) .... sun. This (3) .... have been an extremely sophisticated operation (4) .... heavy labour, organisation and calculation which would challenge engineers even today.

Some of the stones were (5) .... from the Welsh mountains to the southern plains of England and it is still not (6) .... what made ancient man carry these stones hundreds of kilometres (7) .... land and water. There have been many theories. It was once (8) .... to be a monument to a victory in battle. It is now more commonly accepted that there was a (9) .... with sun worship or that it was a temple.

However, two (10) .... are clear. (11) .... , the area was used as a burial ground and second, it was a place of ceremony. (12) .... all, it is the fact that these massive stones have stood for so long that amazes (13) .... who looks at them. Will any monuments from the 21st century still be causing speculation in 4,000 years' (14) .... and if (15) .... , what will they be?

1	A put	B done	C arranged	D laid
2	A falling	B lowering	C setting	D sinking
3	A must	B should	C ought	D could
4	A meaning	B involving	C including	D containing
5	A dragged	B grabbed	C crawled	D crept
6	A understood	B realised	C believed	D recognised
7	A through	B in	C from	D across
8	A mentioned	B said	C told	D known
9	A join	B bond	C connection	D relation
10	A points	B statements	C positions	D arguments
11	A At first	B At the start	C First	D One
12	A Over	B Beyond	C Above	D Almost
13	A people	B them	C those	D everyone
14	A time	B ahead	C in advance	D from now
15	A it	B so	C that	D yes

2 Structural cloze

For Questions 16–30, read the text below and think of the word which best fits each space. Use only one word in each space. There is an example at the beginning (0).

YOUR FIRST DAY AT WORK

Your first day at work will not be as bad as your first day (0) ....*at*........ school. In fact, it will be worse. You (16) .... be the only person wearing a brand new suit (17) .... the price tag still hanging from the back. Nobody will tell you how (18) .... use the office computer systems. You will use the wrong paper in the photocopier. You'll be taken around the office and introduced to at (19) .... 500 people. You'll instantly forget the names (20) .... all 500 people but, without exception, they'll remember (21) .... On your first day, you won't have (22) .... friends but you won't have any enemies either. Just remember (23) .... the first lesson you will have to learn will be to work hard and to (24) .... one of a team. Show concern (25) .... everyone from the managing director to the tea lady (26) .... you will be alright.

It's a strange thing, but (27) .... you wear a suit and carry a business card, people will take you seriously. Your company's clients will want to shake your hand and take you to expensive restaurants. (28) .... nice to people who treat you (29) .... an adult by smiling sweetly and acting responsibly. Then (30) .... home and be a teenager again.

3 Key word transformation

For Questions 31–40, complete the second sentence so that it has a similar meaning to the first sentence, using the word given. **Do not change the word given. You must use between two and five words, including the word given. Here is an example (0).**

Example:

0   You must do exactly what your teacher tells you.

carry

You must .....*carry out your teacher's*..... instructions exactly.

31   Tom found the noise made by the builders unbearable.

put

Tom .... the noise made by the builders.

32   People have broken into Steve's car three times.

had

Steve .... into three times.

33   Alan didn't run in the race because of illness.

been

If Alan .... , he would have run in the race.

34   I'm sure Sue didn't write that letter because it's not her writing.

can't

Sue .... that letter because it's not her writing.

35   People believe that there is a monster in the lake.

believed

A monster .... in the lake.

36   It is my grandparents' sixtieth wedding anniversary next June.

will

Next June my grandparents .... for sixty years.

37   I really need your help to finish this project.

without

I won't be able .... your help.

38   I now regret resigning from my first job.

resigned

I wish .... from my first job.

39   I last saw Tom in 1998.

not

I .... 1998.

40   It's possible that someone has stolen the money.

may

The money .... stolen.

4 Error correction

For Questions 41–55, read the text below and look carefully at each line. Some of the lines are correct and some have a word which should not be there.

If a line is correct, put a tick (✔) in the space by the number. If a line has a word which should not be there, write the word in the space by the number. There are two examples at the beginning (0 and 00).

DOGS FOR THE DISABLED

0	*being*	Lucy Brown is in a wheelchair but she is being determined to be
00	✔	independent. She is helped by her dog Barney, who does
41	....	too many little jobs for her. He collects the post and the newspapers.
42	....	He brings the phone to her when it rings up. When they are out,
43	....	he stands on his back legs for to operate the lifts. If she drops
44	....	something, he picks it up. In shops he puts down the food in the
45	....	basket for her although if other customers sometimes object until
46	....	the shopkeeper explains the situation. If Lucy falls, he will crawl
47	....	under her stomach and stand on command so as that Lucy can push
48	....	herself back up. Barney can to do all these and dozens of other tasks
49	....	after being trained at a special training centre for Dogs for the Disabled.
50	....	Lucy is delighted. She explains us that it is so much easier to accept
51	....	help from a dog than from another person. 'If I will drop a pen, which
52	....	I do so a lot because I have a bad grip, a human will pick it up nine
53	....	times and then get bored. Barney he will pick it up 99 times and
54	....	I know he doesn't care for. It is all a game to him and as long as
55	....	I give him rewards and encouragement, he is happy.

5 Word formation

For Questions 56–65, read the text below. Use the word given in capitals at the end of each line to form a word that fits in the space in the same line. There is an example at the beginning (0).

TAXI DRIVERS' BRAINS

According to a report published (0) ....*recently*......... , there is evidence of	RECENT
(56) .... and adaptation in the brains of taxi drivers	GROW
to help them (57) .... a detailed map of the city they work in.	MEMORY
(58) .... have discovered that the part of the brain that is	SCIENCE
associated with (59) .... in animals is larger in cab drivers	NAVIGATE
than in other people. There seems to be a definite (60)	RELATE
between the work they do and the brain changes. (61)	EXAMINE
of the brains of 16 cab drivers who had had (62) .... training to	INTENSE
remember street names and journey routes showed (63)	NOTICE
development. This could have (64) .... for people with brain	IMPLY
damage as this (65) .... could be used to work out mental	KNOW
exercise programmes to aid recovery.	

Teacher's Book tests · Answers

Unit 1

1 Lexical cloze

1C; 2B; 3A; 4A; 5C

2 Gapped sentences

1 have; 2 going; 3 of; 4 spite; 5 in

3 Key word transformation

1   don't think the film
2   has been showing
3   prefer musicals to
4   do you come
5   does the performance start on

4 Error correction

1 ✔; 2 to; 3 am; 4 been; 5 of

5 Word formation

1 funding; 2 influential; 3 thoughtfully; 4 involvement;
5 inexperienced

Unit 2

1 Lexical cloze

1B; 2C; 3C; 4D; 5A

2 Gapped sentences

1 in; 2 up; 3 when; 4 until; 5 By

3 Key word transformation

1   while I was (staying)
2   after we (had) set
3   if/whether Shackleton wrote
4   be grateful if
5   am (very) keen on

4 Error correction

1 do; 2 ✔; 3 what; 4 was; 5 had

5 Word formation

1 terrified; 2 sensible; 3 irresponsible; 4 activities; 5 instructor

Unit 3

1 Lexical cloze

1D; 2C; 3B; 4A; 5B

2 Gapped sentences

1 on; 2 at; 3 make; 4 would; 5 unless

3 Key word transformation

1   turned down the offer
2   remember studying
3   unless you study
4   provided you do
5   have to do

4 Error correction

1 to; 2 ✔; 3 enjoy; 4 will; 5 to

5 Word formation

1 playwrights; 2 traditional; 3 hopeless; 4 Chemistry;
5 enjoyable

Unit 4

1 Lexical cloze

1C; 2B; 3D; 4B; 5A

2 Gapped sentences

1 which; 2 As; 3 the; 4 from; 5 most/least

3 Key word transformation

1   is/was bigger than
2   whose house was flooded recently
3   has the most efficient
4   some of which we found
5   place I have ever

4 Error correction

1 much; 2 more; 3 ✔; 4 it; 5 ✔

5 Word formation

1 widen; 2 endangering; 3 congestion; 4 friendliest;
5 welcoming

Progress test 1

1 Lexical cloze

1C; 2A; 3B; 4D; 5A; 6C; 7B; 8A; 9C; 10A; 11C; 12A; 13C; 14B; 15A

2 Structural cloze

16 for; 17 be; 18 in; 19 The; 20 with; 21 to; 22 called; 23 as; 24 is; 25 and; 26 at; 27 its; 28 but; 29 of; 30 up

3 Key word transformation

31 were you, I would
32 the cost of the flight
33 fewer theatres in Liverpool than
34 I suggest (that) you go
35 am/would be interested in going
36 have been working
37 when the film starts
38 make a decision about
39 are you going to do
40 worst film I have ever

4 Error correction

41 the; 42 ✔; 43 being; 44 as; 45 been; 46 ✔; 47 up; 48 ✔; 49 to; 50 if; 51 they; 52 more; 53 ✔; 54 a; 55 it

5 Word formation

56 arrival/arriving; 57 beginning; 58 Railway; 59 eastern; 60 traveller; 61 knowledge; 62 possibility; 63 fascination; 64 scenery; 65 connection

Unit 5

1 Lexical cloze

1D; 2B; 3A; 4B; 5C

2 Gapped sentences

1 of; 2 can; 3 on; 4 few; 5 back

3 Key word transformation

1 needn't have bought/didn't need to buy
2 suggest getting/(that) we/you (should) get
3 claimed (that) the fridge would
4 don't have to pay
5 under one

4 Error correction

1 (first) to; 2 an; 3 ✔; 4 of; 5 ✔

5 Word formation

1 spacious; 2 necessities; 3 dissatisfied; 4 complaints; 5 uncluttered

Unit 6

1 Lexical cloze

1B; 2A; 3D; 4C; 5C

2 Gapped sentences

1 for; 2 to; 3 at/for; 4 come; 5 would

3 Key word transformation

1 denied telling
2 to punish me if I
3 advised me to stay
4 to get used to being
5 although they had/led

4 Error correction

1 me; 2 At; 3 of; 4 ✔; 5 was

5 Word formation

1 anxious; 2 reception; 3 personalities; 4 loyalty; 5 privacy

Unit 7

1 Lexical cloze

1B; 2A; 3B; 4A; 5C

2 Gapped sentences

1 up; 2 on; 3 to; 4 from; 5 being

3 Key word transformation

1 are made to work
2 so as not
3 want to be interrupted
4 how to cope with
5 was given

4 Error correction

1 for; 2 them; 3 up; 4 be; 5 ✔

5 Word formation

1 healthier; 2 determination; 3 fitness; 4 weights; 5 strengthen

Unit 8

1 Lexical cloze
1B; 2C; 3D; 4A; 5C

2 Gapped sentences
1 nor; 2 great; 3 any; 4 to; 5 with

3 Key word transformation
1   is surrounded by
2   only a few
3   can go on either/can choose either/
    have a choice of either
4   been/gone abroad
5   should have booked

4 Error correction
1 of; 2 to; 3 ✔; 4 off; 5 ✔

5 Word formation
1 wildlife; 2 scientific; 3 reservation; 4 surprisingly;
5 sensational

Progress test 2

1 Lexical cloze
1C; 2A; 3B; 4D; 5B; 6C; 7C; 8A; 9D; 10B; 11A; 12B; 13A; 14B;
15C

2 Structural cloze
16 the; 17 that/which; 18 for; 19 most; 20 than;
21 buying/getting; 22 from; 23 will; 24 by; 25 to; 26 by;
27 are; 28 too; 29 well; 30 such

3 Key word transformation
31   need not have shouted
32   can be prevented by
33   sofa would be delivered that
34   not got used to driving/to get used to driving
35   in order to get/buy
36   denied borrowing her sister's
37   not wide enough
38   had (the) time, I would
39   prefer the countryside to
40   do not agree with

4 Error correction
41 it; 42 ✔; 43 that; 44 ✔; 45 which; 46 the; 47 and;
48 than; 49 ✔; 50 herself; 51 far; 52 there; 53 at; 54 in;
55 back

5 Word formation
56 Relaxation; 57 addition; 58 overnight; 59 homework;
60 Later; 61 attractive; 62 storage; 63 entertainment;
64 spacious; 65 careful

Unit 9

1 Lexical cloze
1C; 2C; 3B; 4A; 5B

2 Gapped sentences
1 have; 2 so; 3 being; 4 in; 5 of

3 Key word transformation
1   may not have been
2   not realising that/without realising that
3   on seeing
4   can't have come
5   turned out to be

4 Error correction
1 been; 2 up; 3 ✔; 4 ✔; 5 been

5 Word formation
1 behaviour; 2 mysterious; 3 proud; 4 laughter; 5 laziness

Unit 10

1 Lexical cloze
1C; 2A; 3C; 4C; 5D

2 Gapped sentences
1 be; 2 up; 3 had; 4 of; 5 will

3 Key word transformation
1   is due to arrive
2   have an alarm installed
3   gave themselves away
4   to make use of
5   will have been driving for

4 Error correction
1 away; 2 being; 3 ✔; 4 may; 5 for

5 Word formation
1 burglary; 2 network; 3 shoplifters; 4 sensor(s); 5 security

Unit 11

1 **Lexical cloze**

1C; 2D; 3D; 4A; 5C

2 **Gapped sentences**

1 at; 2 on; 3 be; 4 have; 5 the/our

3 **Key word transformation**

1   is said to be
2   will no longer be able
3   face up to the fact
4   had not used dogs
5   wouldn't be short of

4 **Error correction**

1 ✔; 2 been; 3 if; 4 will; 5 ✔

5 **Word formation**

1 threatening; 2 disastrous; 3 lightning; 4 companionship;
5 beneficial

Unit 12

1 **Lexical cloze**

1B; 2A; 3D; 4B; 5A

2 **Gapped sentences**

1 applied/looked; 2 it; 3 did; 4 of; 5 would

3 **Key word transformation**

1   has (got) neither experience nor
2   wish my boss would
3   wishes (that) she had finished
4   have gone on strike
5   regret resigning/that I resigned

4 **Error correction**

1 to; 2 with; 3 the; 4 ✔; 5 in

5 **Word formation**

1 pressure; 2 retirement; 3 variety; 4 memorable;
5 competitive

Progress test 3

1 **Lexical cloze**

1C; 2C; 3A; 4B; 5A; 6A; 7D; 8B; 9C; 10A; 11C; 12C; 13D; 14A;
15B

2 **Structural cloze**

16 will; 17 with; 18 to; 19 least; 20 of; 21 yours; 22 any;
23 that; 24 be; 25 for; 26 and; 27 if; 28 Be; 29 as/like; 30 go

3 **Key word transformation**

31   could not put up with
32   has had his car broken
33   had not been ill
34   can't have written
35   is believed to be
36   will have been married
37   to finish this project without
38   I had not resigned
39   have not seen Tom since
40   may have been

4 **Error correction**

41 too; 42 up; 43 for; 44 down; 45 if; 46 ✔; 47 as; 48 to;
49 ✔; 50 us; 51 will; 52 so; 53 he; 54 for; 55 ✔

5 **Word formation**

56 growth; 57 memorise; 58 Scientists; 59 navigation;
60 relationship; 61 Examination; 62 intensive; 63 noticeable;
64 implications; 65 knowledge

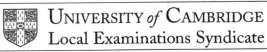

UNIVERSITY *of* CAMBRIDGE
Local Examinations Syndicate

SAMPLE

Candidate Name
If not already printed, write name
in CAPITALS and complete the
Candidate No. grid (in pencil).
Candidate's signature ....

Examination Title

Centre

Supervisor:

[X] If the candidate is ABSENT or has WITHDRAWN shade here ▭

Centre No.

Candidate No.

**Examination
Details**

Candidate Answer Sheet: FCE paper 1 Reading

Use a pencil

Mark ONE letter for each question.

For example, if you think **B** is the right answer to the question, mark your answer sheet like this:

0 ▭A ▭B ▭C ▭D

Change your answer like this:

0 ▭A ▭B ▭C ▭D

	A B C D E F G H I
1	A B C D E F G H I
2	A B C D E F G H I
3	A B C D E F G H I
4	A B C D E F G H I
5	A B C D E F G H I

	A B C D E F G H I
6	A B C D E F G H I
7	A B C D E F G H I
8	A B C D E F G H I
9	A B C D E F G H I
10	A B C D E F G H I
11	A B C D E F G H I
12	A B C D E F G H I
13	A B C D E F G H I
14	A B C D E F G H I
15	A B C D E F G H I
16	A B C D E F G H I
17	A B C D E F G H I
18	A B C D E F G H I
19	A B C D E F G H I
20	A B C D E F G H I

	A B C D E F G H I
21	A B C D E F G H I
22	A B C D E F G H I
23	A B C D E F G H I
24	A B C D E F G H I
25	A B C D E F G H I
26	A B C D E F G H I
27	A B C D E F G H I
28	A B C D E F G H I
29	A B C D E F G H I
30	A B C D E F G H I
31	A B C D E F G H I
32	A B C D E F G H I
33	A B C D E F G H I
34	A B C D E F G H I
35	A B C D E F G H I

142

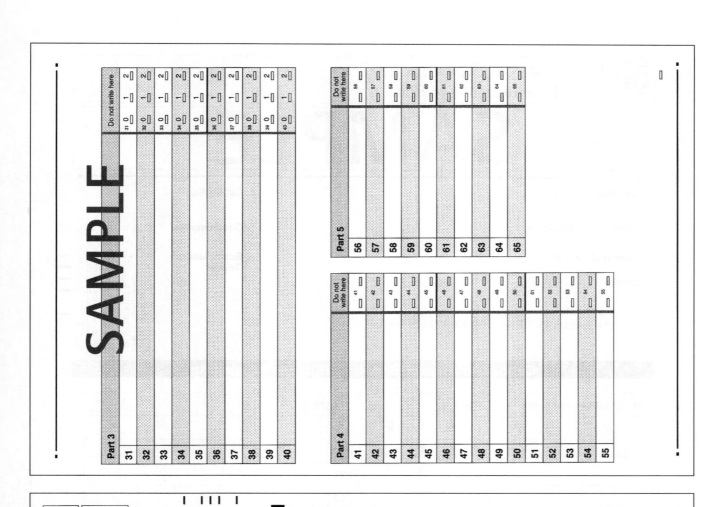

UNIVERSITY of CAMBRIDGE
Local Examinations Syndicate

SAMPLE

Candidate Name
If not already printed, write name
in CAPITALS and complete the
Candidate No. grid (in pencil).

Candidate's signature

Examination Title

Centre

Supervisor:
☒ If the candidate is ABSENT or has WITHDRAWN shade here ☐

Centre No.

Candidate No.

Examination Details

Candidate Answer Sheet: FCE paper 3 Use of English

Use a pencil

For **Part 1**: Mark ONE letter for each question.

For example, if you think **C** is the right answer to the question, mark your answer sheet like this:

| 0 | A ☐ B ☐ C ▬ D ☐ |

For **Parts 2, 3, 4** and **5**: Write your answers in the spaces next to the numbers like this:

| 0 |

Part 1

	A	B	C	D
1	A ☐	B ☐	C ☐	D ☐
2	A ☐	B ☐	C ☐	D ☐
3	A ☐	B ☐	C ☐	D ☐
4	A ☐	B ☐	C ☐	D ☐
5	A ☐	B ☐	C ☐	D ☐
6	A ☐	B ☐	C ☐	D ☐
7	A ☐	B ☐	C ☐	D ☐
8	A ☐	B ☐	C ☐	D ☐
9	A ☐	B ☐	C ☐	D ☐
10	A ☐	B ☐	C ☐	D ☐
11	A ☐	B ☐	C ☐	D ☐
12	A ☐	B ☐	C ☐	D ☐
13	A ☐	B ☐	C ☐	D ☐
14	A ☐	B ☐	C ☐	D ☐
15	A ☐	B ☐	C ☐	D ☐

Part 2

	Do not write here
16	☐
17	☐
18	☐
19	☐
20	☐
21	☐
22	☐
23	☐
24	☐
25	☐
26	☐
27	☐
28	☐
29	☐
30	☐

Turn over for Parts 3 - 5 ↑

FCE-3

DP319/93

SAMPLE

Part 3

	Do not write here		
		0	1	2
31	31	0 ☐	1 ☐	2 ☐
32	32	0 ☐	1 ☐	2 ☐
33	33	0 ☐	1 ☐	2 ☐
34	34	0 ☐	1 ☐	2 ☐
35	35	0 ☐	1 ☐	2 ☐
36	36	0 ☐	1 ☐	2 ☐
37	37	0 ☐	1 ☐	2 ☐
38	38	0 ☐	1 ☐	2 ☐
39	39	0 ☐	1 ☐	2 ☐
40	40	0 ☐	1 ☐	2 ☐

Part 4

	Do not write here
41	41 ☐
42	42 ☐
43	43 ☐
44	44 ☐
45	45 ☐
46	46 ☐
47	47 ☐
48	48 ☐
49	49 ☐
50	50 ☐
51	51 ☐
52	52 ☐
53	53 ☐
54	54 ☐
55	55 ☐

Part 5

	Do not write here
56	56 ☐
57	57 ☐
58	58 ☐
59	59 ☐
60	60 ☐
61	61 ☐
62	62 ☐
63	63 ☐
64	64 ☐
65	65 ☐

UNIVERSITY *of* CAMBRIDGE
Local Examinations Syndicate

SAMPLE

Candidate Name
If not already printed, write name in CAPITALS and complete the Candidate No. grid (in pencil).

Candidate's signature

Examination Title

Centre

Supervisor:
[X] If the candidate is ABSENT or has WITHDRAWN shade here ▭

Centre No.

Candidate No.

Examination Details

0	0	0	0
1	1	1	1
2	2	2	2
3	3	3	3
4	4	4	4
5	5	5	5
6	6	6	6
7	7	7	7
8	8	8	8
9	9	9	9

Candidate Answer Sheet: FCE paper 4 Listening

Mark test version below

| A | B | C | D | E |

Special arrangements S H

Use a pencil

For **Parts 1** and **3**:
Mark ONE letter for each question.

For example, if you think **B** is the right answer to the question, mark your answer sheet like this:

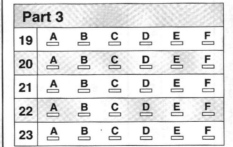

| 0 | A | B | C |

For **Parts 2** and **4**:
Write your answers in the spaces next to the numbers like this:

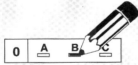

| 0 | EXAMPLE |

Part 1

1	A	B	C
2	A	B	C
3	A	B	C
4	A	B	C
5	A	B	C
6	A	B	C
7	A	B	C
8	A	B	C

Part 2

		Do not write here
9		9
10		10
11		11
12		12
13		13
14		14
15		15
16		16
17		17
18		18

Part 3

19	A	B	C	D	E	F
20	A	B	C	D	E	F
21	A	B	C	D	E	F
22	A	B	C	D	E	F
23	A	B	C	D	E	F

Part 4

		Do not write here
24		24
25		25
26		26
27		27
28		28
29		29
30		30

FCE-4

DP320/94